EDWARD HOFFMAN

SIMON & SCHUSTER

NEW YORK   LONDON   TORONTO   SYDNEY   TOKYO   SINGAPORE

DESPITE

ALL

ODDS

THE STORY OF LUBAVITCH

SIMON & SCHUSTER

SIMON & SCHUSTER BUILDING

ROCKEFELLER CENTER

1230 AVENUE OF THE AMERICAS

NEW YORK, NEW YORK 10020

DESIGNED BY NINA D'AMARIO/LEVAVI & LEVAVI
MANUFACTURED IN THE UNITED STATES OF AMERICA

1 3 5 7 9 10 8 6 4 2

LIBRARY OF CONGRESS CATALOGING-IN-PUBLICATION DATA
HOFFMAN, EDWARD,
DESPITE ALL ODDS : THE STORY OF LUBAVITCH / [EDWARD HOFFMAN].
P.   CM.
INCLUDES INDEX.
1. HABAD—UNITED STATES.   2. HASIDIM—UNITED STATES.
3. SCHNEERSOHN, MENAHEM MENDEL, 1902-.   I. TITLE.
BM198.H57   1990
296.8'3322—DC20
ISBN 0-671-67703-9
90-10115
CIP   9

PHOTO CREDITS
EXCEPT AS NOTED, THE PHOTOGRAPHS ARE BY
S. ROUMANI, Y. FREIDIN, AND Y. VISHINSKY.
PAGE 1 OF PICTURE SECTION, UPPER RIGHT AND LOWER RIGHT: FRIDRICH VISHINSKY.
PAGE 4, UPPER LEFT: COPYRIGHT 1953, KEHOT PUBLICATION SOCIETY.
PAGE 9, TOP: IRV ANTLER. PAGE 10, BOTTOM: SUSAN BIDDLE/THE WHITE HOUSE.
PAGE 15, UPPER RIGHT: VERA ETZION
PAGE 15, BOTTOM: STUDIO 23 PHOTOGRAPHY.

For Aaron Lev and Jeremy Isaac

CONTENTS

PREFACE 11

INTRODUCTION 15

I ENCOUNTERS WITH THE REBBE 29

II WESTWOOD, LOS ANGELES 53

III WALLS OF IVY 65

IV WOMEN OF VALOR 77

V RAISING THE FALLEN SPARKS 103

VI THE CREATIVE FLAME 117

VII BATTLING FOR LIGHT 129

VIII THE HOLY LAND 149

IX A LIBRARY ON TRIAL 177

X DAYS ARE COMING 193

INDEX 215

PREFACE

I have been intrigued by the Lubavitcher Hasidim since childhood in New York City during the 1950s. Though I attended Hebrew day school as a boy, my exposure to the Lubavitchers was only fleeting as none of my teachers or peers were Hasidic. Still, from chance encounters I was curious as to how they lived, and what they were all about. I learned at an early age that they were Orthodox Jews from Eastern Europe who had survived the Holocaust and determinedly held to their Old World garb and customs.

Later, my religious and secular education converged in the late 1960s at Cornell University, a time when new ideas about the mind and spirituality were very much in the air. While majoring in psychology, I also read with considerable excitement Martin Buber's evocative re-tellings of Hasidic tales and legends. The stories touched me deeply and soon led me into the domain of Hasidic history and philosophy. At the same time novels by Isaac Bashevis Singer and Elie Wiesel gave me vivid glimpses into the exotic world of Eastern European Jewry before its cataclysmic destruction a few years before my birth.

While engaged in doctoral work in psychology at the University of Michigan, I managed to find time to deepen my religious studies through the writings of Gershom Scholem. Here I first encountered the dazzling landscape of Jewish mysticism, a vast realm of knowledge and speculation that has fascinated me ever since. Though Scholem was not a psychologist, his meticulous references to Kabbalistic interest in dreams, meditation, the mind-body relationship, and other psychologi-cal topics piqued my curiosity, and I began to read more extensively on Jewish mysticism and its flowering in Hasidism.

Toward the end of my graduate work in 1975, I became a member of Ann Arbor's Hebrew House, a private and independent living cooper-ative for Jewish students. A young Lubavitcher rabbi frequently visited from a Detroit suburb in the evenings to chat with us. He was friendly enough, but I was much too busy completing my doctorate to give him more than a passing nod when he appeared.

A few years passed and, newly married, I moved to southern

Florida to develop my career as a psychologist. There I encountered another Lubavitcher rabbi, who was offering adult classes on Jewish mysticism. By then I had already published an article on Kabbalah and psychology, but was unsure of how to pursue this unusual interdisciplinary field. The timing of the class seemed fortuitous and before long, I found the rabbi's erudition and warm manner most appealing. After the course ended, I enrolled in others that he gave weekly at his home, including one for couples that my wife and I attended for several years.

Through this exposure, I became increasingly interested in the relevance of Hasidism to daily life in contemporary society. It was one thing to read poetic, even inspiring, tales about sages who had lived in remote Russian or Ukrainian villages two centuries ago. It was quite another to see these values enacted and forcefully articulated by the Lubavitchers I met. In part, such contacts spurred me to write my first book on modern psychology and Jewish spirituality, published in 1981, and two others that followed in the 1980s.

As the Lubavitchers gained increasing visibility for their far-flung activities, my interest in their movement began to grow. They seemed to possess a special talent for attracting publicity and media attention, yet I clearly saw that many well-meaning people were confused about Lubavitcher beliefs, practices, and goals. Often in conversations with colleagues and friends, I found myself wanting to recommend a good overview of the movement, but nothing of the sort existed. Eventually I decided to take on the project myself.

The task has been a most enjoyable one. In the role of friendly outsider I have had the pleasure of meeting many of their rabbinic teachers, outreach workers, and administrators across the United States and abroad. From my frequent visits to the Lubavitch headquarters in Brooklyn, New York, I have gained a personal sense of this unique global community that no amount of reading could possibly have provided.

My account is neither exhaustive nor definitive, nor is it designed as a substitute for the many texts written by the Lubavitchers themselves on their movement's philosophy and aims. Rather, my objective is to provide a bridge to this intriguing Hasidic group as it functions in our own time, and to impart something meaningful about the history of the Lubavitch movement and its current programs and aims. If the book succeeds in this respect, it will have fulfilled my purpose.

This book would scarcely have been possible without the valuable cooperation of many persons. Much impetus for the project came from three senior rabbis in the Lubavitcher movement: Yehuda Krinsky, Avraham Shemtov (United States) and Faivish Vogel, director of the Lubavitch Foundation (United Kingdom), who together with his colleagues Rabbi Shmuel Lew and Peter Kalms offered significant assistance throughout. Later, my encounters in Crown Heights with the Lubavitcher Rebbe, Rabbi Menachem Mendel Schneerson, intensified my interest in communicating the unique essence of this Hasidic group today.

Rabbis Yossi Friedman, Daniel Goldberg, and Sholom Ber Levine, provided invaluable assistance throughout my research efforts. For offering their detailed perspective on Lubavitcher programs and aims, I am also grateful to Rabbis Casriel Brusowankin, Chaim Capland, Shlomo Cunin, Moshe Feller, Manis Friedman, Yitzchak Kagan, Sholom Lipskar, Elie Silberstein, Tuvya Teldon, and Sholom Wolpo. Professor Herman Branover of Israel's Ben-Gurion University was likewise a source of valuable information. Appreciation is extended to Mindy Feller and Chaya Teldon for their generous time.

Aaron Hostyk, Irene Javors, and Paul Palnik provided many hours of stimulating discussion related to the topics of this book. Gratitude too is expressed to Gertrude Brainin, Eric Freedman, and Alice Martell. The editorial assistance of Bob Bender is likewise very much appreciated.

Above all, I would like to thank three individuals for their boundless patience and encouragement. My children, Aaron and Jeremy, by insisting that I take breaks and play with them, helped me stay balanced and cheerful. My wife, Laurel, more than any other person, gave me the intellectual and emotional support to complete this project and fulfill my own goals for it.

INTRODUCTION

Hasidism arose in Eastern Europe during the middle decades of the eighteenth century, when the regions of Poland, Belorussia (White Russia), and the Ukraine held the largest concentration of Jews on the globe. Most of them had settled there in earlier centuries. They had fled persecution in areas to the south and east and hoped to establish a new and peaceful life. But relentless economic and political oppression caused most Jewish inhabitants to sink into a morass of poverty and ignorance.

In Broadway plays and Hollywood films, old Jewish *shtetls* (villages) often resemble prosperous New England towns, but the reality was very different and far closer to a collection of dilapidated hovels. Paupers were commonplace, and the aggressive beggar became a stock character in Yiddish folklore and humor. Few people were sufficiently skilled in arts or crafts to earn money at them. Virtually no one was permitted to own his own land.

Because Jews were usually required—on penalty of imprisonment or death—to live in the Pale of Settlement (prescribed areas throughout the cities and countryside)—the most promising business opportunities were usually denied them. Jews had a few privileges, but these could be quickly revoked for failure to pay the rent on schedule: many Yiddish tales hinged on the problem a Jew faced in paying the landlord on time—and the disastrous consequences that ensued for nonpayment.

With political and spiritual salvation removed to the messianic future, Eastern European Jews found few outlets for their creative inner strivings. To the intellectual elite there was one key resource—study and debate over the ancient Talmud and other holy texts. This kind of activity provided a reassuring purpose and structure to daily existence. Scholars derived comfort and meaning from intense discussions about exact Talmudic dicta and interpretations. They were esteemed for their intellectual abilities and enjoyed a corresponding sense of self-worth. Furthermore, since Jews were completely barred from attending the European universities, Talmudic study was virtually the only outlet for an inquisitive mind.

But only a handful in each town could afford the years of intensive study needed to master the Talmud, so all this was of little benefit to the uneducated Jewish masses who were effectively without decision-making power in either religious or secular matters. The tight, hierarchical structure of the *shtetl* accorded most people little opportunity to express their own ideas; most had to accede almost wholly to their better-educated neighbors.

Against this rather bleak social landscape, the Jewish people were ceaselessly confronted with their humiliating poverty and their exile from the Holy Land. The Diaspora had lasted for century after unrelieved century; something would have to change, for life was becoming unbearable for the Eastern European Jewish masses. Slowly at first, then with greater stridency, the *shtetls* began to manifest a growing restlessness.

Some dedicated rabbis, impelled by the memory of past massacres of their ancestors, took to roaming the countryside. Abandoning what little security they had, they traveled incognito—urging their fellow Jews not to lose hope but to observe faithfully their God-given Law. Others journeyed as itinerant preachers throughout the *shtetls*. Preying on fear, they prophesied further nightmares of destruction unless the Chosen People repented of their evil deeds. In vivid contrast, still others searched for a new way to ignite the fervor of the Jewish people once again. Among this last group was Israel ben Eliezer (later known as the Baal Shem Tov or Master of the Good [God's] Name).

Very little reliable information exists about the early life of the Baal Shem Tov, though legends arose about him even before his death. Born around the year 1698 in the small village of Okup, near the Carpathian Mountains, in what is today part of southern Russia, he came from a family distinguished neither by social status nor by education. His parents died while he was still young, and some other village family presumably took him in and gave him a home. For several years the young Israel ben Eliezer served as a teacher's aide and transported children to and from the synagogue school. He was unprepossessing and seemingly uneducated, and when he married, his wife's brother, a prominent rabbi, so disapproved that he urged her to divorce him. She refused, and the couple went to live in a remote village in the Carpathians, where they barely managed to eke out a living. Later they were reconciled with the family and moved to the town of Medzyboz, where they ran an inn.

During this period Israel ben Eliezer gradually became known as a healer and a "miracle worker." According to tradition, he first revealed his spiritual prowess to the world at the age of thirty-six, which would have been in about 1734. Accounts began to circulate about his vast mystical knowledge and his ability to perform apparently supernatural acts to help those in need. Traveling from village to village, the Baal Shem Tov ("Besht" in acronymic abbreviation) cured the sick and those in despair. He also communicated a unique and compelling approach to Judaism.

Relying largely on parables and Talmudic folktales, the Besht used simple language that uneducated people could readily understand. He took classic Jewish mystical themes about the nature of human existence and its relation to the divine, and cast them in the form of appealing stories. His central tenet was that every individual has a specific mission to accomplish on earth. "No two persons have the same abilities," the Baal Shem Tov declared. "Each man should work in the service of God according to his own talents. If one man tries to imitate another, he merely loses the opportunity to do good through his own merit."

Every person, the Besht taught, is capable of reaching the highest state of spiritual enlightenment; the gates of heaven lie open all around us. Declaring that Talmudic study was only one path among many to transcendence, he extolled the power of intense prayer, in joy and happiness, to bring Jews closer to God. "No child can be born except through pleasure and joy," he is credited with saying. "By the same token, if we wish our prayers to bear fruit, we must offer them with pleasure and joy."

Although the Besht drew his early Hasidim (from the Hebrew word for pious ones) as they became known, predominantly from the ranks of the poor and unlearned, he eventually began to attract interest from leading Talmudic scholars, some holding positions of great influence within the Jewish communities of Eastern Europe. Though the Baal Shem Tov had attended no rabbinic academy, these Jewish leaders were impressed with his profound scholarship, his mastery of mystical lore, and his pious yet magnetic personality. Several years before his death in 1760 he carefully chose certain disciples to succeed him in spreading the Hasidic message of the joyful expression of Judaism. Many of these disciples became spiritual teachers themselves and attracted their own followers. Indeed, in its first half century of growth, Hasidism generated its greatest creative energy and produced a galaxy of remarkable leaders known as Rebbes. Fully half of Eastern European Jewry became allied with the Hasidic movement.

The institution of the Rebbe was central to its flowering. Initially, each of the Rebbes was close to the Baal Shem Tov, and highly influenced by his own daily practices. The Rebbes served to provide Hasidic guidance in every sphere of daily life: nothing was considered beneath their purview. Through both group and individual involvement, followers sought out their Rebbe for advice on livelihood, family matters, and health problems. They saw the Rebbe as an intercessor in the heavenly courts, an expounder of mysteries through both study and meditation, and a wise figure who could guide them through the straits of everyday existence. Eventually, as the Hasidic movement spread, individual Rebbes became associated with the places where they lived.

The direct heir to the Baal Shem Tov's leadership was Rabbi Dov Baer of Mezritch. Known as the Maggid (Preacher), he was well known early in his life as a scholar drawn to solitary contemplation. In the 1750s he became won over to the Besht's more exuberant approach to Judaism, and made use of his outstanding organizational abilities to systematize much of his mentor's teachings. He also promulgated Hasidic teachings to initially apathetic or unfriendly Jewish communities.

But some Jews—who called themselves Mitnaggedim (Opponents)—viewed with disdain and even alarm the Hasidic rejection of Talmudic study as the sole path to holiness. In the Lithuanian and northwestern Russian regions, where Talmudic study was highly venerated, rabbinic opposition to Hasidism was particularly fierce and protracted. It was led by the renowned scholar Rabbi Elijah of Vilna and because of his influence Hasidic adherents were publicly excommunicated and their writings burned as heretical. Nevertheless, Rabbi Dov Baer's diligent efforts continued unabated, gaining new supporters with each passing year until his death in 1772.

One of the greatest of Rabbi Dov Baer's disciples was Rabbi Schneur Zalman of Liady, who became the founder of Lubavitch Hasidism. Born in central Russia in 1745, Rabbi Schneur Zalman was a child prodigy in his mastery of the Talmud. When he was ready for advanced scholarship he chose to become a disciple of the Maggid of Mezritch, who had already engendered controversy over his allegiance to the Baal Shem Tov. The Maggid encouraged this gifted young student—more than thirty-five years his junior—to recodify the sixteenth-century Shulchan Arukh (literally Prepared Table, or Code of Jewish Law) and to develop his metaphysical interests within the mystical, experiential realm of Hasidism. The culmination of Rabbi Schneur Zalman's intellectual work was his book, the Tanya *(It has been taught)*. This theoretical but provocative treatise first published in 1796 is still extensively studied by Lubavitchers and others.

In the *Tanya* Rabbi Schneur Zalman held that there is a basic human desire to merge with the Infinitude of God. Each soul "naturally yearns to separate itself and depart from the body, in order to unify with its origin and Source . . . the fountainhead of all life." Nevertheless, Rabbi Schneur Zalman viewed the process of spiritual growth as life-long, requiring tireless self-discipline and the appropriate use of both intellect and emotion. The system was called Chabad, an acronymic abbreviation of the Hebrew terms for the higher faculties of wisdom *(chochmah)*, understanding *(binah)*, and knowledge *(daath)*. For this reason, his followers have for two centuries been known as Chabad Hasidim as well as Lubavitchers, after the town that eventually became their communal base. In the 1960s the Lubavitcher Rebbe chose the name Chabad Houses for the Lubavitch campus centers.

Amid bitter opposition from the non-Hasidic rabbinate, Rabbi Schneur Zalman taught meditative practices designed to help individuals to attain closer communion with God. His anti-Hasidic foes condemned these ideas as heresy and their well-orchestrated opposition was so vicious and prolonged that virtually all other Hasidic leaders in White Russia were overwhelmed and left for other regions. In 1777 a contingent of some three hundred Hasidim, together with their Rebbes, emigrated to the Holy Land. Though they possessed tremendous hope and fervor, not all reached their destination. Eighty were tragically drowned when one ship sank in a storm, and half the survivors returned, forlorn, to Russia. Rabbi Schneur Zalman was to have been among those making the dangerous voyage. But he had fortunately turned back at the last moment on the impassioned pleas of his Hasidic followers not to leave them bereft of spiritual guidance.

Arriving in Safed and Tiberias, the remaining Hasidim found life

in the Holy Land to be unexpectedly difficult. Largely starry-eyed ideal-
ists and scholars, they could find no financially remunerative work in
these backward Arab settlements. Destitute, they appealed for help to
their Hasidic brethren still in White Russia.

But matters were no better there. As a result of the activities of
informers among the anti-Hasidic opponents, Rabbi Schneur Zalman
was twice imprisoned by the czar for allegedly fomenting subversion by
raising funds for enemy Turkey, which then ruled the Holy Land, when
in fact he was collecting donations to support the emigrant Hasidic
community. Though his situation was perilous he was released unharmed on both occasions for lack of evidence and as a result of his own
unbending will. After his second release in 1801 it was clear even to
his antagonists that the Hasidic movement could not be destroyed.
Rabbi Schneur Zalman used his organizational skills to make sure that
his followers would remain unified. Interested in modern science, and
possessed of a sound pragmatic attitude, he established a pattern of
leadership that has been a model for successive generations of Lubavitcher Rebbes.

The Chabad founder's final battle involved Napoleon. Unlike many
European Jews, who welcomed Napoleon for his relatively egalitarian
ideas, Rabbi Schneur Zalman viewed him as a dangerous megalomaniac
and an enemy of religion. He therefore applied his considerable zeal and
influence to helping the czar defeat Napoleon, even planting Hasidim
as double agents within the invading French army in Russia to provide
intelligence to czarist generals. Soon after Napoleon's rout in 1812,
Rabbi Schneur Zalman died, leaving his oldest son, Rabbi Dov Baer,
to become the Hasidic group's new Rebbe.

During the fifteen years of his leadership, though dogged by ill
health, Rabbi Dov Baer accomplished a great deal, both through his
mystically oriented scholarship and by alleviating the material hard-
ships experienced by his numerous followers. Rabbi Schneur Zalman's
staunch opposition to Napoleon was not forgotten, and the czarist government became more sympathetic toward the impassioned Hasidic
group. With czarist backing Rabbi Dov Baer was able to help to resettle
impoverished Hasidic villagers on the land so that they could earn their
livelihood as independent farmers. Maintaining his father's interest in
the Holy Land, Rabbi Dov Baer in 1823 created a Hasidic colony in

Hebron and continued to support it financially until his own death in 1827.

For more than twenty years, Hebron remained virtually the only Chabad community in the Holy Land, until in 1847, a small contingent of Hasidim moved to Jerusalem for its greater economic opportunities. This trend steadily continued, and by the late nineteenth century, the majority of Lubavitcher Hasidim in Israel were living in Jerusalem, with the second-largest concentration in Hebron. Throughout this era, they generally led quiet, religious lives far from the distant shtetls of the Old Country.

It was also under the guidance of Rabbi Dov Baer that the Chabad Hasidim became based in the Russian town of Lubavitch and were consolidated as a coherent and viable religious and social force throughout Eastern Europe.

By the late 1820s, the Hasidic movement had entered a new phase of existence. Gone were the days when those loyal to the Baal Shem Tov or his chosen disciples had to brave the threat of excommunication or witnessed the public burning of Hasidic writings. Yet gone also was much of the initial religious fervor that had inspired multitudes of Jews in Poland, the Ukraine, White Russia, and neighboring areas. In part, this situation reflected the truce that gradually arose between the Mitnaggedim and the Hasidim. Both camps realized that they faced a common adversary in the growing numbers of Jews embracing the Haskalah or Enlightenment. Thus, Hasidism had finally won a comfortable place within the Jewish world, and one manifestation of this victory was the formation of Hasidic dynasties associated with particular locales such as Ger, Chernobyl, and Ruzin.

Leadership was transmitted through lineage, and those who became Rebbes of major groups such as the Lubavitchers were either the sons or sons-in-law of their predecessors. They generally led an ascetic life, supported by the donations of their followers. Many Rebbes developed small teams of support staff to minister to their often far-flung adherents. So too did the Lubavitchers, who valued practical endeavors to help one another materially as well as spiritually. In this respect their present day energetic social-service programs are nothing new.

The new generations of Hasidic Rebbes continued such earlier practices as producing mystically oriented writings and talks, providing

personal spiritual counseling, and utilizing communal singing and dancing for the joyous celebration of Jewish festivals and family events. The
Rebbes were scarcely affluent in comparison to the non-Jewish aristoc-
racy, possessing only modest wealth.

Though early nineteenth-century Europe was changing politically,
culturally and economically the Lubavitchers remained unswerving in
their allegiance to traditional Judaism and its Law. Under their third
Rebbe, Rabbi Menachem Mendel (son-in-law of his predecessor), who
assumed leadership in 1827, and then under his son Rabbi Shmuel,
who became the fourth Rebbe in 1866, the Chabad Hasidim continued
to base their entire way of life on the traditional sources. These comprised the Bible and Talmudic commentaries, and the subsequent legal
codifications by Maimonides in the twelfth century and Rabbi Joseph
Karo, author of the Shulchan Arukh, in the sixteenth century, as well
as thousands of other texts. For centuries, these sources had been
universally acknowledged among Jews as the very foundation of their
religion. But with the inexorable breakdown of ghetto walls the authority of the Talmud and its Law steadily diminished.

First Germany, then other Western countries, witnessed a steady
challenge to Jewish Orthodoxy. In 1819, for example, the long-favored
mystical Sabbath eve prayer "Lekha Dodi" ("Come, my beloved") was
replaced by a Lutheran chorale in the newly published Hamburg Temple prayer book. Many who strongly embraced their Jewish heritage
argued that exposure to Western culture might constitute a healthy
influence, and saw entry into the universities as a desirable and long-
overdue development.

From their stronghold in western Russia, the Lubavitchers
strongly fought this liberalizing trend. They resisted all attempts by the
czar's ministers to introduce secular subjects into religious schools and
seminaries, and held strictly to the Bible as the timeless and literal word
of God. Within their tightly knit communities sustained interaction with
outsiders was seldom necessary, and so like other Hasidic groups, they
remained relatively insulated for many decades.

When increasingly violent and murderous pogroms against East-
ern European Jewry started in the 1880s, Rabbi Shmuel—and his son
Rabbi Sholom Dov Baer, who succeeded him as the fifth Lubavitcher
Rebbe in 1882—energetically sought to protect their fellow Jews, Ha-

sidic and non. Risking arrest, they demanded support from high-level government officials, but to little avail. The anti-Semitic pogroms continued unabated in the face of czarist indifference or even tacit encouragement. Nevertheless, the Lubavitcher leadership stood firmly against mass migration to the United States as millions of Jews left Russia and neighboring areas over the next two generations.

During this era, when science was still transforming Western civilization, the Lubavitcher did not reject technology per se, as did fundamentalist Christian groups such as the Amish or Mennonites. Chabad Rebbes taught that science can reveal the Creator's hand at work in the world, and they encouraged the study of such disciplines as astronomy and mathematics, pointing to Maimonides as an example of how a devout Jew can be a successful scientist. Though they sharply rejected modernist theories such as biblical criticism and Darwinian evolution, they welcomed new inventions such as the steam engine, the locomotive, and electric lighting as means to serve the Almighty more effectively in a time of new historical challenges facing the Jewish people. Provided that this technology was utilized within the appropriate parameters of Jewish Law, it could be seen as a boon, and not as a threat.

The first world war permanently shattered the Lubavitcher way of life. In 1915, as German troops invaded White Russia, the town of Lubavitch had to be evacuated and the Chabad headquarters moved to a series of temporary sites over the next few years. Then came the Bolshevik Revolution in 1917, which overturned the promising yet fragile democratic government that led Russia for several months after the downfall of the czar.

Immediately after consolidating power in 1921, the Communist Party's Yevsektsia or "Jewish section" began stamping out all aspects of Judaism. Hundreds of synagogues and Jewish schools were forced to shut down, and their directors and staff imprisoned if they showed the slightest resistance. In bizarre "show trials" conducted across Russia, Communist officials of Jewish heritage declared war on Judaism and pronounced "the death penalty" upon its basic institutions and rituals. Within two or three years, nearly all Russia's Jewish leaders had fled to Poland, Lithuania, or the United States.

But the sixth Lubavitcher Rebbe, Rabbi Yosef Yitzchak Schneersohn, refused to leave. He had assumed Chabad leadership in 1920, at the age of forty, and his enormous stamina and his indomitable will to protect Jewish religious rights to worship and education made him the unofficial head of all Russian Jewry during this period. He mobilized the remaining Jewish communal leaders, and the legal battles that he spearheaded proved fairly successful within the new Soviet courts. He was therefore able to safeguard at least a modicum of Jewish religious freedom.

By 1927, though, the Yevsektsia's agents had had enough. Rabbi Yosef Schneersohn was arrested as a "counterrevolutionary" and taken for interrogation in Leningrad's Spalerna prison. Initially, the NKVD (secret police) planned to have him executed, but an international protest group that included President Calvin Coolidge and government leaders of France, Germany, and Latvia succeeded in winning his release and gained permission for him to leave Russia with his immediate family and supporters.

Over the next twelve years Rabbi Schneersohn lived first in Latvia, then in Poland where he successfully developed a network of yeshivas (rabbinic academies). The main yeshiva, based in Warsaw, was producing a scholarly journal with editorial assistance provided from a distance by the Rebbe's young son-in-law and distant cousin, Rabbi Menachem Mendel Schneerson, who was in Paris studying engineering part time at the Sorbonne. Though by now suffering from multiple sclerosis, he traveled widely throughout Europe and became the first Lubavitcher Rebbe to visit the Holy Land as well as the United States. Besides promoting the establishment of religious schools and synagogues around the globe, he was a prolific writer who maintained a voluminous correspondence with his followers and with Jewish communal leaders around the world. In the upheaval of the first world war and its aftermath in Russia, many of these were now scattered in countries new to them. Most Lubavitchers credit their sixth Rebbe with initiating the transformation of their Hasidic group into an internationally linked network.

Clearly Rabbi Schneersohn saw no hope for Judaism to flourish within the ruthlessly oppressive Communist system, and he encouraged all Hasidim to emigrate if they could. He realized, though, that most families would be compelled to remain in the country, and left in place his organized underground network of loyal Lubavitchers to carry on

Jewish life autonomously, without synagogues, schools, or communal institutions. Almost all historians of Judaism credit its historical survival within the Soviet Union to these carefully planned efforts. It is hardly surprising that today the Lubavitchers are at the forefront of organized efforts to restore Jewish practice in the fragile new era of "perestroika."

Underground religious activity was extremely dangerous. If the Hasidim were caught by the NKVD, as many were, they faced certain conviction as "counterrevolutionaries." For their "crimes" of teaching Hebrew to children or leading worship services there were two forms of punishment: slow death by hard labor in Siberia or swift death by firing squad.

In September 1939 the Nazis invaded Poland in a blitzkrieg attack. Warsaw fell within days, and Rabbi Yosef Schneersohn and his family were nearly killed during several of the many bombing attacks on the defenseless city of two million people. Rabbi Schneersohn went into hiding for several weeks, while American followers tried frantically to find him. With the concerted help of influential Jewish attorneys in Boston, New York City, and Washington, D.C., the Lubavitchers succeeded in obtaining U.S. State Department help to persuade Germanic authorities to let Rabbi Yosef Schneersohn out of Poland. Accompanied by his wife, his eldest daughter and her husband, and a few supporters, he hastily journeyed through Latvia and Sweden before boarding an ocean liner for New York in March 1940.

Immediately upon arriving, the sixth Lubavitcher Rebbe sought to extricate the remaining members of his family, together with as many other Jews as possible from the calamity that clearly awaited them in Nazi-dominated Europe. Many yeshiva students and faculty managed to leave Poland for Shanghai during 1940. In early 1941, the Rebbe's daughter Chaya Moussia and her husband, Rabbi Menachem Mendel Schneerson, escaped safely from France to the United States via Portugal. But once the United States had declared war on Germany in December 1941, it became impossible for Rabbi Yosef Schneersohn to save his third daughter Sheine and her husband, Rabbi Menachem Horenstein, who were still trapped in Poland. They and the entire Horenstein family died on the second day of Rosh Hashanah 1942 at the Treblinka concentration camp.

Supported by his American followers, Rabbi Yosef Schneersohn established Lubavitch's world headquarters in Crown Heights, then a comfortable, middle-class section of Brooklyn. During the years of the Holocaust, he established a variety of organizations committed to proving, in his words, that "America is no different from any other country in providing a home for traditional Judaism." He appointed Rabbi Menachem Schneerson, also living in Crown Heights, to organize three separate, newly formed Chabad divisions: publishing, educational outreach missions, and social services. Under this impetus a small nucleus of dedicated, young Chabad-trained rabbis also founded yeshivas in more than a dozen cities across North America, circulated new Hasidic texts, prayer books, and periodicals, and promoted national rabbinic conferences.

The Lubavitchers were therefore transforming themselves from an Eastern European Hasidic dynasty to an outward-looking group helping to influence the entire Jewish world. Unlike virtually all other Hasidic groups struggling to survive the Holocaust, the Lubavitchers saw themselves as leading a historic, divinely mandated mission on behalf of all Jewry.

After the end of the second world war, the sixth Lubavitcher Rebbe stepped up the pace of his outreach activities. His first priority was to provide religious support for the beleaguered European Jews, especially those in refugee camps, who had survived the Holocaust. He also sent small groups of rabbinic emissaries to establish Chabad institutions in the Near East, Italy, England, and even Australia, where a group of Lubavitchers who had escaped from the Soviet Union were advised to settle. When the State of Israel became a reality and received a huge influx of Near Eastern Jews from countries such as Turkey and the Yemen, Rabbi Yosef Schneersohn launched a large-scale outreach effort to maintain their religious commitment and observance. This was perhaps the first major effective encounter between Hasidism and Near Eastern Jews.

At the time of their sixth Rebbe's death in January 1950, most of his American supporters were immigrants who spoke poor English, while other Hasidim, newly arrived in Brooklyn from Europe—and indeed almost all Orthodox Jews—belittled the Lubavitcher attempts to instill greater piety in the increasingly assimilated Jewry of the United States and Western Europe.

After the death of the sixth Rebbe it was unanimously agreed that one man possessed the lineage, spiritual depth, character, and intellect required for lifelong leadership: Rabbi Menachem Schneerson, aged forty-eight. At first he refused to assume the position, thinking the responsibility too great. But after several months of persistent, even imploring, exhortations from many Lubavitchers, he reluctantly accepted. In January 1951, on the first anniversary of his father-in-law's death, this gentle rabbinic scholar and Sorbonne-educated engineer was formally "crowned" as the seventh Lubavitcher Rebbe. Though many already recognized his unique blend of spirituality and practicality, Torah learning and scientific prowess, no one could have predicted the rapid growth of this Hasidic group in the forty years of his leadership.

The following chapters provide an insight into the work of the Lubavitchers today, in Crown Heights, elsewhere in the United States and in Israel. As far as possible I have let the emissaries, Chabad House staff and others speak for themselves. For purposes of readability, I have at times combined conversations and events that took place on separate occasions, though such an approach is not strictly historical, I hope that in this way I can better convey the contemporary beliefs and aspirations of the Lubavitcher Hasidic movement.

I

ENCOUNTERS WITH THE REBBE

In Hasidism, the Rebbe by virtue of the strength he incarnates and the majesty he evokes . . . represents the father figure par excellence: someone good yet strict, charitable yet severe, tolerant with others but inflexible with himself. In other words, a singular human being in whom all attributes converge and in whom all contradictions are resolved.

—Elie Wiesel
Somewhere a Master

A Rebbe's task is to teach Hasidism according to the spirit of the times and the needs of the people.

—Rabbi Schneur Zalman of Liady

IT IS A WARM JULY NIGHT IN NEW YORK CITY, AND MANY OF THE streets are still crowded with late commuters and shoppers. People are just getting home from work or sitting down to eat dinner. Both the Mets and the Yankees are playing in town, and the games have already started under the lights. In midtown Manhattan, theatergoers await the rising curtain. Not far off, on the Upper East Side, elegant strollers casually pass homeless men and women huddled in doorways or mumbling to themselves on pavements. For most New Yorkers, it is a muggy summer night like any other.

But in the Lubavitch community of Crown Heights, the mood has been festive. The Hasidic residents have been celebrating a unique holiday, the twelfth and thirteenth days of Tammuz, when, in 1927, their previous Rebbe was released from Soviet imprisonment and near-certain execution for his Jewish activism. Excitement has been mounting since this afternoon, for his successor, Rabbi Menachem Schneerson, will soon be leading the televised celebration.

In preparation for the event, staff at Lubavitch headquarters have been in close contact for days with colleagues making final arrangements with television studios around the world. Less than one hour before the Rebbe is scheduled to begin his discourse, the confirmation calls are coming in from major cities in the United States and overseas. In São Paulo, Brazil, it is late evening; in London, bleary-eyed but energetic Lubavitchers prepare to be up all night; In Israel, it will soon be morning rush hour. Altogether, nearly 150 communities all over the world are tuning in to hear their spiritual leader's inspiring words. In Crown Heights, a team of rabbinic scholars wearing headphones and enclosed in separate soundproof booths, sit ready to begin translating the Rebbe's words into Hebrew, English, Russian, French, Portuguese, Spanish, and Farsi (Persian).

Such a wide audience for the message of a single rabbinic leader is virtually unprecedented, although for millennia, Jews have characteristically turned to their great sages for personal guidance in everyday life. In archetypal terms, Moses stands as the individual who acts as intercessor for his people. Hillel and Rabbi Akiba at the time of the Second Temple became renowned for serving in this capacity, as did many Talmudic scholars. Still later, Maimonides achieved greatness for his unparalleled combination of religious piety, scholarship, and pragmatic wisdom, as exemplified by his daily work as a physician.

It seems no historical accident that the Hasid-Rebbe relationship arose in eighteenth-century Eastern Europe, when the vast majority of Jews lived impoverished and politically oppressed lives. It was the Baal Shem Tov, founder of Hasidism, who stressed that all aspects of mundane life can be elevated to serve God. The institution of Hasidic Rebbe, as it evolved after the Besht's death in 1760, became a unique amalgam of intimate adviser, teacher, scholar, and mystic intercessor.

The early Hasidim also stressed that in every generation there exists a single Jewish leader, a *zaddik,* who is the "Moses" of his time, one whose scholarship, and devotion to others is unequaled. Through his awesome piety, each group of Hasidim felt, their Rebbe could even influence the Almighty's decrees. Not only was he revered as an exemplar through his revelatory discourses, but his very quality of being ("how he ties his shoelaces," as it was put) was seen to exalt humanity and impart subtle indications of the path to the divine. Such a figure is even believed to be the instrument of ushering in the messianic age on earth. While the Lubavitchers readily acknowledge the worthy attributes of other Orthodox heads, they venerate none but Rabbi Menachem Schneerson.

The seventh Lubavitcher Rebbe embodies tremendous paradox. His words and directives are followed by adherents on every continent, yet he has not once left metropolitan New York's environs in over forty years. He exerts a powerful influence on matters inside Israel, yet he has never visited the Holy Land. While still in his twenties, he established a reputation for Talmudic brilliance, at the age of nearly thirty, he began ten years of scientific study at the University of Berlin and at the Sorbonne. He is sought by tens of thousands of people every year for advice on the most personal aspects of their lives, yet he remains an intensely private man without a single peer-confidant in either the Hasidic or the secular world. He has produced millions of printed words through his public discourses and correspondence, but although now in his late eighties, he has never written his memoirs or even the semblance of an autobiography. Much in his leadership style is innovative in Lubavitch history, yet, he ceaselessly stresses the continuity of his mission with that of his predecessor, to whom he always refers in the present tense.

At Lubavitch headquarters on Eastern Parkway, the celebration is about to begin, and the familiar image of their main synagogue's interior now appears on television sets around the world. The pews are filled with men, most wearing dark suits and black hats. The women sit upstairs, watching the scene below through a glass partition. Several large tables covered with white tablecloths have been placed together on a modest-sized platform.

Suddenly, the entire gathering becomes silent, as Rabbi Menachem Schneerson enters the synagogue, preceded by rabbinic aides. He strides to the platform, as hundreds of rabbis and laymen try to make eye contact with him, or simply catch a glimpse of his face. His sturdy bearing is unusual for a man of his age. As befits the festive mood, he nods, smiling, then takes the center seat at the dais. Without a moment's pause, he begins his discourse.

He speaks slowly but almost conversationally, in precise Yiddish without a text or even any notes. "Although the event for which we are gathered together is celebrated each year," the Rebbe observes, "this year it must be celebrated with a totally *new* enthusiasm. Parallels to this may be found in Jewish Law. Although a Jew may perform the same *mitzvahs* from time to time, or even every day, Torah instructs that 'every day they should be new in your eyes.'"

While his comments are being translated and beamed out all over the world, the Rebbe speaks for the next half hour on the importance of remaining vibrant, both physically and spiritually, throughout our lives. Quoting biblical verses, he stresses, "The soul needs food just as the body. To know the nature of such spiritual food, we must ask 'experts' in such matters and follow their directives. When we mature, we will ourselves realize the vital necessity of following such advice."

Recalling past celebrations with satisfaction, the Rebbe comments, "In practical terms, this celebration should cause us to increase in every way our devotion to Judaism with renewed fervor and commitment."

After speaking for several minutes on the theme of personal renewal, the Lubavitcher leader leans back in his chair, and within seconds the entire synagogue resounds with exuberant singing. Rhapsodic swaying accompanies the joyful and wordless Hasidic melody. Here and there, a Hasid stands and, raising a small paper cup with wine, seeks to catch the Rebbe's eye; one by one the Rebbe responds directly to each individual toast with a brief but unmistakable nod of his head. During the break, those in the synagogue are already discussing the Rebbe's early remarks of the evening. Suddenly, all heads turn in his direction, at the resumption of his talk. Silence reigns once more.

The second part of the discourse is much longer than the first. The Rebbe begins by weaving evocative biblical verses with Talmudic interpretations stressing the necessity for all Jews to be part of a religious community. Then, turning to the wider significance of his father-in-law's release from Soviet prison in 1927, the Rebbe says, "The days we are celebrating show that, not only is it possible to engage in Torah study and observance in such a country as the Soviet Union, but also to send an envoy whose appearance proclaims his Jewish identity. We are assured that such efforts will be in the manner of liberation; that is, those envoys will eventually defeat the spiritual darkness in that country. Indeed, we see the fruits of labor of the previous Rebbe's envoys: children and children's children in all parts of the world. Among those present at this celebration, there are many who are the outcome of the self-sacrifice of Jews in the Soviet Union, the results of the mission placed upon them by the previous Rebbe."

Nearly two hours have now elapsed since this session began. Many of the standing men sway, their faces quiet in peace and inspiration.

Speaking further on the implications of his father-in-law's prison release, the Rebbe turns to a familiar subject: the uncompromising necessity for advancing belief in God and Torah-based morality in the contemporary world. Drawing from biblical passages and remarks by sages like Maimonides relevant to this point, the Rebbe offers a rare personal reference to his own life. "If there was ever any doubt whether just and righteous behavior is possible only when based on God's desire versus human-derived behavioral codes, all doubts have been resolved in our era. The same German people who prided themselves on their scientific and philosophical accomplishments, who had so many students pursuing knowledge, these people wrought the most horrific and evil of deeds.

"The Holocaust was not the result of one mentally unbalanced individual who coerced others into helping him. Everyone who was there, I among them, saw how enthusiastically the German people accepted Hitler, expressing the hope that he would bring to realization their heartfelt longing to see *Deutschland über alles.* The only way, then, to ensure that people behave decently and morally is to follow a code of conduct not of human invention but based on the fulfillment of God's will."

After a longer pause filled with exuberant singing, the raising of wine cups, and the acknowledgment of individual toasts with the direct glance and nod of his head, and short conversations among his followers, the Rebbe is ready to resume. His third talk focuses on the practical issue of promulgating spiritual values throughout the world today. After mentioning again his father-in-law's heroism on behalf of Jewish practice within the Soviet Union, the Rebbe emphasizes that closer to home, here, in the United States, spreading religious ideals can be accomplished only if the young "are instilled with belief in God through the public school system that is responsible for the proper education of youth. In this country, parents have neither the time nor patience to devote themselves to their children's education. Yet, for various illogical reasons, no mention of God is permitted in these schools. God is not allowed to enter, as it were, the school premises!"

The Rebbe argues for the necessity of instituting a daily "moment of silence" in every public school classroom in America. "It is important to stress that this should not be a spoken prayer," he hastens to add, "for that situation might lead to all sorts of problems. But the 'moment of silence' will cause children to ask their parents what to think about during that moment, and thereby remind and inspire parents about their own main function—to raise 'a blessed generation of the upright.' "

Clearly and characteristically aiming his televised remarks at non-Jews as well as Jews, the Rebbe reminds his audience of the not-too-distant era when most American families "recited at their dining tables a blessing before eating. There was no need then to open the school day with a 'moment of silence' in which to think about God," he adds, "since the student's parents taught him to thank God for his food *before* he went to school. However, after decades of social turmoil and upheaval, this custom has stopped. A child now hears in his home nothing about the Creator and Ruler of the world. Because the situation has changed, the institution of a 'moment of silence' in schools is for the *good* of the country's citizens, affording their children the opportunity to think about a spiritual value."

The Rebbe now lowers his voice, but maintains its intensity. He speaks for a few more minutes about the current constitutional controversy about religion and the public schools. Then the individual blessings and the joyful singing begins anew throughout the synagogue, and after perhaps ten minutes, the Rebbe is ready to resume.

By now, it is well after one o'clock, and this will probably be his final discourse of the night.

"All that we spoke about concerning the celebration of the twelfth and thirteenth of Tammuz applies every year. In addition, there are aspects that change from year to year—the biblical portion learned during the week of this holiday and, in particular, the section learned on this day itself. Because everything happens by divine providence, we can derive a lesson for service to God from today's biblical portion."

After highlighting the multi-tiered symbolism of Numbers describing the ancient Temple's rituals related to the "burnt offering to God," the Rebbe exhorts his audience that "every morning, we all should be close to the Almighty without thought of reward, and at the end of the day's activities, we should know what to rectify, similar to the evening burnt offering brought by the high priest. The service of every Jew must be in the manner of the burnt offering: that every day, we should devote ourselves totally to God. When Jews act in the proper manner, we thereby merit God's blessing for all things, and hasten the true and complete redemption through our righteous Messiah."

The Rebbe makes an emphatic gesture, and the thousands of Hasidim present burst into song. It is hard to believe that at two in the morning, midweek, they still have such energy. It is even harder to believe that the Rebbe himself, in his eighties, has just spoken for over four hours with only a few minutes rest. The spirited singing continues as his entourage files out the synagogue door. Apparently not in the least fatigued, the Rebbe briskly exits from the platform. He notices a little boy sitting atop his father's shoulders and stops for a moment. Gazing seriously into the child's wide eyes, the Lubavitcher leader vigorously waves his arm in rhythm with the enthusiastic singing, and then is gone.

The dancing and swaying gradually cease, as the synagogue audience slowly disperses, many already engrossed in discussion of the Rebbe's remarks. Though the cable-television broadcast is over, such discussions are now occurring around the globe, and will continue unabated for days: in homes and synagogues, rabbinic seminaries, and Chabad centers. Within hours, a team of Lubavitch scholars will carefully transcribe the extemporaneous discourse and translate it into Hebrew, to be reviewed for accuracy by the Rebbe himself. A second rabbinic group will carry out scholarly research, identifying and sometimes commenting upon all the sources that the Rebbe quoted from memory in his long discourse. Once this research is completed, he may review it again, likewise making any necessary corrections and emendations.

Before the week is out, the Rebbe's discourse will be printed in its entirety in Hebrew. In addition, selected portions of the translations into six languages will be printed and distributed by Chabad's own publishing house. Within days, every word will be read, pondered, and analyzed by the Rebbe's adherents. Then, it will take its place as the twenty-ninth volume of his edited public discourses already in print, an addition to the scholastic output unsurpassed by any other living rabbinic figure.

The Rebbe was born in Nikolaiev, in Russia, on April 18, 1902. His mother, Chana (née Yanovsky) Schneerson was the daughter of the town's chief rabbi. She had been married in 1899 and was now twenty-two years old. Her husband, Levi Yitzchak, was two years her senior and a rabbi drawn especially to mystical studies.

Over the next five years or so, two more sons were born to the young couple: Israel Aryeh Leib and Dov Ber. In 1907, when Menachem Mendel was five years old, his family moved to the larger town of Yekaterinoslav (Dnepropetrovsk) where his father had accepted the position of chief rabbi, a prestigious post he held until 1939, when Stalin's police imprisoned him and sentenced him to internal exile for Jewish activism.

Little information has survived about Menachem Mendel's childhood and adolescence in pre-revolutionary Russia. It is known that he was an exceptionally brilliant student in his Jewish religious studies, and withdrew from Hebrew day school at the age of eleven, since his rabbinic teachers had nothing further to offer him. Thereafter, his father became his sole tutor, and by the time Menachem Mendel was thirteen, he was reputed to be a Talmudic prodigy. Four years later, he was ordained as a rabbi, by virtue of his mastery of the entire Talmud and Codes of Jewish Law.

It seems that Rabbi Menachem Mendel was able to continue his religious studies in Yekaterinoslav during the First World War. He had also pursued his self-taught secular subjects, and he obtained permission from the local university to sit for comprehensive examinations. In deference to his Jewish observance, he was allowed to take the examinations on a weekday rather than on the regularly scheduled Saturday hours.

Rabbi Menachem Schneerson first met the new Lubavitcher Rebbe in 1923, a distant relative and an immensely inspiring mentor for the younger man. The admiration must have been mutual, for the Rebbe chose the youthful rabbinic scholar as worthy to become the husband of his middle daughter, Chaya Moussia. Her older sister was already married to a young Chabad rabbi, Samarius Gourary, who was active in the Lubavitch school system.

Rabbi Menachem Schneerson spent the mid-1920s as part of the Rebbe's inner circle, working to combat governmental suppression of Judaism throughout the Soviet Union. By then, hundreds of synagogues, Hebrew day schools and seminaries, and communal institutions had been forced to close. Nearly all rabbinic leaders had fled the country to avoid harassment, imprisonment or near-certain death in Siberian exile. But, like his father-in-law-to-be, who established a secret network of underground schools, ritual baths, and other communal activities, Rabbi Menachem Schneerson refused to emigrate, even after Communist authorities had compelled them to abandon their headquarters in Rostov and move to Leningrad.

When the Rebbe was arrested by the secret police in the spring of 1927, Rabbi Menachem Schneerson risked arrest himself to ensure that incriminating papers that dealt with their underground efforts on behalf of Judaism could be destroyed before the NKVD found them.

Soon afterwards Rabbi Menachem Schneerson arrived safely in the Baltic Republic of Latvia, where the Lubavitcher Rebbe had established the movement's new headquarters in the capital city of Riga. Once more, the young scholar served as a key aide, helping to maintain the morale of committed Hasidim in Russia now that their spiritual leader was living in foreign exile.

Chaya Moussia and Rabbi Menachem Schneerson were married in late 1928. He was twenty-six, she a year older. The ceremony, which the Rebbe performed himself, took place within the courtyard of the new Lubavitcher yeshiva in Warsaw and was attended by thousands of Hasidim and other well-wishers, including many leading rabbinic authorities.

Several weeks later, the newlyweds moved to Berlin. Neither Chaya Moussia nor her husband had ever lived in Germany before, nor did they have relatives there. Soon after arriving in Germany, Rabbi

Menachem Schneerson enrolled at the University of Berlin. From all accounts, he lived a quiet, scholarly life, devoting most of his waking hours to Jewish study and only secondarily concerned with secular courses at the university. He took courses in mathematics and physics, until Hitler's electoral victory in 1933 forced him and his wife to flee to Paris. When his father-in-law left for a ten-month visit to the United States in late 1929 Rabbi Menachem Schneerson led many religious activities in Riga and presented learned discourses. On several other occasions as well, he traveled to Riga to visit the Rebbe and his family.

Somewhat more information is available about Rabbi Menachem Schneerson's years in France, where he enrolled at the Sorbonne and studied engineering, though he continued his Jewish pursuits remained his highest priority. After he became Rebbe he was questioned by a father unsure of whether to allow his adolescent son to attend college instead of continuing with rabbinic education. "Tell him to stay in yeshiva. The campus environment is very unwholesome for Jewish and moral values," was the Rebbe's unhesitating advice.

A bit surprised and defensive, the father retorted, "How about yourself? You studied in college for years, didn't you?"

"Yes," replied the Rebbe, "but I started when I was almost thirty. So let's make a deal. You agree to my suggestion that he continue with his yeshiva training now. And I agree that when he turns thirty, we'll both let him decide what he wants to do then."

From 1936, Rabbi Menachem Schneerson assumed the key responsibility of editing the Rebbe's letters to his adherents in Russia, Poland, and elsewhere. When his father-in-law transferred Chabad headquarters from Riga to Warsaw during this period, Rabbi Menachem Schneerson served as contributing editor to Chabad's new international scholarly journal, *Hatamim* (*The Upright*), published in Warsaw. Though not yet thirty-five, he was recognized within the Chabad movement as one of its foremost scholars.

By nature, he was quiet and reserved. Observers recall that in his small Parisian apartment, he was always immersed in his study of Torah commentaries.

Though Rabbi Schneerson could not be characterized as aloof or a loner, he seems to have much preferred reading and writing about the Torah to more gregarious activities. In a telling episode, one day at the

Sorbonne his professor noticed the Orthodox rabbi absorbed in a Hebrew text and apparently oblivious to the lecture. Striding over, the professor demanded, "Have you heard a single word I've said?" Thereupon, Rabbi Schneerson repeated the entire lecture, word for word, thus demonstrating the phenomenal memory cherished by students of Talmudic academies for centuries.

In 1939, Germany began the Second World War by invading Poland in a lightning attack. The Lubavitcher Rebbe, aided by influential American supporters, managed to leave the country early in 1940 on the last available ship, while Hitler was still officially at peace with the United States. Arriving in New York City with members of his immediate family and a few aides, he sought to extricate Chaya Moussia and her husband from the Holocaust brewing in Europe.

In May 1940, France was invaded by German forces and surrendered within four weeks. A French puppet regime led by Marshal Philippe Pétain and Pierre Laval was established in Vichy, and the Schneersons, like most Jews, fled to southern France, preferring life under Pétain's government to direct Nazi occupation in Paris and surrounding areas. According to several independent recollections from this period, Rabbi Menachem Schneerson demonstrated amazing and life-risking tenacity to maintain his uncompromising Hasidic way of life. He offered a courageous example of refusal to succumb to the terror that the Nazis instilled in their subject populations.

Later in 1940, upon moving to Nice in southern France, Rabbi Schneerson wanted to observe the festival of Succoth as meticulously as possible, by obtaining prized citrons from Italy. To cross the border was illegal and punishable by death. An older rabbi, hearing of the scholar's plan to travel to Italy by train without proper papers, begged him not to do so. But the next morning, Rabbi Schneerson was gone. Praying for his colleague's safe return, the older man was overjoyed to see him back after a few days, triumphantly holding several beautiful citrons.

In the spring of 1941, they secured a passage from Marseilles to New York. To the grief of Chaya's parents, her younger sister and her husband, Rabbi Menachem Horenstein, were still trapped in Poland when the United States declared war on Germany in December 1941, and all contact with them was lost. It was not until after the war that the Rebbe and his family learned that the Horensteins had all perished in Treblinka, nor is it clear when Rabbi Menachem Schneerson learned that his younger brother, Dov Ber, had been shot by German soldiers when they invaded western Russia in June 1940.

Several months after settling into Crown Heights within walking distance of the Rebbe's residence and office headquarters, Rabbi Menachem Schneerson became deeply involved with day-to-day organizational concerns besides Torah scholarship. During the next few years, he wrote several rabbinic texts, including a Hebrew calendar of Hasidic aphorisms for daily study and a special Passover Haggadah (prayer book).

He also edited many classic Hasidic texts, and in the same period, he began his wide correspondence with Jewish leaders throughout the world. The Rebbe directed his scholarly son-in-law to conduct monthly celebrations with those coming to worship at the synagogue in Crown Heights. Although he remained quiet and reserved, Rabbi Menachem Schneerson became a familiar figure not only in and around New York City but throughout the Eastern United States and Canada. It was a subject that he enjoyed so much that for several months he taught a Sabbath class on it for local rabbinic students. As one recalls, "He would review every single line of the Mishnah, and explain its ordinary significance and then its mystical significance. We were just awed by his knowledge."

In early 1947 he flew to Paris, where his mother, Chana, had just been released from a Displaced Persons (DP) camp. She had managed to escape from the Soviet Union less than a year before, and was now living with several hundred other Russian Chabad refugees all waiting for permanent homes around the world. For three months, Rabbi Menachem Schneerson served as local leader, offering both formal and informal guidance to the refugees, and then returned to Crown Heights with his mother to renew his administrative and scholarly responsibilities.

Rain has been falling since dawn this chilly day in New York City. Most people have refrained from venturing outside, and the traffic is light on many thoroughfares. But here, at an Orthodox Jewish cemetery within the metropolitan area, several police cars are escorting a silver '76 Cadillac through the old wrought-iron gates. After a few minutes, the motorcade departs and the Cadillac moves forward past the cemetery plots until it reaches the Ohel. The engine is turned off, and out steps the figure of Rabbi Menachem Schneerson.

Rabbi Yosef Schneersohn's grave is surrounded by a large marble structure, perhaps twenty feet on each side, open to the sky. Against the back wall is a wooden shelter, built to shield the visiting Rebbe from the elements. Through the window, he can see a low concrete structure filled with bits of paper. Beyond stands the large marble headstone that marks the grave of his predecessor and spiritual mentor with the delicately chiseled Hebrew epitaph:

Here lies buried the holy ark, his holiness—our master, teacher, and rabbi. Light of the world. The crown-glory of the Jewish people. He performed the righteousness of God and His Laws for the Jewish people. He turned many away from sin. Our teacher and rabbi, Yosef Yitzchak, the only son of his holiness—our master, teacher, and rabbi—the godly scholar, saintly one, and ascetic, Rabbi Sholom Dov Baer, of blessed memory, of Lubavitch. He ascended to the heavens on the holy Sabbath, the 10th of Shevat in the year 5710 from Creation. The glory and strength of Israel, and the one who loved it.

Standing facing the headstone, the Rebbe opens a small Hebrew prayer book of psalms and biblical verses. He recites the prayers, though his words cannot be heard outside the wooden shelter. After some time has passed, he opens the large bag. It holds hundreds of recent letters and hand-carried notes, and the Rebbe reads them one by one. Each request from a Jew bears its author's Hebrew name and that of his or her mother, living or not. In the transcendent world, Hasidim believe, this information establishes the soul's link to earthly existence.

Most of the petitions are written in Hebrew, but many other languages are represented. Many are concerned with the personal issues of health, family matters, and livelihood: "I, Samuel, son of Leah, pray that my child David will recover quickly and fully from his illness." Or, "I, Rivkah, daughter of Malkah, pray that my husband and I will be blessed with a child." Or, "I, Sholom, son of Rachel, pray that my son Benjamin will prosper in his business."

Though the Rebbe never says so explicitly, most Lubavitchers believe that at the Ohel he is surely communicating with the departed soul of their previous leader. But, they emphasize, it is God who answers all prayers. The souls of the ascended righteous merely serve as intermediaries, being closer, as it were, to the divine realm.

Though the Rebbe himself discourages such talk, his adherents have for decades circulated countless anecdotes of their leader's uncanny abilities as the primary exponent of Judaism for our generation. Generally, senior Lubavitchers downplay these stories as a trivialization of his essence as a moral exemplar without equal. But they do not deny the truthfulness of accounts that portray Rabbi Menachem Schneerson as the possessor of supernal insights on humanity's grand destiny and our own lives within that scheme.

After nearly seven hours standing at the grave, the Rebbe is ready to return to Crown Heights. He puts the petitions within the concrete structure above the grave and enters his car. Flanked once more by police vehicles, the car swiftly makes its way out of the cemetery.

For more than forty years, the Rebbe has been coming here regularly. Originally his visits coincided with traditional Hebrew or Chabad holidays and took place several times each month, but recently, he has been coming as often as three times a week as well as continuing the previous holiday visits. No Lubavitcher claims to understand the Rebbe's spiritual motives in this matter, but to all who know well his relentlessly demanding schedule, the fact that he spends so many hours here is proof of its tremendous importance to him. These lengthy visits are a clear indication of the mystical foundation of the entire Lubavitch movement.

Rabbi Menachem Schneerson responds personally—either through direct answer relayed by his secretaries, or simply through prayer—to literally tens of thousands of petitions each year from people all over the world. Many are not Hasidic, and not a few are non-Jewish. But they all turn to him as an intercessor capable of imparting inspired guidance to their lives. This is an awesome responsibility for one dedicated to true spiritual leadership, and it was perhaps for this reason that Rabbi Menachem Schneerson at first refused to accept the position of Rebbe upon his father-in-law's death in January 1950.

Though most Chabad Hasidim shared a high regard for Rabbi Samarius Gourary—the previous Rebbe's older son-in-law—few saw him as filling the role of global leader, and by midsummer of 1950 the consensus among most Chabad Hasidim was that Rabbi Schneerson was in fact already their next Rebbe. One Hasid wrote in his diary, "Everyone over here asks him questions on both material and spiritual matters. Day by day, people come to him, and day and night, he answers them clearly, without hemming and hawing, on things that literally involve life and death. He is asked things that cannot be determined by logic alone. Yet he answers them all with very definite guidance."

On the first anniversary of the previous Rebbe's demise, Rabbi Menachem Mendel Schneerson formally agreed to serve as the seventh Lubavitcher Rebbe.

He unquestionably shared his father-in-law's conviction that Chabad Hasidism had a unique mission to accomplish for Jews everywhere and all humanity as well, and initiated no major or even minor shifts in central policy. Besides consolidating the efforts his father-in-law had begun to provide outreach to Jews in Morocco, Tunisia, and Israel, he also encouraged the establishment of Hebrew day schools in Argentina, Brazil, England, France, Italy, Australia, and other countries during his early years as Rebbe.

What was his aim? In a published interview of 1951, he commented, "It is a mistake if we conceive of the worldwide dispersal of the Jewish people as a catastrophe. As a matter of fact, this very lack of concentration of the remnants of our nation was the source of our salvation throughout the centuries of persecution and pogroms. Our history in exile is an unbroken chain of the emergence and disappearance of such centers in country after country. As the Jewish sun set in one land, it had already begun to rise in another. Providence has prepared a new home for traditional Judaism in this country, while the flames devoured the bastions of the strongest Jewish fortresses on the other side of the ocean."

What, specifically, did he see as the Lubavitcher role in rebuilding Judaism after the Holocaust? "The only way American Jewry can live up to its historic task is by self-sacrifice. Everyone must subordinate his own selfish interests and become a Jewish social being. This demands not only a spiritual redirection but a total change of tactics." He added

Orthodox Jewry up to this point has unfortunately concentrated upon defensive strategies. We were always worried lest we lose positions and strongholds. But we must take the initiative and wage an offensive. This, of course, takes courage, planning, vision, and the will to carry on despite the odds.

In an account published in *Commentary* during early 1957, Herbert Wiener described his personal audience with the Rebbe during these early years:

> It was after midnight when a young student ran into the outer office . . . at 770 Eastern Parkway in Brooklyn to announce that the visitor from California, who had flown in to consult with the Rebbe about a business problem, had just left. That meant it was my turn to see the Rebbe and, clutching my notebook, I hurried past several people whose appointments came after mine. Remembering that there are thousands who depend on the Rebbe for every major . . . decision in their lives, and that the worldwide spiritual network known as the Lubavitcher movement, its schools and charities and publications, all wait on the personal attention of this one man, I felt a bit guilty at taking up his time for the sake of a [magazine article]. I resolved not to stay long as I knocked at the door of his private office and entered.
>
> Rabbi Menachem Schneerson . . . was folding some papers at a desk in the far corner of a large, rather bare room. His fedora hat, neatly tailored frock coat, and carefully arranged tie, all black, set off the pallor of his face. The brim of his hat was bent, casting a shadow over his deep blue eyes, which looked with a direct but good-humored expression. . . . He shook my hand and motioned gently toward the chair by his desk, suggesting in a soft voice that I address him in English, although he would reply in Yiddish.
>
> Before I could begin my questions, he asked what kind of work I was engaged in and what I had studied. My notebook with its proposed questions remained closed and I found myself chatting freely about matters I had not expected to discuss. The Rebbe listened, nodding his head from time to time to indicate understanding, and gradually the sense of urgency I had felt in the hallway began to ebb away.

How did the Rebbe's wife, Chaya Moussia, react to her husband's twenty-hour days? No doubt she quickly adjusted to his heightened pace of activity for she had grown up witnessing her father's duties as Rebbe, and was trained from an early age to accept these as vital to Jewish and, ultimately, world betterment. Indeed, Chaya had vigorously urged her reluctant husband to become the seventh Lubavitch Rebbe after her father's death.

Gracious and courteous to everyone, Chaya saw her role as wholly subordinate to her husband's mission of Jewish leadership. In public, she always referred to him as "the Rebbe." When she relayed an answer from him to those seeking his guidance, she always repeated his exact wording and made sure that the listener knew it, invariably refusing either to interpret or elaborate upon his advice. She resisted efforts among the Lubavitchers to bestow public honors on her.

Her death early in 1988 was felt as a deep personal loss by the entire Lubavitch community and occasioned a massive demonstration of affection and regard as thousands came to their home in Crown Heights to share the Rebbe's sorrow and give comfort in his period of mourning.

Lubavitchers also marveled not only at his frequent all-night counseling marathons and his seemingly uncanny powers of discernment among those seeking his help, but also at the fact that he had never taken even a single day's vacation. Aside from three day trips in the late 1950s to visit a new Chabad children's camp in the Catskill Mountains, he had not once left the New York City vicinity since 1951. Nor had he the slightest predilection for acquiring material possessions. He and Chaya still lived modestly in their house near Eastern Parkway.

Such dedication attracted the first postwar generation of American Jews to Rabbi Schneerson's cause. As one midwestern rabbinic emissary today recollects, "I was not originally a Lubavitcher. I had gone to a yeshiva in the New York City area after leaving Minnesota in the mid-1950s, and started hearing more and more about the Lubavitcher Rebbe. He clearly seemed such a model of selflessness, with such remarkable devotion to Judaism, that I decided to enroll in their Crown Heights seminary. It was not easy for me, you must understand. It was one thing to read about great Jewish sages of history. That I could relate to, from my years of study. But to accept that there is such a person living in our own time: that was different. Yet, the more I learned about Lubavitch, the more I could see that it was true."

Although Rabbi Menachem Schneerson repeatedly claimed that his father-in-law retained his unique place as a leader of the Jewish world, his own style as Rebbe was certainly different. For one thing, his public discourses and correspondence concentrate almost entirely on philosophical and metaphysical concepts within Judaism, whereas those of the sixth Rebbe's were lightened by many historical anecdotes and stories.

Of great significance to the Lubavitchers, the present Rebbe is no less demanding of his many rabbinic emissaries. As one older Hasid remarks, "When you give the Rebbe a report about something you've done to advance Judaism, he may be pleased for a few moments. But he always moves on quickly to discuss what *hasn't* yet been accomplished." Through a series of specific "mitzvah campaigns" aimed at strengthening Jewish ritual observance everywhere, the Rebbe transmitted his zeal and urgency to thousands of followers. He also succeeded in impressing upon them the need to awaken greater Jewish study among all age groups, from young children through the elderly.

In late 1974 Rabbi Menachem Schneerson sharply curtailed his individual counseling, after he had already reduced such activity from three to two nights per week. To his dismayed followers, he explained: "Our movement has grown a thousandfold since the early 1950s. I cannot possibly perform the same services that I did when I began." After he suffered a heart attack in 1977—for which he insisted on home rather than hospital treatment—it was clear that he had to guard his health more carefully. Since then, advice has been sought by either mail or telephone, through the Rebbe's secretaries. At the same time, however, the Rebbe increased the frequency of his public celebrations, and since 1986, introduced the custom of bestowing blessings and dollar bills for charity every Sunday morning.

Summers in New York City are usually uncomfortable, and the heat wave this past week in mid-August has been especially unbearable. The highways out to Long Island and the New Jersey shore are already jammed with summer traffic heading for the beaches. On such days, Manhattan resembles a ghost town. Its famous skyline is nearly wholly obscured by haze and its usually teeming streets are now empty and still. The streets in the outer boroughs—the Bronx, Queens, Staten Island, and Brooklyn—silently shimmer in the heat and resemble a desolate scene in an Edward Hopper painting.

But on this particular Sunday here in Crown Heights, things look very different. In front of Lubavitch headquarters on Eastern Parkway, thousands of men and women stand separately in two very long lines that stretch all the way around onto Kingston Avenue, the adjoining side street. The line of women is slowly moving through the entrance to the Lubavitch world headquarters. The majority are not Lubavitchers. Most of the women are young and well-dressed. They are extremely relaxed in the hazy Brooklyn sunshine and chat quietly in small groups. Some hold infants in their arms, or gently rock carriages with small sleeping children. Since ten o'clock this morning, many of them have received a Hebrew blessing and a dollar bill to give to charity, symbolizing the holiness of charity in daily life. Only when all the women in line have met the Rebbe will he begin to see the men.

In the other line, which isn't moving at all, the men appear more restless. Their ages span three or even four generations; stooped and gnarled aged figures clasp the hands of preschool boys. Most are obviously not Hasidim. A few men carry briefcases, others are dressed very casually. Several carry airline flight bags with address labels for numerous American cities and distant countries. But despite their disparate backgrounds and residences, occupations and ages, manner of dress and foreign tongues, they—like the women—are united in purpose this morning—to experience a personal moment with the Lubavitcher Rebbe. Although in recent years Rabbi Menachem Schneerson has nearly discontinued formal private audiences, he has instituted a custom by which literally anyone willing to wait in line on a Sunday morning can meet him for a brief encounter.

In the line there is minimal jostling for position, and the mood is convivial. Everyone knows that he will get to meet the Rebbe, who will not leave for his regular visit to his predecessor's grave until he has seen every one of the men and women. They pass a row of wooden tables in which vendors who are not Lubavitchers are displaying trinkets with the Rebbe's picture. One of the Lubavitchers remarks, a bit ruefully, "Sometimes, I feel that this business of presenting the Rebbe in this way has got out of hand. We in Lubavitch certainly don't encourage it."

"But what about the portraits and photographs of the Rebbe that his followers hang in their homes and offices?" asks a visitor, now that the subject has been broached.

"The answer to that is simple. The custom started in the 1940s, when the previous Rebbe came to the United States. After the war, when some of his Hasidim were able to leave Russia for other countries in Europe, he wrote and asked that they send him photographs of their families. He hadn't seen them for many years, since he had been exiled from the country. One elder Hasid wrote back, somewhat perturbed, saying, 'Hasidim sending photographs of their families? Whoever heard of such a thing!' And the previous Rebbe answered, 'Here in America, everyone keeps photographs of their family and people whom they love. That's why I am requesting pictures of your families.' So we hang our Rebbe's portrait in our homes, because we admire and love him. But there's more than that, of course. His portrait helps us to remember that there's more to life than just ordinary, everyday existence. It reminds us that there's something higher to which we all can aspire."

Until recently the trinkets served another purpose: they were one of the only things that visiting Lubavitch emissaries to Russia could take to Jews waiting to get out of the country at a time when the Russian government wouldn't allow any of the Rebbe's published writings or tape-recorded talks to be brought into the country.

By now, the line has reached the entranceway. In the foyer, before his closed office door, stands the Rebbe, speaking softly in French to a middle-aged man. His words are inaudible several feet away, but the man in his tan raincoat with his flight bag beside him, has an imploring demeanor. The Rebbe offers advice and a blessing, accompanied by a crisp dollar bill. The man suddenly smiles, though weakly, and takes the bill. Then, reaching for his bag, he moves on.

Next comes a Hasidic father, carrying his young son, who is obviously neurologically handicapped. The father speaks earnestly in Yiddish to the Rebbe, who then turns to look at the boy. Their eyes meet and hold. Abruptly, the Rebbe breaks into a smile. Bestowing words of advice and à blessing upon son and father, the Rebbe hands each one a dollar bill for charity, patiently waiting for the smiling child to grasp the bill with his trembling hands.

Then an Israeli, perhaps in his late twenties, with a nervous, almost apologetic air, clutching a small paper speaks to the Rebbe, who looks at him closely, and after a moment's pause gently asks a question in Hebrew. The man stiffens and pales, his voice rises anxiously, and he begins speaking rapidly and somewhat disjointedly. The Rebbe nods and, extending his hand, accepts the paper and puts it down carefully on the table. He looks calmly at the man, who is less anxious now, and then bestows a blessing and a dollar. Holding the bill gingerly, the Israeli straightens up and leaves. His note will be opened and read by the Rebbe at the Ohel, as the grave of his predecessor is known. And so the line moves on as the number of waiting men on Eastern Parkway grows fewer and fewer.

The sleek, expensive automobiles parked alongside Lubavitch headquarters appear incongruous amid the aged tenements and row houses of Brooklyn's Crown Heights, but the residents are long familiar with such sights. Many are aware that today, less than a week before Yom Kippur, some of North America's wealthiest men and women have flown or driven here to meet with the Rebbe. Many are well-known to the national media, their names appear regularly in the financial sections of magazines and newspapers. Every year at this time, they come to participate in an annual gathering of major financial donors to Machne Israel, the Chabad social-service organization that the Rebbe has directed since the early 1940s.

The breakfast program at the Oholei Torah Center on Eastern Parkway features several Lubavitch emissaries followed by a young Soviet refusenik who finally obtained permission to emigrate to Israel this past year. In halting English that conveys an awkward sincerity, he praises the movement first for providing him with years of underground Jewish education and now for expediting his adjustment to Israeli society. Following this moving speech, Rabbi Avraham Shemtov, a Hassid with a full red beard and piercing eyes, makes an impassioned plea for help from his audience.

"We have more than one thousand Chabad institutions around the world now. Nearly every month, another one is opening. Whether in Hong Kong or Argentina, Switzerland or Australia, we are there to reach out to every Jew at every age. On a scale the world has never seen before, we have been bringing the light of Torah and our sages like Maimonides to tens of thousands, even youngsters, on every inhabited continent. But I don't have to relate everything Lubavitch is doing. By being here in this room this morning, you are making a commitment. You already know, of course, or else you wouldn't be here. With God's help, each of you has found his way to this moment. But let us aid others not yet aware of Lubavitch and what it does to find their way to this moment too. But if I told you the sacrifices that our emissaries make, the sacrifices of their families in far-off places of the globe, maybe you will spread the message. For what are they making these sacrifices? What do they get out of it? Nothing for themselves. Absolutely nothing. And yet, there is something. What is it? To serve their fellow Jews. To serve the Jewish people as agents of the Rebbe, who, by his own living example has inspired such devotion."

Rabbi Shemtov motions in the direction of Lubavitch headquarters across the street. "It is one man: the Rebbe, who inspires us. And in a few minutes, we will all be privileged to merit meeting with him as a group, and then as individuals. But let me tell you, from my own experience, I have known the Rebbe since I was a youth. My father was a Lubavitcher Hasid who came out of Russia and served the Rebbe as an emissary in England. And I tell you this: sometimes I looked at the Rebbe. But I wonder, did I really see him? Sometimes I listened. But I wonder, did I really hear him? And it has always been my fault, my mind and thoughts being elsewhere in his presence. It has never been the Rebbe—perish the thought—who was not fully there in the moment with me."

The audience listens intently as Rabbi Shemtov continues. "So when you meet with the Rebbe in just a few moments, and each of you will have the privilege of talking with him personally, I ask you: be sure that you are fully there for him, so that he can be fully there for you." He concludes his remarks with an appeal to their generosity, and then all disperse to Lubavitch headquarters.

Some fifteen minutes later, the group has reassembled in a large room on the ground floor. Many have been here before; but for a few it is the first visit and nearly all are genuinely excited, almost nervous with anticipation. Machne Israel's Development Fund Chairman, David Chase, makes some informal comments. He is a Holocaust survivor and is also ranked among *Forbes*'s four hundred wealthiest persons in the United States.

Suddenly, in a flurry of flashbulbs, the Rebbe enters the study room and moves to a lectern. His audience stands silently at attention as he speaks slowly in English for several minutes, and then repeats his remarks in Yiddish. "I may look like an old man," he says, "but I hope that my actions are youthful, for I have many new plans and projects in mind." He briefly highlights the importance of "spreading Torah and mitzvahs among the Jewish people dispersed throughout the world," and emphasizes that in this way, the Messiah "will come speedily in our time." Before addressing his audience in Yiddish, he adds. "If you are not accustomed to hear this language, remember that it is what your mothers and grandmothers spoke."

One by one, each of the visitors is escorted by a Lubavitch emissary or local administrator to speak personally with the Rebbe for a couple of minutes. A few are joined by their wives, and they hand him small papers for his later reading and prayer at the Ohel. He smiles broadly at some, seemingly engrossed in light conversation about their family celebrations, like weddings, the birth of a child, or bar mitzvahs. Others relate more sobering matters of a personal nature. The Rebbe is fully attentive to everyone, his manner unhurried.

Soon after, the black limousines are gliding out of Crown Heights and carrying their passengers to metropolitan New York City's sprawling airports, towering office buildings, or more distant destinations. For them the occasion is over.

But Rabbi Menachem Schneerson will not be resting. Despite his advanced years, his decades of leadership and devoted Torah scholarship, rest for him is unthinkable until he realizes his goal of inspiring Jews everywhere and all humanity to attain the spiritual heights of unending joy and harmony.

It is a stirring image, one which the Lubavitcher fully recognize will involve tremendous effort to attain. The extent of the challenge is nowhere better exemplified than in the new frontier of American society, the state of California.

II

WESTWOOD, LOS ANGELES

*A soul may descend to this world and live a lifetime of seventy or eighty years,
for the sole purpose of doing a favor for another, materially or spiritually.*

—The Baal Shem Tov,
founder of Hasidism

THE SKY OVER THE CITY IS ALREADY FILLED WITH HAZE AND
smog, yet the air feels invigorating; in the distance rises
the gleaming steel-and-glass skyline of Los Angeles. Across the street
from the sprawling UCLA campus in the Westwood section stands an
attractive new five-story half-timbered building, its façade an exact
replica of Lubavitch headquarters in Crown Heights, with a small sign
in front that reads "Chabad House." In a top-floor office, gazing out the
window while waiting for his first meeting of the day, sits Rabbi Shlomo
Cunin, a boyish-faced man of forty-nine. At this early hour of the day
he sees only a lone cyclist and two or three students ambling along the
outskirts of campus.

Shlomo Cunin's office is pleasant and comfortable. A big mahog-
any desk is almost overflowing with reports, brochures, memos, and
publicity releases—the essence of contemporary organizational life and
scarcely unusual. But one striking feature of the room identifies the
nature of the enterprise. On the rear wall, facing a black couch and a

coffee table, hangs an impressive portrait of a bearded, patriarchal figure with an intense, determined expression: Rabbi Menachem M. Schneerson. Shlomo Cunin, the Lubavitch West Coast director in the United States, is one of the Rebbe's thousands of emissaries who have devoted their lives to promulgating traditional Judaism.

After morning prayers in the large third-floor synagogue end at 7:30 am, Rabbi Cunin allots his usual half hour to religious study before the start of his twelve-hour working day. He reviews the biblical section for the week together with some of the classic commentaries. Next he considers a Hasidic treatise on the struggle for inner perfection. He only has time to scan the latest printed discourse of the Rebbe before Rabbi Chaim Dalfin enters the office.

Rabbi Dalfin has flown up from San Francisco's suburban Marin County for a few days' visit, and has several matters to discuss with Cunin, the busy administrator for ninety Lubavitcher rabbis involved with more than forty separate Hasidic institutions in California. These include a fast-growing array of Hebrew day schools and synagogues, adult-education programs, summer camps, and social-service agencies. The two men have not seen each other for several months and briefly exchange pleasantries and news about their families. Rabbi Cunin proudly mentions the birth of his third grandchild, and recounts his recent trip to Crown Heights, the Lubavitch headquarters in New York City. Though he has served the Jewish community in Los Angeles for twenty-five years, Shlomo Cunin has lost little of the accent and rapid-fire speech of his native Bronx.

"And how are things 'up north?'" he asks the younger man. Chaim Dalfin shrugs, smiling. Like many regions of California, Marin County across the Golden Gate Bridge from San Francisco, has sprouted tremendously in recent years and has long been satirized in the popular media as the center of America's countercultural trends and fads—from health foods and encounter groups to hot tubs and open marriage. During the 1970s, it seemed that scarcely a month passed without some new movie, novel, or comic strip ridiculing Marin's indolent inhabitants as they sought sensual perfection or enlightenment among its quiet cafés and leafy redwood hills. If California was rightly called "a state of mind" in those days, then the hilly towns overlooking San Francisco Bay were its quintessence.

But during the mid-1980s San Francisco became a major financial center of the West Coast and an entire downtown area of high-rise office buildings went up almost overnight. This development, coupled with an acute regional housing shortage, quickly drew Marin County into the city's ever-widening commuting orbit. Though remnants of the relaxed countercultural mood linger in places, increasingly clogged roads now link residential areas and shopping malls, as thousands of young families have moved into their new neighborhoods.

Among them have been many Jews, drawn to new professional and business opportunities in the San Francisco area. Many have moved from elsewhere on the West Coast; some are originally from the Midwest or the East Coast. Common to nearly all of them, apart from their college backgrounds and affluence, is a minimal involvement with Judaism. It was to alter this situation that idealistic young Chaim Dalfin left New York.

Since his arrival in 1985, Rabbi Dalfin has led Jewish study courses and traditional services at his home in an unincorporated section of San Rafael. Attendance has steadily grown, and it seemed that the Rabbi's home study center might be expanded. Then, suddenly, he was notified that the local homeowner association had filed a complaint with the Marin County Planning Commission on the grounds that he was breaching county ordinances by using a private home for public activities. Drawing upon Hasidic teaching, Chaim Dalfin decided to see the complaint as serving a higher end. It spurred him to postpone expansion no longer, but to purchase much larger and properly zoned premises immediately.

Within San Rafael he has found an attractive property known as the Nunes Ranch, a large, two-story house on a half-acre of land that lies on a main thoroughfare and had access to a nearby school parking lot. The purchase is scheduled to take place in a few days, and the two men are reviewing the financial details, as well as their future ideas for the site. They both hope that what was once the Nunes Ranch will become the focus for all Lubavitch outreach activities in both Marin County and in Sonoma County to its north. Besides the expansion of traditional Jewish classes and worship, their plans include the construction of the first *mikveh* (ritual bath) to be built in the region.

As Rabbi Cunin escorts Rabbi Dalfin to the elevator, it is nine o'clock, and most of the administrative and support staff are in the building. The switchboard is already busy, and messages on the fax machine are coming in from the Lubavitch network of centers throughout the USA and Europe. Rabbi Cunin returns to his office for his next appointment, with Dr. Susan Oppenheimer, the psychological director of Lubavitch's Homeless Program for Los Angeles.

Dr. Oppenheimer's office and the Homeless Program's residential unit are also housed in Chabad House, and she and Rabbi Cunin meet frequently to discuss administrative and other issues. Dr. Oppenheimer has instituted individual and group counseling as part of the rehabilitation provided for each participant in the Homeless Program. The residential program, now in its sixth year of operation, runs smoothly and has acquired a laudatory reputation among Jewish and nonsectarian agencies throughout the city. It has many more applicants than can be accommodated in the twenty-one-bed, sixty-day program in Westwood.

When the young Rabbi Cunin began his outreach work in Los Angeles upon the Rebbe's request in the late 1960s, he found himself confronted with the depressing problems of young Jewish men and women without any regular lodging. In the vernacular of twenty years ago, they were known as "street people," mainly casualties of the drug revolution. Now the problem seems far more serious and pervasive. Just after the Lubavitcher launched their Homeless project in 1985, the Jewish Federation Council Task Force on the Homeless estimated that each night there were as many as fifteen hundred Jews on the city's West Side streets: some 3 to 5 percent of the city's total homeless population.

Drawing upon two centuries of Hasidic philosophy and Jewish precepts about charity, the Lubavitchers have aimed at rehabilitation, not the fostering of dependence, among their clients. Outreach activists such as Rabbi Cunin strongly believe that true charity involves strengthening the recipient's self-worth and dignity through real accomplishment. Consequently, clients are given two meals a day and a clean, comfortable place to sleep, and are expected to be out looking for work by early morning, pursuing job leads discovered on their own initiative or supplied to them by staff. Not all those living on the streets possess sufficient mental stability for such self-direction, and Dr. Oppenheimer carefully selects those who can best benefit from the program.

Today's short meeting concerns the coming holidays of Rosh Hashanah and Yom Kippur. Though Rabbi Cunin seeks to avoid proselytizing, several clients have recently expressed a wish to attend services during the holidays, but lacking proper synagogue attire they feel embarrassed and reluctant to come. Cunin and Oppenheimer agree that suitable clothing should somehow be obtained, since participating in synagogue services will be a good boost for the clients' self-image. Rabbi Cunin can think of several retailers who might be willing to donate clothing and he jots down a reminder as Dr. Oppenheimer leaves to direct a group counseling session downstairs.

Pausing a few minutes to consult his day's schedule, Cunin returns a phone call from his son Mendel, a rabbinic student in Buenos Aires. Mendel reports that a young Jewish man he knows will be flying tomorrow morning to Alaska, with an afternoon stop-over in Los Angeles. Would it be possible for a Lubavitch staff member to meet the man at the airport and take him for a friendly kosher lunch in town? No problem at all, says the elder Cunin. If he can make time tomorrow, he promises Mendel, he'll escort the man himself.

Next, Cunin receives a call from Rabbi Manis Friedman, Lubavitch's educational director in Minnesota. The two discuss the arrangements for a talk Rabbi Friedman will be giving to UCLA students and faculty entitled "Love and Intimacy: A Hasidic Perspective." For many years, Lubavitchers in Los Angeles have sponsored lectures and cultural events for Jews on local college campuses, and their Minnesota colleague has proved a popular speaker. The talk is scheduled for a weekday evening during Chanukah in December, and Cunin and Friedman make tentative plans to meet when both will be visiting Crown Heights in several weeks' time. Like many Lubavitch emissaries, the two are frequent travelers, especially to the Rebbe's headquarters where they both hear his inspiring discourses and participate in the synagogue services he leads.

It is now past midmorning and Rabbi Cunin has scheduled two visits to local Lubavitch programs before returning to his office to finish the day's work. With his young colleague Rabbi Mendel Fogelman driving, the car heads for the Beverlywood section of town. Even though the rush hour is officially over, traffic soon slows to a standstill and the two discuss the Rebbe's latest printed discourse. This week's talk contains several references to the coming of the Messiah and the necessity for individual Jews everywhere to hasten the event through greater devotion to religious study and observance. Though both enjoy administrative problem-solving, the subtleties of Hasidic philosophy still occupy the most important place in their busy lives.

Suddenly, Rabbi Cunin's car phone rings. The caller is Jerry Weintraub, the Hollywood film producer of several box-office hits including *The Karate Kid* series. Since 1980, Rabbi Cunin's staff have hosted a highly successful annual telethon to raise funds for Lubavitch nonsectarian humanitarian programs, and Jerry Weintraub has become informal chairperson of this well-publicized event. Though neither Hasidic nor Orthodox, Weintraub openly explains, he became a committed ally after undergoing a mystical experience in the Rebbe's presence during synagogue prayers a few years ago. (Interestingly, many other worldly figures have privately reported similar encounters with the Lubavitcher leader.) For the past few years, the telethon has been broadcast throughout the United States on local cable-television channels, and has featured such prominent entertainers as Bob Hope, Richard Dreyfuss, Elliott Gould, Jon Voight, Whoopi Goldberg, Lionel Ritchie, and Bob Dylan. With his connections to the Hollywood entertainment community Weintraub has been an invaluable supporter of the Lubavitchers' California social-service programs.

Cunin and Weintraub discuss the theme of the approaching telethon, which usually lasts seven hours and takes place on the Sunday between Rosh Hashanah and Yom Kippur. They also discuss which celebrities might still be available at this late date to confirm an appearance on the show. Weintraub promises to make a few more calls and contact Rabbi Cunin by Monday.

Traffic has let up somewhat on the Santa Monica Freeway, and before long, Shlomo Cunin and Mendel Fogelman have arrived at the Lubavitch Residential Drug Treatment Center for Men, a large, one-story institutional structure in Beverlywood. The neighborhood of run-down homes on tiny plots of land is very different from UCLA's sophisticated Westwood area, but its streets seem safe enough at this hour.

With its thirty-two beds, the Center is the only Jewish-sponsored facility of its kind in the United States. Rabbi Cunin greets the clients enthusiastically as he is shown inside by Dr. Stephen Bailey, clinical director of the program. A bearded man in his forties, Dr. Bailey looks like an archetypal psychologist except for the knit yarmulke perched on his head. A former tenured professor at the University of Maryland, Dr. Bailey has served in this capacity since 1979, when the residential drug-treatment program, then in its infancy, occupied a dilapidated three-bedroom house and was largely a bootstrap operation. At first, the addicts had been housed in the Lubavitch's administrative center in Westwood where the rabbinic staff had naively assumed that all that their clients needed was old-fashioned Jewish affection and caring. One morning, however, they found that all the typewriters in the building had been stolen, apparently by the clients to purchase drugs.

Far more horrifying was the burning to the ground of the entire center. Three of the young men undergoing drug rehabilitation died in the fire, which police considered to have been started deliberately. Emotionally and financially, nearly fifteen years of struggle seemed to have gone for naught. The same year the clients were temporarily moved to the three-bedroom facility and Rabbi Cunin started the annual fund-raising telethon that now supports the Center, as well as the Lubavitcher Homeless Program in Los Angeles and the new women's residential drug-treatment program.

At today's luncheon meeting, Shlomo Cunin, Dr. Bailey, and administrator Dennis Brown once again discuss arrangements for the coming High Holy Day. Though nearly all the clients are Jewish, most come from nonobservant families and have had little previous exposure to traditional Judaism. As with Lubavitch's residential program for the homeless, Rabbi Cunin and his staff are careful to avoid urging religion on the recipients of their help. (More than a third of the clinical staff of counselors, psychologists, and social workers are non-Jewish, but in a house where all food is strictly kosher and where there are no formal activities on Saturdays, and since both the clinical director and the administrator are clearly Orthodox, it is not difficult for some clients to become interested in heightening their own Jewish identity.) As usual, Dennis Brown, who became a Lubavitcher Hasid several years ago, will be inviting several interested residents who have attained "privilege" level to a pre-Rosh Hashanah dinner in his home, and will then escort them to synagogue services.

Shlomo Cunin has a few minutes left and strides down the hall to chat with Stanley Goldstein, director of Project Pride. Goldstein has directed Lubavitch's national nonsectarian drug-education program since it started in 1986. Under his supervision the small staff has put together a package of printed materials and videotapes distributed through the Lubavitch network of twenty Project Pride centers across the United States. These materials, already translated into half a dozen languages, include coloring books for young children, though most of the booklets are aimed at adolescents and young adults. They carry the message: you can avoid succumbing to drugs as a means to "feel good," if you keep yourself emotionally balanced by practicing honest communication, rational decision-making, and stress-management techniques. Besides such national distribution work, Project Pride staff based in Los Angeles provide dozens of yearly classroom presentations about drugs for public and Hebrew day-school children.

Goldstein is organizing another training seminar on drug education for Lubavitch rabbis around the United States, and he and Cunin briefly discuss logistical issues. The seminars typically take place at an Orthodox Jewish seminary in Morristown, New Jersey; Project Pride's last seminar drew more than a hundred Lubavitch rabbis and inspired several to obtain public grants for their drug-education efforts. Cunin inquires whether certain emissaries have yet participated in Project Pride, and encourages Goldstein to contact them again.

Cunin sees that he is getting behind schedule, for he has one more important visit to make before returning to Westwood: to inspect the newly opened Lubavitch Drug Rehabilitation Center for Women, located in distant Culver City.

While the Lubavitch car crawls through the midday traffic jam on the Santa Monica Freeway Shlomo Cunin converses on the car phone with rabbinic emissaries in Berkeley, Stanford, and San Diego, to discuss their campus plans for Rosh Hashanah and Yom Kippur. While new Lubavitch centers—known as "Chabad Houses"—have opened at several colleges across California in recent years, there has generally been a decline in student interest in nonacademic activities, including religious involvement. The emissaries agree on the need to generate more publicity and to pool their resources in order to do so.

Rabbi Cunin next phones the coordinator of Lubavitch's newest center planned for California, in the exclusive community of Bel Air. Because the area consists solely of private houses, no zoning for a synagogue or educational center would be permitted and Cunin has authorized the renting of a tennis club for Saturday religious services. Since he knows several famous Bel Air residents, Shlomo Cunin is optimistic that the Hasidic presence will be well received in the wealthy community.

The Chabad Women's Center for Drug Rehabilitation has just opened this week, and Rabbi Cunin is making his first appearance. Although the Culver City facility is modeled along the lines of the successful men's residential program in Beverlywood, it differs in one major respect: it is entirely privately funded. This means that Orthodox Jewish—even Hasidic—content can be explicitly included in the daily treatment routine, which is not permitted in the publicly funded men's program. The Culver City staff are still in the middle of admissions. As Shlomo Cunin enters the lobby he notices a haggard woman, apparently a potential resident, nervously sitting beside her teenage son.

"Do you have anything to do with this place?" she asks him anxiously.

"A little," he replies noncommittally.

"Who are you?" she sharply asks.

He looks at her pallid complexion and drawn expression for a moment. "Oh, I'm one of the rabbis," he slowly answers.

"You must have a very low opinion of me, then," she says, as her son frowns, glancing at the floor.

"Not necessarily," she hears, quietly spoken. "We don't know what we would look like in your shoes."

"I would like to tell you that both my parents were graduates of the Auschwitz concentration camp. I can't remember a single night from my childhood when my mother didn't lie awake crying. And I, a child, had to comfort her, instead of her comforting me. And my father would come home every night so crazy that he'd slap me without reason. I'm not saying this justifies why I became a drug addict, but it may help you to know something about me."

Rabbi Cunin excuses himself for a moment, and goes out to his car. He returns holding Sabbath candles. "Have you ever lit these?" he asks her gently.

"No," the woman replies a bit self-consciously. "I was raised without religion because of the Holocaust background of my parents. Because of their bitterness."

Cunin reassures her that nobody could blame them. Then he places the candles before her and explains the reason for lighting them, and the accompanying Hebrew blessing. They talk for a few more minutes and she agrees to light the candles for the next Sabbath.

Rabbi Cunin spends the next two hours meeting staff and clients at the Center. His warm manner seems to animate everyone. A little later Dr. Bailey arrives from Beverlywood and there is a palpable air of enthusiasm that the long-awaited opening has finally come. One of the key topics of staff discussion is how best to publicize the new residential program. Rabbi Cunin is able to tell them that he has already been working on this challenge: he has funded the printing of a quarter of a million copies of their annual telethon magazine which carries the news. One hundred and fifty thousand will be circulated in southern California; the rest will be sent to Lubavitch headquarters in New York City for distribution on the East Coast and in the Midwest.

The freeways back to Westwood are especially busy on the return journey, and Rabbi Cunin seizes the opportunity to make several phone calls. He chats with his wife about the day's activities, then with screen actor Jon Voight about details for the coming telethon. Though he is not Jewish, Voight has become one of Rabbi Cunin's most loyal supporters and the two men are now personally close. They exchange news about mutual acquaintances in the entertainment community.

On their return journey, Cunin and Fogelman resume their earlier discussion of the Rebbe's recent discourse in which they agree he has specifically encouraged his followers to foster the utmost joy in their lives. "We are close to the end of the present Hebrew year. Now, nothing in this world is coincidental. Everything is guided by the hand of God. This is especially true in all aspects of Torah, even Jewish customs recognized by the Torah. Since the Hebrew letters denoting this year are connected with the subject of joy, it follows that this year's general theme has been one permeated with joy. As we approach the new year, we need to take with us this year's theme: joy! Let us call upon all Jews to increase their religious devotion and joyousness in order to bring the Messiah!"

By the time they have analyzed the implications of the Rebbe's emphasis on joy as the key to redemption, they are back at Lubavitch's Westwood headquarters and Rabbi Cunin is handed a stack of phone messages and fax transmissions. Several of the latter concern pressing budgetary and financial matters. Money is a never-ending source of worry for him, and he glances with dismay at some of the bills. But taking strength from the Rebbe's recent remarks, he deals with the mass of paperwork for the next couple of hours. Glancing at his wristwatch, he sees that it is now just after seven o'clock, and dials the familiar phone number of Lubavitch headquarters in Brooklyn. As he afterwards explains to a visitor, "I listen to the Rebbe's prayers by live hookup every weekday evening here. This practice originated only a few months ago, after the Rebbe's wife passed away and the synagogue couldn't accommodate everyone who wanted to pray with him as a mourner." He adds that Lubavitch centers around the globe, not just his own office in Los Angeles, are linked for the services.

A few minutes later Rabbi Cunin is ready to go home. He grabs a sheaf of papers, including copies of several recently issued public talks and letters from the Rebbe to his worldwide followers. Looking up for a moment, Shlomo Cunin sees that the sky has started to darken over the sprawling city. A couple of stars are already visible, and he is glad his day is over after only thirteen hours of work. With the national telethon soon approaching and several new Lubavitch centers opening throughout California, there will be much to accomplish tomorrow.

Rabbi Menachem Mendel Schneerson

The Early Years

The present Lubavitcher Rebbe, in his forties.

The Rebbe as a child in Russia.

The Bridge Between Generations

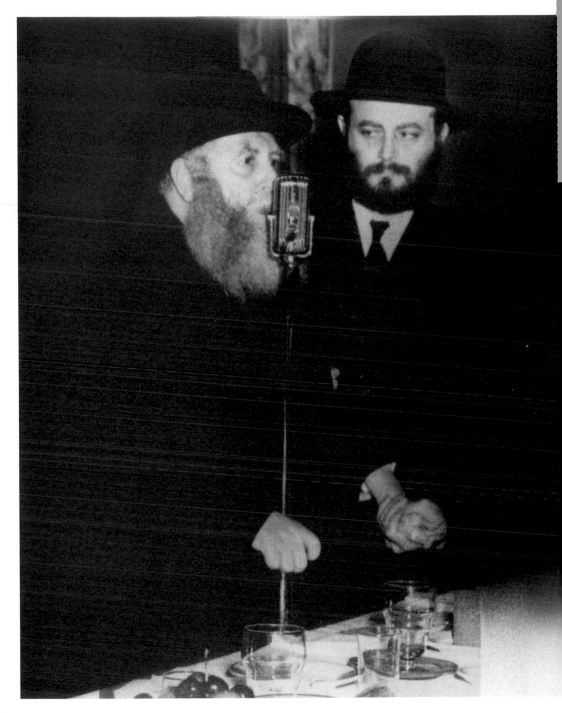

The Rebbe in the 1940s, supporting his father-in-law, Rabbi Yosef Yitzchak Schneersohn

Four Rebbes of the Lubavitch Dynasty

Rabbi Shneur Zalman of Ladi, 1745–1812

Rabbi Menachem Mendel, 1789–1866

Rabbi Sholem Dov Ber, 1860–1920

Rabbi Yosef Yitzchak Schneersohn, 1880–1950

The Rebbe in Action

The Rebbe distributes coins for children to give to charity.

(Below left) The Rebbe with former President of Israel, Zalman Shazar

(Below right) The Rebbe with Rabbi Adin Steinsaltz [Evan-Yisrael]

The Rebbe and former Prime Minister of Israel Menachem Begin

A Farbrengen at Lubavitch Headquarters in Crown Heights, New York

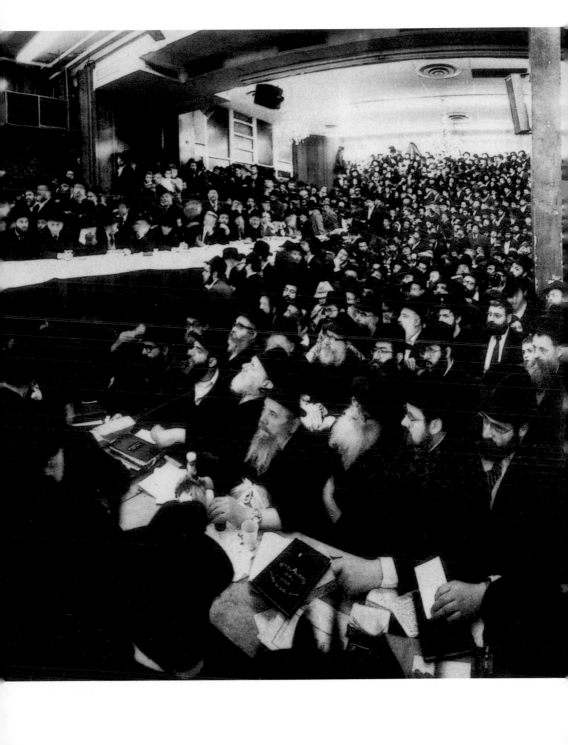

Lubavitch Centers around the World

Chabad–Lubavitch World Headquarters in Brooklyn, New York

Chabad–Lubavitch Headquarters of the United Kingdom in London, England

Chabad–Lubavitch Center in El Paso, Texas

Bet Rivkah Seminary Campus in Paris, France

Chabad-Lubavitch Center in Houston, Texas.

Chabad House School and Yeshiva Gedolah, in Yeoville, Johannesburg, South Africa

Actor Jon Voight at the auction of the annual Lubavitch telethon in California

Chabad counselor and new arrival at the Los Angeles program for the homeless

Education Day
Dedication

Education Day, U.S.A., 1989 and 1990

By the President of the United States of America

A Proclamation

Ethical values are the foundation for civilized society. A society that fails to recognize or adhere to them cannot endure.

The principles of moral and ethical conduct that have formed the basis for all civilizations come to us, in part, from the centuries-old Seven Noahide Laws. The Noahide Laws are actually seven commandments given to man by God, as recorded in the Old Testament. These commandments include prohibitions against murder, robbery, adultery, blasphemy, and greed, as well as the positive order to establish courts of justice.

Through the leadership of Rabbi Menachem Schneerson and the worldwide Lubavitch movement, the Noahide Laws—and standards of conduct duly derived from them—have been promulgated around the globe.

It is fitting that we honor Rabbi Schneerson and acknowledge his important contributions to society. Our great Nation takes just pride in its dedication to the principles of justice, equality, and truth. Americans also understand that we have a responsibility to inspire the same dedication in future generations. We owe a tremendous debt to Rabbi Schneerson and to all those who promote education that embraces moral and ethical values and emphasizes their importance.

In recognition of Rabbi Schneerson's vital efforts, and in celebration of his 87th birthday, the Congress, by House Joint Resolution 173, has designated April 16, 1989, and April 6, 1990, as "Education Day, U.S.A." and has authorized and requested the President to issue an appropriate proclamation in observance of these days.

NOW, THEREFORE, I, GEORGE BUSH, President of the United States of America, do hereby proclaim April 16, 1989, and April 6, 1990, as Education Day, U.S.A. I invite Governors from every State and Territory, community leaders, teachers, and all Americans to observe these days through appropriate events and activities.

IN WITNESS WHEREOF, I have hereunto set my hand this fourteenth day of April, in the year of our Lord nineteen hundred and eighty-nine, and of the Independence of the United States of America the two hundred and thirteenth.

Gy Bush

Presenting a Chanukah Menorah to President Bush

Rabbi Feller observing afternoon class at Bais Chana in St. Paul, Minnesota

Rabbi Manis Friedman, Principal of Bais Chana

Farbrengen for women at Lubavitch Headquarters in New York

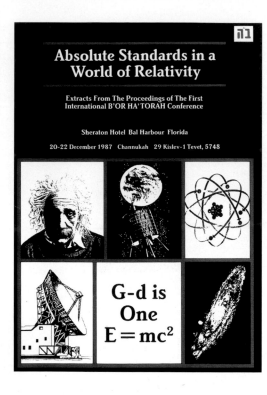

Absolute Standards in a World of Relativity

Extracts From The Proceedings of The First
International B'OR HA'TORAH Conference

Sheraton Hotel Bal Harbour Florida

20-22 December 1987   Channukah   29 Kislev-1 Tevet, 5748

G-d is
One
$E = mc^2$

Program from First
International B'or Ha'torah
Science Conference in Bal
Harbour, Florida

Some of the distinguished B'or
Ha'torah speakers

<table>
<tr><td colspan="4">THE   B'OR   HA'TORAH   CONFERENCE</td></tr>
<tr><td colspan="4">PARTICIPANTS</td></tr>
<tr><td>Education</td><td>Mrs. Laya Block
Director of Education</td><td>Author/Lecturer</td><td>Rabbi Nissan Mangel
Educator, Translator of Classics</td></tr>
<tr><td>Philosophy</td><td>Prof. Yitzhak Block
University of Western Ontario</td><td>Author/Lecturer</td><td>Rabbi Zalman Posner
Author, Translator of Classic Chassidic Texts</td></tr>
<tr><td>Physics</td><td>Prof. Herman Branover
Ben Gurion University</td><td>Physics</td><td>Dr. Avi Rabinowitz
Ben Gurion University</td></tr>
<tr><td>Physics</td><td>Prof. Cyril Domb
Bar Ilan University</td><td>Education</td><td>Mrs. Miriam Rhodes
Lecturer in Education</td></tr>
<tr><td>Biology</td><td>Dr. Aryeh Gotfryd
University of Toronto</td><td>Mathematics</td><td>Prof. Paul Rosenbloom
Columbia University</td></tr>
<tr><td>Psychiatry</td><td>Dr. Miriam Grossman
Child Psychiatrist</td><td>Artificial Intelligence</td><td>Dr. Zvi Saks
Carnegie Mellon</td></tr>
<tr><td>Mathematics</td><td>Prof. Avraham Hasofer
University of New South Wales</td><td>Philosophy</td><td>Prof. George Schlesinger
University of North Carolina</td></tr>
<tr><td>Applied Technology</td><td>Mr. Peter Kalms
Solmecs Corporation</td><td>Author/Lecturer</td><td>Rabbi Dr. Immanuel Schochet
University of Toronto</td></tr>
<tr><td>Sociology</td><td>Dr. Menachem Kovacs
Montgomery College</td><td>Economics</td><td>Dr. Meir Tamari
Bar Ilan University</td></tr>
<tr><td>Education</td><td>Rabbi Sholem D. Lipskar
Rabbi - Educator - The Shul - Aleph Institute</td><td>Biology</td><td>Prof. Eliezer Zeiger
University of California Santa Cruz</td></tr>
</table>

Participants at the
Conference

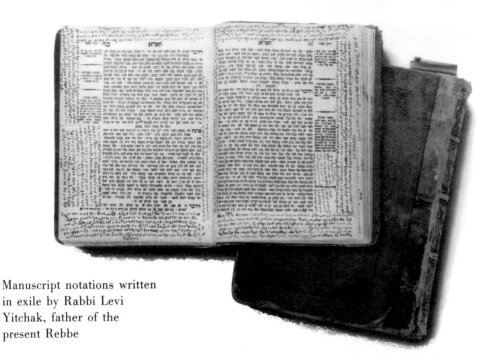

Manuscript notations written
in exile by Rabbi Levi
Yitchak, father of the
present Rebbe

Schoolroom in Leningrad synagogue

A Russian student.

Rabbi Mendel Futerfass, a renowned Chasidic elder, conducts a farbrengen

Prime Minister Shamir at Satec with Josef Gutnick.

Convoy of Mitvah tanks

Chabad soldiers in the Yom Kippur War of 1973

The Rebbe observes a Lag B'omer parade near Lubavitch World Headquarters in Brooklyn, New York.

III

WALLS OF IVY

No two persons have the same abilities. Each one should work in the service of God according to his own talents. If an individual tries to imitate another, he merely loses the opportunity to do good through his own merit.

—The Baal Shem Tov

FAR ABOVE LAKE CAYUGA IN ITHACA, IN PASTORAL CENTRAL NEW York State, Rabbi Elie Silberstein is steadily climbing a steep hill toward Cornell University. It is a location far removed in every way from the high-voltage glitter of Los Angeles, but the Lubavitchers deem it no less important in their devotion to promoting traditional Judaism throughout the Jewish world.

Silberstein pauses to catch his breath for a moment, then continues his ascent. Although he has been a Lubavitch emissary in Ithaca for five years, he still finds that the hilly terrain affords him more than ample daily exercise. Glancing at his watch, the energetic young Hasid sees that the faculty luncheon he is sponsoring will not begin for another half-hour, but he does not want to be late. Relentlessly hardworking, he has built up a reputation for reliability in his work: bolstering religious self-identity among the thousands of Jews associated with Cornell University and Ithaca College, as well as those in the local township.

Autumn arrives early this far north, and the trees have already changed color. A few students can be seen ambling on the hill below and an occasional car can be heard, but the Ithaca landscape is quiet and rural, far from Elie Silberstein's native city of Antwerp, Belgium, and far, too, from the noisy pavements of Brooklyn, where he obtained his Lubavitch rabbinic training. Soon after being ordained, he was invited by the Lubavitch regional director in Buffalo to establish the first Chabad House in this scenic, college community among the Finger Lakes.

Though young Rabbi Silberstein originally knew nothing of up-state New York, he knew a great deal about Chabad Houses including the fact that they had first been organized in the late 1960s, when the Lubavitcher Rebbe had decided that the time was right to initiate Hasidic outreach on America's college campuses. Too many Jewish youngsters seemed to be floundering spiritually, the Rebbe had declared. Cast adrift from their tradition, they were losing direction and becoming attracted to destructively shallow values. "Today, we must strengthen the spiritual equilibrium of our youth, and such is the psyche of every Jew that the only way to accomplish this is through religious study and practice. Jews cannot survive in a life devoid of Torah, just as fish cannot live without water."

Inspired by the Rebbe's message, a new generation of largely American-born Lubavitch emissaries began opening Chabad Houses. Since the early 1970s, literally scores of such locally administered and decentralized centers for Jewish study and prayer had been established in such places as Ann Arbor, Berkeley, Buffalo, Columbus, Denver, Milwaukee, Phoenix, and Pittsburgh to serve communities and universities with significant Jewish populations.

Starting a Chabad House is a very demanding job, reflecting the Rebbe's view that each such operation must be as locally oriented as possible to become truly effective. Seed money would certainly be given to Rabbi Silberstein, but he would have to do most of the fund-raising himself in wholly unfamiliar territory.

Financial problems were not the only ones. There was no Hasidic, or even Orthodox Jewish, community living within the Finger Lakes, an industrially abandoned region whose aging, predominantly rural population was struggling to survive economically. The Silberstein family would therefore have a lonely life; they would not have a single religiously observant neighbor within sixty miles. Furthermore in a few years, Elie Silberstein and his wife, Chana, would be confronted with another, even greater, difficulty—one facing many Chabad House emissaries: securing adequate daily Jewish education for their children.

Uncertain whether to accept the invitation from Buffalo, Rabbi Silberstein wrote to the Rebbe for advice. Although by then the Rebbe had delegated most administrative details to others in the Hasidic movement, within fifteen minutes of receiving Silberstein's anxious letter, he returned his message: "Take the position without delay." Silberstein took the Rebbe's unusually swift reply to mean that he viewed the new outreach post as extremely important.

Arriving along with thousands of undergraduates in the fall of 1984, the Silbersteins felt that they needed to be sufficiently close to Cornell's campus for Jewish students to be able to walk easily to the Chabad House on Sabbaths and holidays, when mechanized travel is forbidden by Jewish Law. They quickly rented half a house in the student area known as Collegetown, a quiet, tree-lined section of small stores, student bars and restaurants, and wooden frame houses converted to apartments and furnished rooms.

From the beginning, the rabbinic directors of Chabad Houses have found certain programs particularly effective in drawing Jewish college students and faculty alike. Besides offering traditional worship services and lessons in classic subjects like the Talmud, Silberstein also attracted interest with his provocative lectures on the mystical aspects of Hasidism. He would often read aloud a Hasidic tale about the Baal Shem Tov or another Jewish historical luminary, and spirited group discussion would follow. Lubavitchers know that for those unfamiliar with the intricacies of Hasidic philosophy, such stories have long been the means of introduction to their evocative worldview.

Before long, Rabbi Silberstein began sponsoring leading scholars to lecture on Hasidic thought. One such presentation, on the meaning of Chanukah, by Professor Rabbi Immanuel Schochet of Toronto, attracted several dozen Cornell faculty. Inspired by this interest, Silberstein next initiated informal courses on contemporary social problems from a Hasidic perspective. When the name of New York City's controversial "subway vigilante," gunman Bernhard Goetz, dominated the mass media, Rabbi Silberstein taught a course entitled "Self-Defense in Jewish Law." Much to his delight, he learned that Cornell University's library director wished to videotape these presentations for their intellectual appeal. Encouraged by similar remarks, he and his small staff have begun publishing an annual Hasidic periodical for the Ithaca community.

Today's talk and faculty luncheon have been planned to coincide with the holiday period of Rosh Hashanah and Yom Kippur, and the Silbersteins have prepared the kosher meal themselves. Though Chana's two young children keep her busy, she also teaches classes at home on such subjects as "Women in the Jewish Tradition"—lecturing on biblical figures like Ruth and Esther. Academically, the month of September is probably the busiest time of year, and the group of fifteen is considerably smaller than the forty or fifty professors that Elie Silberstein usually draws to his Hasidic events on campus. As he enters Anabel Taylor Hall, the very archetype of a venerable, ivy-draped college building, Elie Silberstein greets his guests and soon begins his discourse.

The topic is a thorny one in Jewish thought: the famous passage in Genesis narrating the "binding of Isaac" by his father Abraham. It is a passage that Jews have read in synagogue each Rosh Hashanah for millennia, but which modern sensibilities cannot easily accept. Though the well-educated men and women at the luncheon have probably heard many philosophical interpretations of the challenging passage, none of the professors seems familiar with the Hasidic perspective. Weaving Talmudic commentary and legend with Hasidic exegesis, Rabbi Silberstein holds his audience's attention.

"We hear a lot of different ways to understand this section of the Torah," he says, "and, frankly, most of these are just nonsense. For example, some modern Jewish writers make a big deal out of the supposed fact that Isaac is a child of five or six when Abraham takes him into the wilderness. But the Talmudic sources clearly say that Isaac was thirty-seven years old. So that immediately changes our outlook at least somewhat, doesn't it?"

He pauses for a moment. "The Hasidic view is that the *akaidah* [Hebrew for "binding"] was actually Abraham's tenth and final spiritual test. In all his other tests, Abraham had shown tremendous devotion to God in his righteousness. But he was by nature a kindly and loving person. Such feeling came naturally to him; it was his inborn temperament, we might say. For this reason, Abraham's nine earlier spiritual tests weren't so significant—even the one involving his willingness to throw himself into a furnace rather than renounce his faith in God. The binding of Isaac was a much greater test, for Abraham had to transcend his basic kindly nature by being ready to sacrifice his son.

The faculty audience seems satisfied with Silberstein's discourse, and only one hand goes up. A literature professor asks, "How about the view that this account is supposed to teach the world that human sacrifice is wrong? After all, the Bible says that God commanded Abraham to take a ram and slaughter it, after he lets Isaac go."

Rabbi Silberstein shakes his head. "That is definitely not the Hasidic explanation. We are told elsewhere very specifically in the Torah that human sacrifice is forbidden. So we don't need this portion from Genesis to tell us that. Rather, what Hasidism wants us to learn from this account is that we can change our inborn nature—and overcome our ego—to serve our Creator. In our own era," Silberstein says pointedly, looking at a psychology professor sitting near him, "we tend to think: 'I'm born an angry person, or a bitter person. That's my nature. That's who I am. I can't change it.' But Hasidism teaches us differently—that no matter what kind of temperament we are born with, we can and should try to change it as Abraham did with his test involving Isaac, to better serve God in holiness. So the real question is: Why aren't we doing it?"

Several days have passed. It is now Monday morning, and Elie Silberstein has to stop at the bank before heading to Cayuga Heights to lead his weekly luncheon class for the Cornell psychology faculty. Parking his car downtown, he sees a couple of familiar Jewish faces: a local social worker and a bookstore manager who have frequently attended Chabad House activities. They stop and chat on the street corner before going their separate ways. Then an Ithaca College student greets him and the two briefly discuss arrangements for the coming festival of Succoth. Though the local Jewish community is tiny by major metropolitan standards, such casual everyday friendship has a satisfying quality for Rabbi Silberstein. Inside the bank, he exchanges greetings with familiar staff; by now, his full beard and Lubavitcher garb (Black Stetson, conservative suit) no longer evoke surprise or curiosity.

But things were not always this way. Soon after arriving in town, the Silbersteins realized that they faced a challenge quite distinct from simply conducting outreach among Jewish students and academicians. Cornell University and Ithaca College stand watch on opposite hills, with Ithaca nestled below, and historically, town-and-gown relations have been strained, at times exceedingly so. They have, at best, represented two completely separate worlds. At worst, there was angry local backlash against campus antiwar and civil-rights demonstrations in the 1960s, it even became physically dangerous for students to venture through remote backwater areas of the county. While the sight of Elie Silberstein wearing his traditional Hasidic garb was not wholly unfamiliar to most college faculty and students—who hail mostly from large urban areas like New York City and Boston, Tompkins County's natives were a different group entirely.

On Halloween Day in his first year in Ithaca, Rabbi Silberstein recalls, he was standing in line at this same downtown bank when an old man began to stare at him intently. Smiling at last, the elderly figure exlaimed appreciatively, "That's quite a costume you've got there, young man!" A few months later, when Chana Silberstein lay in Tompkins County General Hospital after giving birth to a child, her nurse asked casually, "Will your husband, the minister, be giving a church sermon this Sunday?"

After encounters like these, Elie Silberstein contacted the *Ithaca Journal* (the town's sole daily newspaper), whose editor agreed that a feature article about Hasidism might be interesting. The piece that followed generated favorable publicity and episodes of misunderstanding are no longer commonplace.

Though it is now beginning to drizzle there is a cozy atmosphere inside the home of psychiatry professor. Rabbi Silberstein begins the Jewish study session promptly. He knows that everyone is busy with teaching, research, or administrative duties, and that several people must hurry off at one o'clock to get to their own classes on time.

As usual, the springboard for the faculty group is the biblical portion of the week read in synagogues throughout the Jewish world. Silberstein offers his Hasidic interpretation, filled with symbolism and legend. Rather quickly, it seems, the discussion becomes tangential to the initial subject matter, but Silberstein does not seem bothered by the group's digression. To teach stimulating classes like these, Lubavitch rabbis such as Elie Silberstein undergo a rigorous seminary preparation that belies the popular stereotype of Hasidim as simple pietists celebrating God through song and dance. Chabad's core curriculum of Hasidic philosophy comprises dozens of analytic Hebrew tomes written by generations of Rebbes. As already mentioned, the foundation of all these books is the *Tanya* published in the late eighteenth century by the founding Lubavitcher Rebbe Schneur Zalman who wrote on a variety of mystical, theological and psychological topics, including human motivation and capacity for inner growth.

Silberstein explains to his group that the Chabad model of the mind focuses extensively on man's highest nature, linked step by step all the way to God. Yet it is only through our daily actions that we can actually bring that holiness into the mainstream of our lives.

The professors seated around the room seem intrigued, and Rabbi Silberstein realizes that the subject of Judaism's traditional ritual observance has at last emerged for open discussion. Since the class began the previous year, he has deliberately refrained from emphasizing this pragmatic aspect of Jewish mysticism, but he now finds it opportune to do so.

"Hasidism teaches us that we can relate to the presence of God in our lives at two levels: the rational and that which is called 'the mystery of God.' Eastern religion lays much emphasis on direct spiritual experience, and that is important also in Judaism. But in seeking spiritual experience, we're still on the human level, trapped by our limited mental framework. Hasidism therefore emphasizes that the more important level is the 'mystery'—that which lies totally beyond human understanding and comprehension. How do we do this, if we as humans lack the mental capacity for it? God created tools for us, and that's what Judaism's ritual laws—the *mitzvahs*—are all about. Think of these as divine instruments or channels to enable us to reach God's mysterious qualities. These qualities are even more alluring than the rational, because they are wrapped up in a mystery beyond human comprehension. That's why it's only through performing the *mitzvahs* that we as Jews can attain a certain closeness to God. No amount of study or learning can bring us there."

Rabbi Silberstein is aware that few faculty members who attend these classes are religiously observant or even give the matter much thought. The issue of spurring Jewish commitment in Ithaca to ritual observance has been a delicate one. "I have to be especially careful not to push religious observance on them. But even though they come primarily to explore Hasidic philosophy and metaphysics, some are quietly becoming more observant as well."

Today's class therefore marks something of a breakthrough in this realm, for after further discussion each member of the group decides to perform one *mitzvah* on a permanent basis. For the men, donning phylacteries seems appealing; the sole woman in the group agrees to begin lighting Sabbath candles without fail. Rabbi Silberstein is delighted, yet also a bit surprised by this sudden display of religious conviction. "I guess I'm finally communicating effectively," he says, as he steps into his car. "Or maybe it's because they're more conscious of their Jewishness, now that Rosh Hashanah and Yom Kippur are on their minds."

Away from Ithaca's well-groomed college campuses, Rabbi Silberstein has also become involved in reaching a surprisingly large local subcommunity: disaffected Jews who have sought inspiration for two decades through Eastern religion and "New Age" books and audio tapes. In the late 1960s, the bucolic Ithaca area became home to several rural communes, additional groups of craftspeople, and a loose community of self-proclaimed political radicals and counterculture devotees. When their communes collapsed and political causes evaporated, many of these young people and ex-students simply stayed on and became part of Ithaca's economy as they moved into their thirties and forties, opening small businesses or working at social-service or teaching jobs.

Though this subcommunity has seen countless gurus, yogis, and swamis pass through Ithaca over the years, it remains open to new ideas about religion and transcendence. Having been inspired since the 1960s by innovative and spiritually oriented psychologists like Abraham Maslow and Richard ("Ram Dass") Alpert, they have a ready context for relating to contemporary Hasidism, and many are becoming curious about Elie Silberstein's Chabad House.

"One of the things we have discovered in this area is that there are a lot of people who are essentially Jewish only by birth," he admits. "They may have been bar-mitzvahed or even attended Hebrew school as children. However, for the vast majority Judaism has become an insignificant or even negative experience. You ask such persons, and they say, 'Sure, I'm proud to be Jewish.' But what does being Jewish really mean? The question confuses them. Then, they are surprised to see how much fulfillment they can find in traditional Judaism."

By stressing such topics as Jewish meditation and the nature of the soul, in his weekly Chabad House classes or one-to-one sessions Silberstein has begun to affect some of these alienated Jews. He often mentions the Lubavitcher Rebbe's encouragement of authentic Jewish meditative practice as distinct from cultish behavior. Though long unaffiliated with any Jewish institutions, Silberstein's audiences are both spiritually hungry and intellectually active. No matter how sarcastic or bitter they become in recounting their past exposure to Judaism, Chabad's emissary is unruffled and even sympathetic.

"What you unfortunately experienced as a child wasn't authentic Judaism," he tells a small group of would-be Jewish meditators who have sought serene lives in Ithaca since the late 1960s. "What you were given was the product of people who were uneasy with real Judaism and who tried to give you some kind of empty substitute. I don't blame them. They probably meant well, figuring, 'At least, let's give the youngsters *something* Jewish, even if it's not much.' But that approach didn't work, and it still doesn't work. You know that, and I know that. Now let's see what authentic Judaism is all about."

Elie Silberstein's gentle message seems effective. A recent example that he cites is Susan, a former Cornell student and professional woman now in her late thirties, who had purchased a ticket to India to visit a famous guru. After attending a Passover seder with the Silbersteins, Susan became keenly interested in Hasidism, canceled her flight, and began taking classes at the Ithaca Chabad House. Rabbi Silberstein proudly adds, "She is now planning a trip to Israel."

It would be inaccurate to say, though, that Ithaca's Jewish counterculture community has embraced overnight the strict, traditional lifestyle of the Silbersteins. Though they are eager to insist on the legitimacy of young women studying to be physicians, attorneys, or business executives, Chana and Elie Silberstein maintain an uncompromising adherence to Jewish Law as codified in the Talmud and later works. For instance, these delineate strict observance of the Sabbath and the dietary laws, and also stipulate a host of restrictions concerning the mingling of men and women. Such strict self-discipline is not easily accepted by those who have been so firmly shaped by the permissive values of campus life during the past generation.

But even here, Rabbi Silberstein seems to be effective in shattering stereotypes about Hasidism. For example, he acknowledges in his classes that some people are indeed born with widely variant sexual desires. While emphasizing that sexuality within marriage is the only permissible and holy expression of this God-given urge, Silberstein makes it clear that every Jew is welcome at Chabad House. "We don't categorize people," he insists. "We each have our inner struggles. I don't view anyone as really being that different from me."

Despite Rabbi Silberstein's steady success, monetary problems have continued to hinder his program. Early in 1986, it seemed that his entire operation might have to be suspended as a result of inadequate financial backing. While in Chicago, Detroit, or Miami, Lubavitch emissaries are able to tap the ample resources of sympathetic local multimillionaires, in rural and academic Ithaca Elie Silberstein has faced serious problems

In June 1986, a group of Cornell and Ithaca College faculty members wrote directly to the Lubavitcher Rebbe about this crisis situation: "Over the last two years, Elie Silberstein and his wife, Chana, have been shining lights of the beauty of Orthodox Judaism on our campuses," they commented. "We understand that there is a real possibility that, due to lack of funding, their influence may be absent next year. Ithaca is a small community removed from major metropolitan Jewish centers. The town has no organized Orthodox Jewish presence. However, the campuses are populated by over six thousand Jewish students from all over the United States. It is critical that in this important stage of their educational and emotional development these students have an Orthodox Jewish example to emulate."

The letter cited the Silbersteins' success in assisting and even unifying the local Orthodox Jewish community. It praised their accomplishment in building the first *mikveh* in the town's history, as well as in advancing religious study among Jewish college students. "But it is in the area of marriage and family life that the Silbersteins contribute most importantly," the writers noted. "They must continue to serve as examples to these students who are about to make their own marital choices." The letter ended with a plea that the Lubavitcher Rebbe help keep the Ithaca Chabad House alive.

Several weeks later came the Rebbe's reply. He advised the writers to relay their sentiments about the Silbersteins to the Lubavitch regional director in Buffalo, under whose aegis the Ithaca facility was founded. He devoted the rest of his letter to broader issues. "I was particularly gratified to note how closely you have been involved with Chabad activities in your community," he wrote. "Your profound concern for the future of Judaism among your students and in the community at large, gives me confidence that you will do your utmost to ensure their continuation and steady expansion."

In keeping with the Rebbe's long-standing emphasis on the potential of every individual's capability to affect the entire world, he stressed the tremendous import of the professors' own influence upon their students. "Each of you has a special responsibility and extraordinary opportunity through personal conduct to reinforce the Jewish identity of your students. Know too that God does not bestow a responsibility on anyone without providing the ability to carry it out in the fullest measure, with joy and gladness of heart."

Since then, Silberstein has been able to obtain extra funds from Lubavitch regional headquarters in Buffalo, and his programs have continued to expand. In early 1987 he purchased a big house across town, closer to graduate student and faculty residences. The Silbersteins' open-house celebration drew over one hundred people, a sizable crowd by Ithaca's small-town standards. Soon after, in entrepreneurial fashion, the Hasidic couple purchased a second building, converted half to a new *mikveh*, and rented the other section for income purposes.

Obtaining adequate funding, however, remains a perpetual problem and limits the Silbersteins' ability to hire additional outreach staff. Elie Silberstein concedes that he may even have to seek donations from Jewish Cornell alumni, most of whom have only indirect knowledge of Lubavitch and the Silbersteins, and what they represent. For the future, Rabbi Silberstein plans a variety of projects, though lack of money continues to limit what he can realistically accomplish in this university town. "My goal would be for every Jew in this area to draw closer to traditional Judaism. But on a practical level," he says, "I want to continue to work with this population of intellectual and spiritual people. It's very challenging and the sky's the limit."

Certainly, no less challenging to the Lubavitch movement has been its effort to strengthen Jewish family stability. In this crucial domain, the Lubavitchers have been at the forefront of Torah outreach to Jewish women today.

IV

WOMEN OF VALOR

Let her works praise her in the gates.

—Proverbs 31:31

THE QUIET MIDWESTERN STREET HARDLY SEEMS LIKE THE SITE of an international Hasidic study center. With bicycles sprawled on wide, trim lawns and basketball hoops visible behind spacious Colonial homes, the setting could not be more suburban and quintessentially American. If the Lubavitcher world nexus is the concrete landscape of Brooklyn, it is hard to imagine a more striking contrast. But appearances are often deceiving, as the Talmud reminds us. From the outside, the Bais Chana Women's Institute looks like a fraternity or sorority house, though this serene neighborhood is not near any college. Aside from the small wooden sign "Chabad-Lubavitch" fastened above the entrance, there is nothing one can see from the street to indicate that the building is a Jewish, let alone Orthodox and Hasidic, institution.

The inside front lobby Bais Chana also resembles a college residence, but here the similarity ends. Beside a table near the entrance hangs a portrait of the Lubavitcher Rebbe. On another table sit several dozen Sabbath candles. In the dining room at the center of the first floor a group of some thirty women of varied nationality and age are seated, listening to Rabbi Moshe Feller telling a Hasidic story. It is Saturday evening, and he wears full Hasidic garb. As the humorous tale reaches its climax, most of the women chuckle or smile. Not surprisingly, others seem fatigued; it is nearly ten o'clock, after a sweltering summer day.

The tale is attributed to Reb Nachman of Bratslav, the late-eighteenth-century Hasidic master. It symbolically depicts the human tendency to seek fleeting pleasures while ignoring higher duties. After he has finished, Rabbi Feller invites questions, then launches into a brief discourse on the Hasidic attitude toward the stresses of daily life. Finally, he thanks the women for their time, and from a side room enters Rabbi Yitzchak Barash, a young Lubavitch emissary who has come to lead the concluding Sabbath service.

Little booklets with both Hebrew and English lyrics are quickly passed around. The singing gradually becomes more exuberant and within a few minutes, the women are pounding the dining tables Hasidic style for rhythmic emphasis. When the service ends, one young woman calls out, "Remember, morning prayers are at nine o'clock tomorrow!" Mock groans resound, and within a few moments, the dining room is empty as a weary Rabbi Feller sits down.

Rabbi Moshe Feller, a small, gentle, man in early middle age, looks as though he has just stepped out of a Sholom Aleichem novel. But he speaks with the flat tones of his native American Midwest. Born and raised in the Twin Cities of Minnesota, Feller attended a non-Hasidic yeshiva in New York City before choosing rabbinical training at the Lubavitcher seminary. Shortly after ordination and then marriage in 1961, he was ready in his mid-twenties to go wherever Lubavitch requested. Moshe Feller half expected an outreach assignment somewhere like Afghanistan or Tunisia, having already served as a temporary Lubavitcher emissary in Latin America where his full beard often led people to mistake him for a Marxist revolutionary. Sometimes as he walked down the street he was greeted with a "Viva Fidel!" as strangers with upraised fists saluted him. But to young Rabbi Feller's surprise, the Rebbe suggested that he establish Chabad's new midwestern regional office in his own hometown of the Twin Cities.

Lubavitch's grass-roots people-to-people approach was still quite new. Emissaries had by then been established in only three American cities: Detroit, Miami, and Philadelphia, all with much larger Jewish populations than the Twin Cities. Feller's mother had just died, and his father was preparing to move to New York City to be near his son. But the Rebbe advised Feller senior to stay put: "We want Moshe in Minnesota."

"I wasn't invited by the local Jewish population," Rabbi Feller recalls frankly. "I was sent here. People had known me since I had been a small child, and I wasn't really into this 'prophet-in-your own-country' type of thing. But the Rebbe wanted me to go, and so I went."

At the time the Twin Cities had only one remaining Orthodox Jewish congregation. Feller recollects, "The epitaph for traditional Judaism here had already been written. People thought I was crazy for trying to buck the tide." The Rebbe hadn't given much specific advice either. "We weren't encouraged specifically to set up Hasidic synagogues or day schools, Hebrew day camps or community centers. In the broadest terms, my mandate was simply to bring individual Jews to their religious roots and identity. How? The Rebbe had said something to the effect of, 'Moshe, you've got a good head on your shoulders. Use it.' But I still remember his exact parting words twenty-nine years later, and I've even written articles about them. He said, 'Be flexible.' Not meaning, be flexible about Jewish observance—God forbid—but about setting up programs. If something doesn't work, try something else."

Over the next decade, the Lubavitch presence in the Twin Cities steadily grew. Rabbi Feller and his wife Mindy developed a host of activities including a summer camp, and in general, substantially revitalized the Twin Cities Orthodox Jewish community. By 1971 they had acquired a mansion known as the Bremer Estate in an attractive residential area. With further growth, additional staff were recruited, and there now exists a thriving Lubavitcher community of nearly a hundred families. With the generous financial support of benefactors like Minnesota's former U.S. Senator Rudy Boschwitz, they have exerted a strong presence wherever Jews live in the Midwest. This past year, a local Lubavitcher opened Minnesota's first kosher restaurant, the Old City Café.

Bais Chana (literally meaning The House of Chana, named in memory of the Rebbe's mother) was started in 1971. Young Rabbi Manis Friedman and his wife, Chana, had just arrived in the Twin Cities from Brooklyn following his ordination. Several of his relatives had begun Jewish outreach work in the Detroit area, and he asked whether any local Detroit women they knew might like a "Hasidic experience" in Minnesota. Eighteen attended that first summer, forty-three the next, and one hundred and ten the year after, in 1973.

There has never been any need to advertise. Rabbi Friedman quickly gained a reputation as a lively and charismatic Hasidic teacher, and soon initiated a winter study program as well. The format became standard by the mid-1970s: nine weeks in the summer and four weeks during the winter. Since Bais Chana was started, over seven thousand Jewish women have already passed through its doors, from all over the United States and abroad. For those unable to afford the cost of tuition and board, work-study scholarships are offered. No woman is rejected for financial reasons; and every effort is made to accommodate those whose schedule does not precisely fit Bais Chana's. Local Lubavitcher families are glad to have interested women as guests because "a career woman with a two-week vacation per year can't be kept waiting," observes Rabbi Feller. "We have a very welcoming Lubavitch community here in the Twin Cities. Even with this huge mansion, we're always filled to capacity."

A relaxed mood pervades Bais Chana this morning. In the dining room, a few women are finishing their coffee or tea. Upstairs, some are reading from Hebrew prayer books or Bibles, or talking quietly in small groups. Rabbi Friedman is scheduled to begin his lecture at eleven o'clock, but at ten minutes before the hour, no one is even near the upstairs meeting hall that doubles as Bais Chana's synagogue. Finally, at about eleven-forty, he enters the building, and within moments, the group of about thirty women quickly seat themselves classroom style.

Manis Friedman, a youthful-looking man with a full beard, medium build, and an air of good-natured vitality, has become a major Chabad speaker in the United States on family life and related contemporary issues. His schedule frequently takes him around the country to speak at synagogues, Jewish community centers, and college campuses. He sits down at a desk with a microphone connected to a recording device across the room. Each of his talks at Bais Chana is taped live, and the best of them are commercially produced and distributed by Chabad Houses and other outlets throughout North America's Jewish communities. Friedman has recently gained an international audience as his talks have been translated and rerecorded into French, Hebrew, Portuguese, and Russian.

The class is a mixed group of women mostly in their twenties and early thirties, although some are middle-aged or older. Judging by their dark complexions and style of dress, a few would seem to be of Sephardic backgrounds. British accents reveal others who came originally from England or South Africa. Nodding to the group, Rabbi Friedman turns on the cassette recorder. As the students prepare to take notes, he begins today's class with a Hasidic story.

There was once a poor man named Shmuel who was invited to a wealthy man's home. Shmuel was thrilled to be there, and felt highly honored, not only because the wealthy man offered wonderful hospitality and a sumptuous meal, but also because he had an interesting custom. He would deck his tables with the most expensive settings, and each poor guest like Shmuel was invited to take home any item of his choice after the meal.

Now, Shmuel was not very bright. While being served the lavish meal, he knew that soon he would be encouraged to select an item as he left. So he observed everything carefully. He noticed that whenever the wealthy man wanted something, he would lift a crystal bell from the table, and ring it. Two butlers would instantly appear and give the wealthy man whatever delicacy he wished.

After the meal, he asked Shmuel what he would like to take home. Shmuel paused for a moment, then replied: 'I want the bell.' It seemed like a bizarre request, but his host thought to himself, each to his own. If he wants the bell, so I'll give him the bell.

Bell in hand, Shmuel eagerly returned to his nearby village. He invited everyone to a feast he was having the next evening. The entire village turned out. Long tables had been set up, and benches. But everything was bare. There was not even a single tablecloth or napkin, let alone food and beverages. As the villagers began to protest, Shmuel smilingly assured them that he would reveal all in due time. Finally, everyone was seated and hungrily awaiting dinner.

Shmuel now appeared with the crystal bell and with a great flourish rang it repeatedly. Nothing happened. He rang it again, this time more loudly and insistently. Again nothing. Seeing his shock and confusion, the angry villagers almost ran him out of town.

That very night, Shmuel breathlessly ran to the wealthy man's mansion. Enraged, he pounded on the door until a servant opened it. "You tricked me!" Shmuel screamed as he saw the wealthy man in nightclothes standing astonished on the balcony. "You switched bells on me! Your bell worked! The one you gave me doesn't work!"

The wealthy man smiled and patiently explained, as though talking to a child: "It isn't the bell that causes fancy food and lavish plates and expensive silverware to appear. It's what lies *behind* the bell, wealth that has been accumulating for many years." As Shmuel slowly left the doorway, he could still hear the wealthy man's final words: "Just to lift the bell and shake it accomplishes nothing."

It is an engaging story, and the women smile a bit dreamily. But what exactly does it have to do with Judaism and modern family life? Knowing that he has the group's attention for the moment, Rabbi Friedman explains, with a decidedly Yiddish inflection to his voice. "As Jews, we have been very spoiled. If we go back just two or three generations, all we needed to do was to ring the bell. Our grandparents and great-grandparents seemed to have raised healthy children just by ringing the bell. The kids grew up. No problem. They got married. No problem. They had children. No problem. Everything worked fine. Fathers were fathers, mothers were mothers. Children were children, Jews were Jews. Everything seemed to work. You rang the bell, it worked.

"You needed to get married? You got married. You needed to have children? You had children. You needed to be a mother? You became a mother. You needed to be a father? You became a father. The children needed to grow up Jewish? They grew up Jewish. When the children needed to get married, so they got married.

"We started taking a lot of things for granted. The bell worked. In our time, we try taking the bell home, and we ring it, but it doesn't seem to work anymore. We ring it this way. We ring it that way. Neither way it works. We came to America from Europe, and all we saved from our Jewish communities was the bell. We now have to rethink how the bell works."

For the next two hours, Rabbi Friedman's talk ranges across Jewish history, biblical exegesis, and Talmudic commentary, as well as the terrain of modern psychological thought. He sardonically analyzes the foibles of the contemporary American social scene: singles bars and nightclubs, psychotherapy and personal-growth seminars. Sometimes, the thread linking all these diverse subjects seems tenuous, and the faces appear to be straining to follow a specific point that Rabbi Friedman is trying to make. Speaking without notes, he stresses an interesting Hasidic precept concerning self-direction: "Whenever you have a real urge to change something about yourself, do something concrete, anything—even move the furniture about in your room—so as to strengthen the urge for change."

Rabbi Friedman's main point this morning seems to be that men and women generally have two fundamentally different approaches to life: the man yearns to "slay the dragons" of injustice and inequity, to bring about perfection through his labors. The woman, in contrast, seeks to protect, nurture, and sustain the godliness and perfection that already exist on earth. Both are needed, Rabbi Friedman insists. Both are equally important.

He speaks too about the humbling, ego-effacing benefits of marriage. "I can talk to you about life, and sound very high-minded," he asserts. "Then I return home to my family, and whom am I kidding? I can announce to them, 'From now on, I'm going to be a more perfect human being!' And they say, 'Who are you kidding?' They know me too well. With my family and friends, I can't play games."

The question-and-answer period begins, and the students seem animated once again. Many questions involve problems of marital discord, or relations with in-laws—others Hasidic or Biblical concepts he has mentioned. It is one-thirty in the afternoon as the Torah class ends. Most of the group will be leaving shortly for a day's outing in Minnesota's summer countryside. They file out of the large room in spirited conversation.

By late afternoon, most of the Bais Chana participants have returned from the outing. They are now meeting in small groups or one-to-one sessions for tutoring throughout the building. All Bais Chana instructors are committed Lubavitcher women who spend the summer teaching a variety of subjects, including Jewish prayer and rituals, the

Hebrew language, and Bible study. Hasidic philosophy is closely inter-
woven into the lessons, complementing Rabbi Friedman's discourses.
More important, perhaps, the instructors provide visible role models
exemplifying how Hasidic women behave in their daily lives. Though
their outlook is certainly different from that of most contemporary
Jewish women, these instructors cannot easily be reduced to facile
stereotypes.

Bais Chana's chief instructor this summer is Chaya Zern, who
graduated in June from Harvard University. Born and raised as a
Lubavitcher in Springfield, Massachusetts, she attended women's yeshivas until the age of eighteen. Upon soliciting and receiving the
Rebbe's blessing for her to enroll at Harvard, Chaya lived with a
Lubavitch family in Boston and taught at the local Chabad-Lubavitch
day school while obtaining an undergraduate degree in psychology. She
is soft-spoken, exuding quiet confidence, and she seems accustomed to
being challenged about the seemingly subordinate status of women in
the Hasidic community.

"I am asked about that all the time," Chaya comments mildly, "by
college students and others, and not just here at Bais Chana. I tell them
that, personally, I know it's not true. It is true that women's main
fulfillment is through the home, especially making its foundation. Unfortunately, that's something that isn't prized very much in our society
today. Therefore, many Jewish women feel discontent being entrusted
with the responsibilities of being a mother and a wife. They feel that
such work is trivial compared with the status of having a career.

"In the Hasidic world, our whole mind-set is different. We feel that
the holiest thing, and that which commands the most respect, is family
life, even to the extent that whether or not someone is Jewish is totally
dependent on the woman. It's the woman who makes a home a Jewish
place. Also, today there seems to be a tremendous overemphasis on
outwardness: that if something is louder, it's automatically better. Or
if something can be very showy, then it's superior. That may not
necessarily be true. What happens inside the home, in a quiet way, may
be the more important thing."

Chaya has a busy schedule at Bais Chana, supervising the other
instructors, teaching small classes, and making sure in a general way
that the atmosphere remains true to Lubavitcher values of decorum and

modesty. She seems both respected and well liked among the students, many of whom are unaware of her Harvard background. Perhaps Chaya deliberately downplays its significance, or avoids mentioning her secular education altogether either through modesty or because she has not yet resolved in her own mind exactly what Harvard has meant for her life. Though in her gentle way she firmly adheres to traditional Hasidic values, the influence of Chaya's college experience becomes apparent when she is asked about her plans for the fall. She hesitates before listing several differing possibilities, then offers the contemporary refrain, "I haven't committed myself to anything yet. I want to keep my options open."

The chief female presence at Bais Chana is now exerted largely behind the scenes by Mindy Feller. Raised in an observant Jewish family in Brooklyn, Mindy graduated from Hunter College in New York City at the age of nineteen, a Phi Beta Kappa with a degree in mathematics. After moving to Minnesota she held professional positions until her children were born; she worked as a statistical research analyst for the Kenny Rehabilitation Institute and later as an educational consultant devising mathematics achievement tests for the state of Minnesota. At the same time she taught daily classes—especially Bible and Commentaries—at Bais Chana.

Nowadays, Mindy Feller has a host of administrative duties serving the hundred-family Lubavitch community in the Twin Cities. As a result, apart from offering informal supervision to Bais Chana's teaching staff, she mainly appears on the premises to give lectures about the Hasidic emphasis on physical modesty for Jewish women. "I teach that we should look on ourselves as princesses," Mindy relates, "not in the 'JAP'y manner, but in the way King David alludes to in the Psalms. Royalty has both privileges and obligations. Jewish women must see themselves this way, and through Jewish eyes look at being physically modest as something refined and beautiful."

A forceful organizer and educator for more than a quarter century, Mindy Feller is often consulted by a new generation of women serving as emissaries in the Lubavitch movement. Virtually every day, she spends time offering practical advice and emotional support to her younger counterparts in new Chabad Houses across the United States and abroad.

Representative of such Hasidic activists is Chaya Teldon, who grew up in a Conservative Jewish household in suburban Detroit. She gradually became drawn to Chabad and decided to make Jewish outreach her lifetime activity. She and her husband, Tuvya, became emissaries in their mid-twenties, serving the far reaches of New York City's suburban Long Island.

A poised and self-confident speaker who chooses her words carefully, Chaya emphasizes the egalitarian nature of Chabad's emissary couples. "People think of Hasidism and immediately conclude that everything is run by men, and the women just sit around taking orders or are banished to the kitchen. That's simply not true. My work complements my husband's, but we do different things, reflecting the local need and our personal interest.

"I teach two classes each week for women. One class is studying *Pirkey Avoth* (*Ethics of the Fathers*, a third-century text) and the other revolves around the Torah portion of the week. We also do frequent hospital visitations and have a monthly program with a different woman speaker for each occasion. Not all the topics are specifically religious," Chaya concedes, "but I always try to make Jewish teachings relevant. For instance, last month we had a nurse speak about health and wellness awareness. It seemed like a perfect opportunity for me to speak about the traditional Jewish view of spiritual health and wellness. I could mention examples of activities. We reach out through programming by women, about women, and for women."

Like most Lubavitcher women, Chaya Teldon has a large family that makes great demands on her time. How does she cope with all the traditional responsibilities as well as maintain the lifestyle of a "professional" woman? It is no easy matter, she readily admits. "Sometimes, the stress level of women emissaries really becomes extremely high. In such instances, I find networking with other women who do this work to be my greatest support outside the home. Especially helpful is the Lubavitch Women's Organization.

"It's not a sisterhood, it's not an extension of the synagogue or an imitation men's club. Every year, the Women's Organization holds several conventions, geared strictly for Lubavitcher women and their particular challenges as part of this worldwide Jewish movement. It's a chance to let your hair down with other women, to share frustrations as well as programming ideas. But I want to emphasize," Chaya says pointedly, "that no one made me go into this outreach work. It's difficult and demanding, especially with young kids at home. But strengthening Judaism is what I have chosen to do."

The issue of women's responsibilities and desires is frequently raised at Bais Chana. Rabbi Friedman finds that it often comes to the fore, such as tonight in his discussion of Jewish religious practice. "Our tradition has always emphasized," he says, "that we're not to act righteously because it makes us feel noble, or lofty, or spiritual. Rather, we should act righteously, in accordance with the tenets of Judaism, because God says so."

"Is it easier for men or women to do this?" someone asks.

"For women, it's generally easier," answers Rabbi Friedman. "It's a more feminine reflex."

Suddenly, though the hour is late, all eyes are open. The discussion is now arriving at something immediate and tangible: the inward differences between men and women, and the nature and goals of modern feminism. In response to what they think he is intimating, several students quickly insist that "women don't want traditional goals in life anymore, they're not like their mothers or grandmothers."

Rabbi Friedman shakes his head. "No, I'm sorry to inform you that I think women haven't changed at all. This whole uproar and disturbance and feminist revolution is really a backlash against what men have done—desert the home."

The faces now appear a bit puzzled. This immediate condemnation of modern men isn't what they were expecting, as he addresses the subject of feminism.

"In olden times in Europe, men went to war, or went to work, because of the family. Whenever the husband left the home, it was because the family needed something, and he was the one who was supposed to go out and get it. If the man was away from home for a day, a week, even a month or a year, the family still felt that they had a father and a husband, and that it was a family, even if he was absent for a long stretch of time.

"Then came the Industrial Revolution, and men suddenly started leaving home. Not because the family needed the husband to do so, but because work had become his devotion in life, his status symbol. All of a sudden, children and mothers found themselves alone. So for several decades, maybe longer, women said, 'We'll try to care for the home, you go out and do your work.' But it wasn't a family anymore. Not only did the husband leave home to get away from the family, but even when he came home, he wanted to be left alone.

"So the family fell apart. After enough decades had passed of taking this situation, the women said, 'Wait a minute! What am I staying home for?' So if you take this situation to its final conclusion, the women aren't saying, 'We want to work.' Women are saying, 'We want to have families.' "

One perceptive woman, raises her hand. "But I remember reading somewhere that one of the earlier Rabbis, I don't know if he was Lubavitcher or not—said something like, 'The important thing in life is your relationship with God through prayer and study.' "

"Where did you hear that?" asks Rabbi Friedman. As the woman starts to look defensive, he replies, "Yes, one of the Rebbes did say that. Because in those days, Jewish life had become so parochial in the village that your wife and your hut and cow, that was as broad as your horizons got. And the Rebbe was saying, that's not healthy either. Your life has to be more than your little hut. The Rebbe was trying to loosen up that kind of grip. But today, the emphasis has to be the complete opposite. We've become totally estranged from the family."

As though suddenly aware of the hour, Rabbi Friedman leans forward, then prepares to rise. "So in the final analysis, women are actually saying: 'Give me back my family. And if not, then let's see how you feel when I leave the home, when I come home at the end of the day and say, 'I'm tired. I can't be bothered to take care of the kids.' Because nobody is benefiting from this."

From the satisfied, even delighted, expressions on the faces of most students, it seems that Rabbi Friedman has scored with this argument. It is now two hours past midnight. Morning prayers begin in just a few hours, and then another class led by Rabbi Friedman. The fatigue on some of the faces is understandable.

As the class breaks and Rabbi Friedman heads for home, he seems the very model of the zealous academician who devotes all his waking moments to the intellectual work he loves. He may be teaching Hasidic philosophy rather than physics, chemistry, or constitutional law, but it is two in the morning, nevertheless, and his family has gone to sleep without seeing him return home. None of the women students appears to detect this apparent contradiction between his message and his own conduct, or at least nobody raises the issue with him. Perhaps, they are all too tired.

Even the most fleeting visit to Rabbi Friedman's home indicates that the Lubavitcher hold a very different view of family life than that popular in American culture today. He and his wife, Chana, have reared fourteen children, ranging in age from several months to twenty-one years. The proud parents laugh when asked if this number constitutes any sort of record for their Hasidic group. "On the contrary," Chanah replies, "In some of our communities, it's not even worth boasting about." Though reliable statistics do not exist, most Lubavitcher families have four or more children these days, and very large families, like the Friedmans' mini-clan, carry high status. He finds that many women at Bais Chana question how he and Chanah can possibly raise fourteen children adequately. "The best answer I can give is to bring my kids over. That usually ends the discussion."

The Lubavitch predilection for large families originates in their literal adherence to the biblical injunction "Be fruitful and multiply." They believe that the Torah is timeless, and therefore applies as equally to the contemporary world of six billion people as it did to that of ancient times. Indeed, the Lubavitcher Rebbe has strongly criticized the very concept of family planning—that is, attempting to limit family size or seeking to space the conception of one's children—as a wholly misguided effort.

In a public discourse during 1980, he declared: "It is an unfortunate fact that all too often people are influenced by popular opinion rather than by what is right. While many social issues are nothing more than harmless trivialities, there is currently one issue of vital significance that is being treated casually: family planning. It is a destructive practice that has become so widespread as to affect all but the strongest individuals. The ills of family planning cannot be overstated, for it involves such crucial issues as emotional stability, marital harmony, and the entire husband-wife relationship. Ironically, the practice of family planning masquerades under the guise of benevolence, proclaiming concern for the well-being of married couples, and indeed, all humanity."

Sharply condemning the common attitude that child rearing is a worrisomely expensive undertaking, the Rebbe went on: "An appraisal of real motives might be in order. Is it possible that the concern of financial limitation may be a rationalization for living in a particular lifestyle? Contemporary society demands a material standard that is, to say the least, excessive. Is it possible that we have adopted indulgences as necessities and this causes our worry about finances?"

In the same discourse, the Rebbe strongly criticized the popular view that having children limits mobility and freedom. "The real problem is not one of insufficient personal resources, but rather one of priorities. In many other aspects of life, such as careers and personal achievement, people accept inconvenience and even self-sacrifice to attain their goals. The real problem is that children are regarded not as sources of joy and happiness, but as burdens and impediments to pleasure and 'fulfillment.' "

The Rebbe likewise stressed that those who deliberately choose to be childless are being shortsighted. While children may interfere with youthful pursuits, we are not young forever and a life without children becomes increasingly lonely and sterile as we pass through middle age and then our elderly years.

The Rebbe was equally critical of the contemporary emphasis on spacing the conception of children. He alluded to the lesson that many Jewish couples today are learning the hard way. "A child is not a faucet to be turned on at will. No power on earth can guarantee the birth of a baby." Stressing that "such power is God's and God's alone," he added, "the blessing so disdained earlier may not be available later. Take His blessings when He offers them, gratefully, and rest assured that this third Partner is benevolent . . . and can be trusted to know the best time."

These beliefs certainly challenge the dominant consensus of present-day American society that small families, or marriages that are voluntarily childless, are admirable developments. Other critics of the small-family outlook contend that it essentially represents a secular ideology concerning children. For example, sociologist Allan C. Carlson, president of the Rockford Institute, terms this ideology "anti-natalism." This anti-natalist ideology was generated by the eighteenth-century English economist Thomas Malthus. His *Essay on Population* of 1798 presented an early example of the penetration of science into what had been religion's exclusive domain.

Using crude biological and anthropological evidence, Malthus cited "the constant tendency in all animated life to increase beyond the nourishment prepared for it." His implicit message was that the biblical injunction to "be fruitful and multiply" collided with the mere arithmetical expansion in available resources, and led to human misery. Malthus expressed hope for human progress by voluntary abstinence from sex through delayed marriage. The English philosopher John Stuart Mill went one step further in urging the use of contraceptives that would allow men and women to enjoy both uninhibited sexual relations and smaller families.

Feminism presented a second challenge to the biblical imperative. Modern feminism has generally sought to shift women into roles other than those of wife and mother. While fertility per se was not the primary feminist target, it became so, since the task of raising children remained a formidable obstacle to full emancipation. In the twentieth century, most feminists have consistently criticized organized religion for emphasizing women's childbearing capacity, and urged an end to religious pronatalism.

Scholars today have noted that the impulse to marry and raise children has varied considerably among America's diverse ethnic and religious groups during this century. For Jews, the guiding principles have not overtly changed, but social behavior has definitely altered. The overwhelming trend has been a steady erosion of Jewish fertility from generation to generation.

The marked exceptions have been the Orthodox and, more dramatically, the Hasidim, although Jews as a whole have consistently shown the lowest fertility of all American religious groups. Indeed, they have already achieved the dubious goal of "zero population growth," and are now diminishing in total population size.

The contrast with Jews in Israel is startling. In general, Israeli fertility is significantly higher. In 1975, the average Jewish woman in Israel under forty-five had 2.83 children, compared to the 1.86 figure for her American counterpart. Several surveys have shown a dramatically high, positive correlation between religious observance and family size. The least religious Israeli Jewish woman had an average of 1.39 children; those moderately religious, 2.62; and those highly religious, 4.48.

In Israel, this situation may be related to the grim legacy of the Holocaust: a desire to affirm Jewish identity no matter how hostile the surrounding world. Many observers have also noticed a joyful acceptance of children in Israeli culture, an ethos perhaps also reflecting the strong commitment to nation-building and to unspoken anxieties about the possibility of losing a child to war or terrorism. Such attitudes have yet to make a statistical dent in Jewish America. The recent establishment of the Task Force on Jewish Population in New York, coupled with numerous synagogue sermons and magazine articles on "The Coming Shrinkage of North American Jewry" are signs of belated recognition of this significant problem.

Within the walls of Bais Chana, the issue of raising a large family is one of several that are frequently debated informally. Staff members have noted that this topic is a relatively new one; ten and fifteen years ago, students were concerned with abstract matters that seemed far more weighty, today's students tend to be interested less in world-shattering change than in balancing their own careers with the rewards of family life.

"When we began in the early 1970s," observes Rabbi Friedman, "we were getting political activists and radicals, and the dropouts from the sixties. Then came those who had been into Eastern religions like Buddhism, Hinduism, and Yoga. Then came people who were into food fads like macrobiotics and vegetarianism. Now we're getting a new group for us: successful women who have good jobs and careers, and are looking for something else."

But what can the Lubavitchers really offer those who wish to pursue satisfying professional careers? What if a woman wants to keep her career as an accountant, attorney, or physician, yet devotedly raise children? "The question comes up a lot," concedes Rabbi Friedman, "and the only answer is the subjective one. It all depends on the individual. A woman came along recently and asked me, 'Can I be a painter?' My answer was, 'I don't know. It depends on what talents you have.' There are some who can handle it all, and do very well. Others can't, and they drive themselves crazy trying. It's really a very individual thing."

Another emotional issue that staff often encounter is intermarriage. Rabbi Friedman comments, "Some of the women who come here are engaged to non-Jews, and it's likely they come here saying, 'I dare you to convince me not to.' " By talking about Judaism in general terms, staff members find that the issue's whole context changes for most coming to Bais Chana. He estimates that in four out of five cases the women either discontinue the relationship, or that it soon becomes merely a station on the way to a more lasting bond with a Jewish man.

Middle-aged and older women pose a different sort of challenge to Bais Chana's staff. "Some come because they have a lot of free time, and they've always wanted to do something like this, to learn more about Judaism," notes Rabbi Friedman. "Some come because their daughters or sons have become more observant, and they feel totally inadequate, and want to learn how to handle it. Still others come because they feel guilty that their children have married non-Jews or are floundering emotionally. It can be a very sad and painful thing to see these older women eagerly learning about Jewish philosophy and observance, and then hear them suddenly start talking about how they can't get their adult daughters to come here."

In these cases staff recommend that the women try to persuade their children to contact someone observant, to break the ice, as it were, and if a warm, positive relationship develops, the daughter or son may draw closer to Jewish self-identity. "The important thing is to get them over the self-blaming," Rabbi Friedman comments. " 'That I should have done this or that' or 'If I only knew then what I know now.' That kind of feeling doesn't do anyone any good."

To what extent does the national background of students affect their involvement in Bais Chana's program? From their appearances alone, it would seem that the women from a Sephardic upbringing have differing needs and expectations from those raised in the affluent American suburbs, and Rabbi Friedman agrees. "Generally, with the Sephardic community and outlook, they're more faithful as Jews. Faith comes to them much more easily. Their beliefs are very strong and tangible: in sages and miracles, in God, in the coming of the Messiah. They never have a problem with faith. American and European Jews are different. They always have a problem with faith. But they're often more knowledgeable about the details of Jewish observance, its nuts and bolts."

For the Bais Chana staff, nearly all of whom have been raised as Hasidim, one common aspect of the students' backgrounds continually startles them: the breakup of the proverbially rock-solid Jewish family unit. "So many of the women who come have had such negative and at times nonexistent relationships with their own mothers," Rabbi Friedman observes. "This unraveling of the Jewish family is really a shocking thing. I thought we were immune to such things."

Bais Chana draws a relatively self-selected group of women committed to learning about Orthodox Judaism in a structured Hasidic milieu, so in a way its apparent success is not unexpected. How effective would its message be in the larger world of mainstream American society? It is not an unfamiliar issue for the Lubavitchers, and for this reason, Rabbi Friedman often travels around the country, giving talks on Hasidism as it relates to contemporary social issues. Over the past year, he has spoken before campus audiences at Berkeley, UCLA, and elsewhere.

For many of these occasions Rabbi Friedman draws frequently from the Rebbe's public discourses (sichot) for specific material. These talks, delivered at Lubavitch gatherings in Crown Heights, vary tremendously in scope. In recent years, the Rebbe has addressed such diverse domestic issues as prayer in the public schools, care of the disabled, the nature of retirement, and penal reform.

Several months ago, on a bitterly cold winter evening in upstate New York, some sixty students and faculty associated with Vassar College assembled at Poughkeepsie's local Chabad House to hear Rabbi Friedman discuss "Homosexuality: A Hasidic Perspective." Apart from a few regulars people had come specifically to hear the provocative lecture.

In essence, Rabbi Friedman presents the view that homosexuality is a natural and probably inborn tendency. He suggests that most people undoubtedly possess at least the potential to become physically attracted to members of their own sex. He further informs the gathering that whether homosexual or not, "a Jew is still a Jew," and that, "in Lubavitch synagogues, we don't exclude anyone from joining with us, whatever their proclivities." Nevertheless, Rabbi Friedman gently insists, "Homosexuality is wrong. Not because I think it's wrong, but because the Torah says so. It's a sin, just like other sins. And people are supposed to stop sinning if they haven't yet. Just because something seems natural, that doesn't mean it's okay. There are children born crippled or with speech defects, or with many other kinds of disorders, and they're all natural. That doesn't mean we don't try to cure the person, just because it's a condition that's natural. And to form congregations of Jews who are homosexual makes as much sense as having a congregation of adulterers, or any other kind of sinners."

Citing the Lubavitcher Rebbe's recent public remarks, Rabbi Friedman stresses that homosexuality can be overcome, and that an individual with such tendencies can nevertheless marry, raise children, and remain faithful to his or her spouse. He concedes that such a person may have to struggle through an entire lifetime to control the homosexual urge, but states, "As long as they physically abstain from the act, they haven't sinned. A thought is not a sin. And yes, people who have to struggle with this tendency are not in a very happy state of affairs. They need all the compassion and support and love we can give."

During the question-and-answer period, Rabbi Friedman seeks to dissolve some of the room's tension with banter. When one young man earnestly asks, "What does the Torah say about sexual pleasure, assuming that it's between husband and wife? Is it permissible to have pleasure when you engage in intercourse?"

"I don't know of any other way," Rabbi Friedman teases.

He is challenged by several women who appear irritated with his comment that Orthodox Jewish law defines male homosexuality as sinful, but regards lesbianism merely as "immodest." He holds his ground with only a trace of tension.

"I don't understand something," says one woman student a bit testily. "If all people are born with the potential to be attracted to both men and women like you said, then why does the Torah forbid us to touch or shake hands just with members of the opposite sex? Why isn't it forbidden concerning both sexes?"

"Well, it would certainly make things a lot easier for us," Rabbi Friedman concedes, smiling. Later, he evaluates his audience's response to the talk. "You know," he laughs, "I was really bracing myself for an onslaught when I finished my lecture. Yet there wasn't any. But I hadn't expected the attitude among some of the women when I explained the Torah's distinction between male and female homosexuality. It's as though the women felt I was trying to cheat them out of a sin."

There is little doubt of the sincerity and warmth of Bais Chana's staff, but what do the participants really think about the program? Are they ready to embrace not only a rigorously Orthodox, but also a Hasidic, lifestyle? Do some ever feel they are being given something of a hard sell, however well-meaning, in the intense daily atmosphere? Generally, the students' reactions vary a great deal according to their previous experience with Chabad, as well as their expectations and goals in joining the program.

It is Sara's first visit to Bais Chana. She heard about the Institute from Lubavitcher friends in Milwaukee. In her mid-twenties, and friendly but shy, she speaks hesitantly about herself. Sara grew up in Buffalo with minimal Jewish exposure. But from an early age, she had been curious about the community of Lubavitchers who lived in the area. Later, she attended the Cleveland Institute of Music, where she majored in the cello. Though Sara has played a bit professionally, she has never devoted herself sufficiently to music to become a full-time performer and has yet to establish herself in satisfying work. After moving to Milwaukee, she became involved with a Modern Orthodox Jewish outreach program, and eventually boarded with a Lubavitch family. After hearing Rabbi Friedman give a series of lectures in Milwaukee, she decided to try Bais Chana.

Sara has been a student for two weeks and will be leaving today. She has enjoyed learning the prayers and liturgy, and the warmth and intimacy of her Bible study group. Rabbi Friedman's classes have been the most stimulating, particularly a recent one on the Hasidic view of loyalty. "To me, it was an extremely relevant talk, because he made an important point: that we need to develop loyalty in our lives to be complete men and women. We need to be more loyal—to our husband, to our rabbi, to our synagogue, and not keep searching forever for perfection. This is a big personal issue for me, to decide on something and stick with it. His comment has helped me, so I can now go back to my rabbi in Milwaukee and the Jewish community there, and not look for nirvana."

But Sara is not about to become a Lubavitcher. She is troubled by their tremendous veneration of the Rebbe. This is an aspect of Hasidism almost totally without counterpart in the liberal suburban Judaism of her Buffalo upbringing. Hence, it is scarcely surprising that Sara finds it hard to fathom, much less to accept, as valid for her own life. "It's hard for me to understand," she admits, "and it's still over my head as to what it really means. But you can speak your mind here and express your concerns about the idea of the Rebbe: that he is so much higher, closer to God, than all the rest of us.

"When I'm with these people and see their sincerity, I don't give it much thought, but when I'm in my own head, it's hard to understand. I see perfectly normal people leading normal lives and it gives me a sense of what the Rebbe concept is. They've been brought up since day one with the Rebbe concept. But for others, I think, it's very hard."

After being encouraged by her Chabad friends in Milwaukee, Sara wrote to the Rebbe for advice about a personal problem, and received this reply: "Be more careful with your eating and drinking in accordance with Jewish law." He then gave her his blessing.

"Frankly, I can't see how that kind of advice relates to my personal problem," Sara remarks. "But Rabbi Friedman said something interesting to me: 'Maybe the Rebbe is suggesting that you look at your problems through the Jewish part of you. That you shouldn't forget the needs of the Jewish part of your soul.' To someone wanting to connect more with Judaism, that's an important piece of advice."

It is nearly time for Sara to leave for the airport. "I have learned a lot here," she says, suitcase in hand. "But I'm not saying there aren't other [Jewish learning] places available too."

Justine is from quite a different background. A willowy blonde in her late twenties, she displays a sharp, analytic mind and her odyssey to Bais Chana has followed a convoluted path. Born to non-Jewish parents in a small Maine town, she was raised as a Unitarian. At Swarthmore College, near Philadelphia, she met Jews for the first time in her life. As a result of such encounters, Justine gradually found herself attending Jewish services, study groups, and religious-related activities. Two years ago, she went through a conversion to Orthodox Judaism. She now lives in Boston. Like Sara, Justine has struggled to establish an adult identity for herself, and has drifted through a series of clerical jobs. Having chosen the profession of landscape architect, she will begin study toward her degree this fall.

Like virtually all other participants at Bais Chana, Justine heard about the program through personal recommendation. Last summer, she and her boyfriend were planning a cross-country trip together. The journey would take them right through Minnesota, and she obtained Rabbi Feller's phone number through Lubavitch headquarters in New York City. Her plan was to stay overnight for the Sabbath before moving on. But the Lubavitcher community intrigued her so much that she spent nearly a week with a host family and decided to return alone this summer for a month at Bais Chana.

Justine quickly describes what she likes about the program: its mystical teachings. She finds the transcendental aspects of Hasidism quite appealing. The emphasis on the Orthodox laws of family purity also appeals to her. "It's pretty clear that like some other women here, I've run the gamut in relationships with men, so to speak," she comments, "and we don't want to get bored with our husbands one year after marriage. The family-purity laws seem very sensible on all levels, physical and otherwise. We've all seen the damage done when too much mingling [between the sexes] is encouraged, and the phenomenon of women losing themselves in their men, their marriage. It's great to immerse yourself in a relationship, but not to the point where you forget who you are. I feel that this type of marriage encourages your exploration of yourself beyond your family: with God and with other women."

Justine is referring, of course, to the complex and demanding set of ritual observances between husband and wife in traditional Judaism. For approximately twelve days per month—corresponding to the woman's menstrual cycle—all physical contact between husband and wife is strictly forbidden and they must sleep in separate beds. But nonphysical contact is allowed, and many Lubavitch couples insist that this arrangement revitalizes their marriage every month. It is interesting that this arrangement, long abandoned by nearly all modern Jews, has an appeal for some who have been on the front lines of the sexual revolution.

Justine is not impressed with everything that Bais Chana represents. She readily expresses her unease about the Orthodox separation of men and women in synagogue seating. "I don't like sitting behind the synagogue partition between men and women. I resent that the men get to be where the action seems to be. I'm sick of having to strain in synagogue to hear what's being said, and of getting lost in the prayers. I'm sick of the chitchat of women and children crying in the back. But this is not strictly a Lubavitcher problem. In fact, it's better in Lubavitch than in other Orthodox places.

"I also believe in family planning and birth control. They're not even issues with me, they're so obvious." When informed that the Rebbe has explicitly criticized these practices, she seems surprised and interested, but comments, "Sometimes, I wonder why all the sages were men. Why couldn't they have included some women when they had those round-table discussions? Yet, the very fact that this school exists shows a tremendous respect for women. It's very rigorous academically. It has nothing to be ashamed of, compared to Swarthmore. Lubavitch wouldn't have put the time and money into a school for beings they consider intellectually inferior.

"But why do men have to thank God every day that they weren't born a woman? That issue was raised during Rabbi Friedman's very first class, and he gave several explanations. Some of these just seemed preposterous to me.

"And yet, I feel drawn to a great deal in the Hasidic way of life. And certainly, the instructors here feel no tension at all with that prayer, and even help their little sons learn to recite it from memory. You know, I was very interested in the feminist message when I went to Swarthmore. But I now see that the whole basis of that message was secularist.

Can I reconcile this conflict? I'm not sure. The degree to which I can reconcile it—the feminist versus the religious sides of me—will determine the degree to which I'm immersed in the Hasidic world. Because the minute I feel something clipping my wings, I'm going to balk."

Sara and Justine might both be characterized as being in a transitional state in their lives. Both have completed college, yet are uncommitted to a career and are also unmarried. They have traveled a bit, and though they speak with some confidence about their growing self-direction in life, neither can be considered settled down by any contemporary definition. For such women, who seem indicative of many at Bais Chana, their encounter with Chabad Hasidism may offer an unconscious way to connect with something enduring, stable, and disciplined.

But not all at Bais Chana have been at the forefront of feminism and the sexual revolution. Some, like Helene, grew up at a time when marriage and children, not a fulfilling career, comprised most women's expectations. Consequently, Helene never had to undergo the struggles for self-identity that have marked today's generation of young women. Her parents were Russian-Jewish émigrés, and she was born in Cuba just before the second world war. She emigrated to Miami in 1960 just as Castro was consolidating his power. There are thousands of middle-class Cuban Jews like Helene now living in south Florida.

While raising several children, she discovered the Lubavitchers and since the early 1970s, has been a friendly outsider to their community. Over years that have included a divorce and the death of a son, Helene has taken classes given by its local emissaries, and even hosted study groups in her own home. As for Bais Chana, she heard about it through acquaintances in Miami. Helene has a warm sweetness about her, and offers only praise for her experience this summer. What she finds most encouraging is the supportive atmosphere—a place to experience Judaism away from her regular daily life.

When casually asked if she has ever been to Crown Heights to see the Rebbe, Helene's face becomes radiant. She had two private audiences with him more than a decade ago and has corresponded with him intermittently since then. It was because of his advice that Helene opened her home to Hasidic classes, and she describes him as, "the most wonderful and inspiring person I have ever met in my life. The first time I met him, I felt in my own being a holiness in being a Jewish mother and a Jewish wife. I felt I understood my purpose in life.

"Many things have happened to me because of that first encounter with him more than fifteen years ago. His final words to me were: 'If you want God to be good to you, then you must be good to God.' " Though not rigorously observant, Helene feels committed to helping the Lubavitchers spread their message throughout the Jewish world. Her Bais Chana instructors are "so patient, I can't begin to tell you."

Like most Chabad emissaries Rabbi Friedman has ambitious hopes and dreams for the future. Speaking for his colleagues at Bais Chana he observes, "We'd like to see a full-time campus with more comfortable facilities, not only for college women, but also for women with children and married couples. We'd like to see a full-time staff, with several married women teaching full time, as role models for participants." He adds that his personal vision "is that we should have certain courses complementing the Jewish focus, like an exercise room or health club, a diet plan, and a holistic physician on staff."

Rabbi Friedman does not measure Bais Chana's success in terms of how many of its students decide to become Hasidim or even wholly Orthodox in their Judaism. "It is our belief," he says emphatically, "that God exists, that every word of Torah is literally true and correct. If a student moves even an inch closer toward that direction, it's not only a success, it's wonderful."

Rabbi Feller has a parallel but somewhat differing outlook. He sees Bais Chana's growth as part of the larger achievement of Chabad's twenty-seven-year presence in Minnesota. "To create a worldwide center for Jewish women, we didn't need to live in New York City or Los Angeles. Right here in my home town, we have been able to make this happen.

"And we will continue to make things happen here 'Jewishly' in the Twin Cities," he adds. "The Rebbe doesn't believe in moving people around. What makes Chabad—and Bais Chana—unique is that we don't have the situation that pervades other Jewish organizations in this country, where a smaller community is viewed as a stepping-stone to some larger, more prestigious, and more important one. Nothing is a stepping-stone to something else. Your growth is vertical, not geographic. Just because a Jew is part of a small community of a few thousand, doesn't make your work less important in the slightest. Minnesota was hardly known as a bastion of world Judaism, and look what we've accomplished here."

Perhaps the most significant thing about the Bais Chana Women's Institute is the opportunity that it offers bright Jewish women for serious and unadulterated exposure to traditional Hasidic Judaism. There are other sections of society faced with prejudice where Lubavitch encounters quite a different challenge. In a similar context nearly two centuries ago, a famous Hasidic rabbi once said, "If you want to help someone who has fallen into a ditch, you must be willing to step into the mud." And so the Lubavitchers strive to realize their vision through outreach to some of the most despised and rejected members of today's Jewish community.

V

RAISING THE
FALLEN SPARKS

One who saves a life is as though he has saved an entire world.

—The Talmud

ALTHOUGH MIDWINTER IS THE HEIGHT OF THE TOURIST SEASON, this formerly popular resort area of Florida has deteriorated badly over the past fifteen years, and few tourists venture this way anymore. Inside the aging Raleigh Hotel on Miami Beach, some two dozen Jewish men and two women of varying ages are listening to Rabbi Sholom Lipskar deliver a Hasidic discourse. Most of the audience seem keenly absorbed in the topic of ethics, and a few people are taking notes. Though Hasidim in Miami Beach were once very few, the Lubavitch community of south Florida has now become a permanent and visible presence, promulgating all kinds of outreach activities throughout the state.

But this is no ordinary adult-education class, and these are not typical students. All are Jewish federal prisoners, serving sentences for such white-collar crimes as drug smuggling, insurance or mail fraud, and tax evasion. After careful screening they have been chosen to participate in a federally approved two-week Torah seminar led by Lubavitcher administrator Sholom Lipskar and his Aleph Institute staff. Nearly all have already shown a serious interest in Jewish study and observance through Aleph's varied programs, and it is expected that they will serve as religious leaders among their prison peers when the retreat is over.

In the quiet, almost chilly, air-conditioned banquet room of the Raleigh Hotel, Rabbi Lipskar expounds on a theme of the *Tanya:* every person has a higher nature linked to God that can totally transcend external surroundings, even prison. By tapping into this inner source, we become able to control time instead of passively serving it. "You're not your prison number or your prison file. That's just your environment," he says earnestly. "And you needn't let being in prison limit your own growth. You can direct it at all times. How? By observing the lifestyle of the Torah that God has given us."

After a few questions have been asked, Rabbi Lipskar goes on to offer his audience some words of inspiration. He cites the examples of former Lubavitcher Rebbes who maintained an unswerving self-assurance and dignity even when they were imprisoned by brutal regimes and faced possible execution for their religious activity. He briefly tells of the courage shown by the previous Rebbe during his imprisonment by the Soviet secret police in 1927. "I can't even begin to tell you the number of Chabad Hasidim who have proven this point. You can rise above your surroundings when you leave here and go back to complete your sentences. You have an essence in you that's Godly and that no one can take away from you."

Soon it is time for lunch, and the three-hour class is over. The break will not be long lasting, for a full schedule of classes and prayers is ahead, until ten at night. As the tightly scheduled group disperses, Rabbi Lipskar sits down and smiles at each one leaving the meeting room. He is a portly man in his mid-forties, with an intense and determined air about him. Born in Russia and raised in the Lubavitch communities of Toronto and Crown Heights, he arrived in south Florida in 1969 soon after receiving rabbinical ordination. He had a special interest in enhancing Jewish education and quickly rose to become dean of the new Lubavitch yeshiva on Miami Beach. In this capacity he played an active role in helping Chabad's influence to grow tremendously in the region during a period in which Florida had established itself as a leading Jewish population center in the United States.

By 1981, Rabbi Lipskar felt ready for a new challenge. But he felt a restlessness, a yearning to accomplish something different and innovative within the field of Jewish education. He privately sought the Rebbe's advice that fall and was told with a gentle, encouraging smile: "The Almighty will soon give you a good thought."

That same Sabbath weekend in Crown Heights, the Rebbe's public discourse emphasized the fact that "Hasidim must reach out to all Jews, no matter how out of the way they may be. The Hebrew word for redemption is *geulah*, whereas the word for imprisonment or exile is *gola*. The difference between the two is merely the single letter aleph, first in the Hebrew alphabet and a symbol of energized activity."

As Sholom Lipskar listened to this lecture, a "good thought" indeed came to him. He recalled that several years before, the Rebbe had stressed the importance of providing spiritual direction to Jews in prison. Yet no real follow-through of that remark had taken place. Suddenly a link between these two, seemingly disparate, matters became clear. Why not bring religious education to Jewish prisoners? Of course individual rabbis here and there were making occasional prison visits around holiday time, but these tended to be isolated and perfunctory affairs. There was nothing even remotely organized or systematic happening in terms of real outreach. The fact that these Jews had committed criminal offenses did not justify spurning them. As the Rebbe had constantly stressed in his talks, a Jew is still a Jew, no matter what his or her station in life. The Rebbe was particularly fond of remarking, "Nine Jews of the caliber of Moses cannot make a *minyan* (prayer quorum), but ten of the most ordinary Jews can."

After flying back to Miami Beach, Sholom Lipskar gave further thought to the subject. Library research revealed the figure of approximately fifteen hundred Jews in federal prisons, not a large number. He also discovered that some professionals in the penology field recommend taking into account the prisoner's entire social network: his or her spouse, children, parents, siblings, friends, relatives, co-workers, neighbors, and others. Some researchers calculated that up to twenty or thirty people are directly affected each time someone is imprisoned for a sustained period. As Rabbi Lipskar quickly calculated, this figure translated into nearly fifty thousand Jews, hardly a trivial number at all. He saw that it might even be double that if he added those affected by state and county jail imprisonment.

Yet, as Lipskar enthusiastically spoke about his findings and their implications, few rabbis or lay people seemed concerned or even interested. He realized that "historically, Jewish communal leaders in the United States have been reluctant to become involved with Jewish prisoners on more than a superficial basis." The general Jewish community "was viewing this work as a burden, not as something representing a rich resource of human beings who, if given the opportunity, could lead meaningful lives and even contribute something to the rest of society."

Undeterred, Sholom Lipskar decided to heed the Rebbe's guidance and initiated his work alone. He began by planning Jewish outreach not only for prisoners but also for the isolated elderly. Members of both groups had a lot in common: Both suffered from marginal or pariah status and both experienced a great deal of empty or "dead" time in their daily lives. Lipskar was familiar with the spiritual needs of the Jewish elderly; Miami Beach had the largest concentration in America of what gerontologists call the "old-old," thousands of men and women, mostly poor and frail, in their late eighties and nineties. It was the Rebbe's faith in their untapped capacity to benefit from Jewish learning that sparked young Rabbi Lipskar's plan to include them in his new-found mission.

Indeed, during the next few years, the Rebbe spoke more forcefully on the theme. He emphasized that the concept of retirement does not exist in traditional Judaism, and that all individuals, regardless of chronological age, need to remain physically and spiritually active to fulfill their purpose on earth.

Taking his cue from the Rebbe's public talk, Lipskar called his venture the Aleph Institute. He knew that the first Hebrew letter symbolically conveys many things, such as belief in God. He also remembered that Lubavitch's founder had once characterized the aleph as comprising three aspects: the dot on the top, which represents the essence of God; the dot on the bottom, which stands for the essence of each Jew; and the line in the center, which connects the two.

Sholom Lipskar's first visit to a federal prison in Miami was a memorable one: "I can still see myself slowly walking from the parking lot. It felt like a cemetery, which was the only other place I had ever felt this way in my life. There was a stillness that was pervasive. Even the birds didn't chirp right. There was an eerie stillness that dominated the environment. It wasn't the sound of vibrancy or vitality. It was the sound that you might hear at the back of a funeral parlor, as though instruments were being readied for some final, macabre ending.

"I passed through sets of big gates in that medium-security facility," he recalls. "At the first, I was searched by guards, and went through a metal detector. My pockets were emptied. Then a second set of gates automatically opened and shut, and then a third set, which did the same. And then, I found myself in a pleasant environment, almost a Shangri-la. There was a little lake in the center of the grounds. It was nicely landscaped. I almost felt that I had passed into another world. And in a way, I had."

"Every feeling I had about prisons turned out to be a misconception," he recollects. "I didn't see people who dressed alike and looked alike, as soon as I began talking with them, I sensed each as a lost human soul inside the shell of a prison inmate."

Gradually relaxing, Rabbi Lipskar found the afternoon passing comfortably. It was only upon leaving that the "reality and the horror of the truth emanated. I looked behind me, and I saw the men standing about two hundred feet from the front gate, because they were forbidden to stand any closer. I saw the look of yearning in their eyes as they watched me leave, and their gaze followed me right to my car."

Sholom Lipskar began with a nucleus of twenty Jewish convicts at the single Miami prison. He decided to innovate immediately, and become a consultant or resource person to complement the study of Judaism that the group was undertaking on the other days. In this way, "their exploration of their Jewishness became an ongoing affair, of which one day per week had a special rabbinic interaction."

Rabbi Lipskar continued to act in this role for almost three years, often advising the prisoners on personal problems. Family difficulties involving marriage and children were pervasive, and he felt hampered by being able to offer little more than a sympathetic word. More useful, he felt, was his role as religious adviser, and he gradually encouraged the group to become more observant.

Many had been raised with minimal Jewish education, and had not even been bar-mitzvahed. They had never opened a Hebrew prayer book, let alone attempted the traditional rituals. But moved by Sholom Lipskar's conviction that embracing the "Torah lifestyle" would help them in every way, most adopted a positive attitude and overcame fears of ridicule or ostracism from their fellow convicts. "In the beginning, when we started putting on phylacteries while praying, there were a lot of questions," said Joseph, a thirty-one-year-old bank robber from Palm Beach, who was serving a seven-year sentence. "The non-Jews around us thought it was something like voodoo. But it has turned around. They respect you for it if you are consistent and they see you are living your religion."

Eventually, having come to know many of the convicts' spouses, children, and other family members, Rabbi Lipskar decided to sponsor informal support groups. It had become apparent to him that few penologists had fully recognized the profoundly disruptive effects that individual imprisonment has on families. Through vigorous fund-raising, he was able to hire enough part-time staff, assisted by volunteers, to carry out this much needed help.

By early 1984 Sholom Lipskar had conceived the ambition of expanding his outreach work with prisoners to create a "retreat," in which some could actually leave their prisons for a two-week furlough period and participate in a highly concentrated program of Jewish study and prayer. It was his belief that their rehabilitation could be greatly accelerated in this way. He submitted the proposal to the scrutiny of several federal judges and, with their endorsement, succeeded in winning official approval for his new program. Though there were religious furloughs for Christian prisoners, this was the first time that any Jewish organization had successfully orchestrated an effort of this kind.

That November, a group of nine Jewish federal convicts arrived at Miami Beach. All were serving time in East Coast penitentiaries, for nonviolent offenses such as bribery and fraud, and had been selected from among some two dozen applicants for their motivation and ability to benefit from the program. On the first evening they were greeted by a formidable rabbinic lecture on "Torah Values as a Source for Rehabilitation," and early the next morning they were required to participate in Hasidic prayer. The program proved so demanding to this initial group that two men asked to be allowed to return to their prisons immediately. With Aleph staff assistance, however, both were able to continue successfully, and over four years, not a single person has quit a retreat.

Indeed, after the first retreat ended, the prison grapevine spread encouraging word about it, and for each retreat that Project Aleph sponsors, it receives over eighty applications from federal prisons around the country. To be eligible for the two-week furlough, now held at several national locations besides Miami Beach, participants must be serving the final two years of their sentence. All applicants are carefully screened by prison officials; some are forbidden to be in particular places; others may not associate with certain of their peers.

Like all Chabad programs in the United States and abroad, the Aleph Institute is rooted in traditional Judaism, specifically Hasidism. They base its approach to convict rehabilitation on concepts in the Talmud, Maimonides' writings, and Chabad tracts such as the *Tanya*. They believe that the Torah contains timeless wisdom for every age's particular moral and social concerns, including the contemporary field of criminology. Though the Lubavitchers are often categorized as ultraconservatives or fundamentalists for their uncompromising positions concerning public morality, their stance on treating criminal offenders is surprisingly liberal by contemporary political standards.

While the Lubavitchers are vigorously fighting liberal groups like the American Jewish Congress and the American Civil Liberties Union (ACLU) on religion-state separatism they are now *allied* with the ACLU in battling for the religious and social rights of prisoners. Such a situation underscores the difficulty of applying simplistic political labels to a religious movement as complex as Lubavitch.

In essence, Lubavitch argues that the Torah decisively rejects extended confinement as a means for dealing with crime. Allusions to prison can be found in Genesis and other books of the Bible, for example, the story of Joseph's imprisonment after Potiphar's wife accused him of making sexual advances to her. However, these instances refer either to non-Jewish penal systems or to the Jewish practice of placing the accused in a temporary holding cell until trial and sentencing. Lubavitch interprets biblical accounts of individuals placed in towers and denied adequate food as forms of execution rather than punitive incarceration.

"A clear indication that the Torah does not advocate the use of prisons," explains an Aleph Institute brochure, "is the fact that it deals in minutest detail with all sorts of punishments, types of instruments used, duration of whipping, doctors' participation, and the amounts of fines. Yet, the Torah does not give a single detail on punitive incarceration."

Lubavitchers find the closest parallel to modern punitive incarceration in the Torah-mandated "cities of refuge" (penal colonies) during ancient Jewish times. These cities served the purpose of "protective custody" by preventing a victim's relatives from resorting to vigilante-style vengeance. But an offender was also supposed to atone in the city, and this was deemed possible only in a humane milieu. Thus, the Torah stipulates the geographic and physical requirements necessary for a proper city of refuge, such as proximity to market towns and sources of fresh water. Moreover, these cities were full-fledged communities, where not only the offender's wife and children, but also his teacher would live.

Lubavitch makes it quite clear that, "Once prisons are established, particularly in countries where human rights are respected and governments advocate the betterment and freedom of their citizens, Jews must obey the laws of the land. The guiding axiom must be that everything in creation exists for a purpose, and that we are to find meaning and purpose in prison to the fullest extent possible."

What can be the positive worth of imprisonment? The Lubavitchers argue that aside from the benefits of deterrence and societal safety, incarceration can serve a useful purpose if the offender undergoes genuine rehabilitation (in Hebrew, *teshuvah*). But for this process to occur, three features must be present. First, the prison environment itself has to be humane and accord the possibility for growth. Second, the miscreant must truly acknowledge personal flaws and reject them as undesirable. Third, he or she must make a firm and disciplined resolve for change and self-improvement. *Teshuvah* also involves remorse for one's past and a resolution to behave differently in the future. Therefore, when the miscreant is separated from society by imprisonment, an intense process of self-evaluation and self-improvement can occur.

The Lubavitchers extol Judaism's many ritual laws as the specific disciplining force that enables Jewish convicts to accomplish this process. Through religious study and observance they can not only effect self-rehabilitation, but become moral exemplars to peers and even staff within the prison. Aleph Institute activists contend that typical imprisonment accomplishes none of these aims.

"Prison inhibits and limits individual potential, destroys the miscreant's family, and breeds bitterness, anger, insensitivity, and eventual recidivism. Consequently, it is of tremendous importance to make it possible for inmates to transform a period of suspended life to vibrant life, thus fulfilling their purpose in the universe. As Ecclesiastes reminds us, 'From the darkest moments and deep loss can come the greatest light and ultimate gain.' "

Though prison outreach is arduous and time-consuming, each Aleph staff member or local Lubavitcher affiliate seems to have at least one success story to relate that makes the effort worthwhile. Yet, the activities of most of them are not confined solely to providing guidance to individual Jews in prison. Sholom Lipskar has broad ambitions and wants to bring Hasidic values to bear on the way in which criminals are treated in American society. Guided by the Torah's rejection of imprisonment as a means of punishment, he has recently been pressing for governmental support for alternatives to imprisonment for nonviolent criminals. One Aleph position paper lists more than half a dozen other options for sentencing judges.

The Aleph Institute's efforts have been getting results: new arrangements allow nonviolent offenders who commit minor offenses to serve a short prison term followed by community service. And Aleph's alternative-to-prison program now has dozens of graduates. Its staff seek as clients those prisoners who genuinely want to change and who have a family that can offer them support.

One arrangement is typified by the case of Carol, a Fort Lauderdale woman who had served time for marijuana trafficking. After a conviction for shoplifting resulted in her being sent back to prison, she heard about Project Aleph through a friend. Rabbi Lipskar persuaded the local judge to give Carol another chance with the help of the Aleph

Institute. She was placed on "community control," a strict form of probation in which a person may not go out except for work and other activities approved by the parole officer. Aleph staff members are already counseling her husband and child, and are planning to provide counseling for Carol as well. It is interesting to note that she is not Jewish.

Recently, the Aleph Institute helped to sponsor a national symposium on "Alternative Punishments under the New Federal Sentencing Guidelines." Held in New York City, the symposium was co-sponsored by the Brooklyn Law School and the Judges of the Eastern U.S. District Court of New York. Rabbi Lipskar was among the six presenters, who included the U.S. Sentencing Commissioner, the Director of the Federal Bureau of Prisons, and former Chief Justice of the U.S. District Eastern Court Judge Jack Weinstein.

"The Aleph Institute," he commented, "primarily operated by Orthodox Jews . . . is doing extraordinarily fine work. Its pre-prison counseling, in-prison education, and post-prison assistance to defendants and their families provide standards of compassion and assistance worthy of emulation. . . . They understand and force us to face the fact that each person is entitled to be treated as an individual personality and not as a faceless number."

In a similar vein, a director of chaplains for the federal corrections department has stated, "It's the kind of volunteer organization that we like to see. It has become a resource for our entire system. Rabbi Lipskar is really making an effort to be the support group for incarcerated Jews to get them in touch with their Jewishness and to help them through this experience [of imprisonment]."

But Lubavitch prison outreach work has had its difficulties. Some emissaries seem more willing than others to admit the frustrations of advising Jewish prisoners, but nearly all divide their problems into two distinct categories: those related to the large bureaucracy of the penal system, and those involving individual prisoners.

One major obstacle that all the Chabad emissaries face is logistic. Few federal prisons are close to metropolitan areas; many are not even near major airports. Because most emissaries are based in the larger cities of their respective states, a single prison visit to a handful of Jewish inmates can take up a half day or longer. Once an emissary arrives at the prison gates, he must wait to be escorted by the prison chaplain and wait, too, for the inmates to be brought from their work assignments. Even in the best of circumstances, such bureaucratic exigencies prove frustrating to those accustomed to busy and autonomous daily schedules. For example, Rabbi Lipskar recalls arranging an elaborate trip to meet a group of Jewish inmates in a Texas federal penitentiary only to be told on arrival that the chaplain was on vacation and that no religious visit with prisoners could take place without him. Eventually Lipskar was able to persuade the warden to allow the meeting to take place, but it is not an episode he would like to repeat. On another occasion, he traveled for hours to visit a single Jewish prisoner in a Florida state prison, only to learn that the man had been transferred to a distant facility earlier that same day.

The issue of contraband poses a constant problem to those working in prison outreach. Though penal officials generally permit matzos and grape juice to be brought in for Passover, they remain wary of sanctioning other foods or religious items for Jewish inmates. One midwestern Chabad emissary relates how his attempts to bring in honey cake for Rosh Hashanah and dreidels for Chanukah were both denied on the grounds that the items might contain contraband. Even phylacteries are suspect, since prison authorities are reluctant to allow the admittance of little black boxes that can't be opened at the gate.

On one occasion, a group of Jewish inmates in a Florida state prison decided to hold their daily prayers with phylacteries in the fields outside their cell building. As they stood in prayer they were startled to hear, "Freeze! Stop in your tracks! Don't move!" and see several nervous prison guards pointing loaded revolvers at them. One guard shouted, "What have you got on your head? Who are you communicating with?"

Their explanation of the phylacteries did not convince the guards, who marched the group, hands raised above their heads, into individual solitary-confinement cells for attempting to escape. There they remained until Aleph staff confirmed the religious nature of the black straps and little boxes seized by the guards.

Another difficulty for the Lubavitchers in their outreach work with prisoners is those who claim to be Jewish but are not. "They feel that if they ally themselves with a rabbi, they may be better off," says Ohio's emissary Chaim Capland with an ironic grin, "and you can't throw them out. As long as you don't have to count them in a minyan, it's not a tremendous problem. However, I do try to spend more time with the ones I know are Jewish."

More problematic has been the way some inmates have attempted to manipulate the Chabad rabbis over the issue of kosher food. Many prisoners—some clearly not Jewish—demand kosher food as a way to strike back at the hated system or simply because they want better fare. "When you're in that kind of subculture," Chaim Capland comments, "and everyone is telling you what to do, and particularly if you've been the kind of person who's kicked others around, you just don't change your personality overnight. I remember one fellow, built like a tank, who was appealing for kosher food rights. 'Look at me,' he said, 'I'm weak, withering away to nothing like a rabbit. All I eat is lettuce!' "

Pressured on one side by prisoners demanding their support to obtain kosher food and on the other by officials unwilling to be bothered, even in cases that seemed legitimate, Aleph staff and their local associates felt beleaguered. Eventually, Aleph formulated and distributed a set of guidelines for chaplains and prison authorities alike. "If the inmates say they're now keeping strictly kosher," Rabbi Lipskar says, "we tell them to try eating only fruits, vegetables, and bread. After a few months if they're still following that diet, then of course we'll help them out. But if they think that just by saying they're 'kosher,' they're going to get kosher steaks from the butcher, or bagels and lox for Sunday breakfast, that's a different trip."

Most Lubavitch emissaries mention the necessity of drawing a moral distinction between a crime and its perpetrator, who may suffer genuine remorse. But this is not always easy and many emissaries prefer working with well-educated Jewish inmates guilty of financial crimes like income-tax evasion, which lack obvious victims. Yet the Chabad rabbis do not shun the criminally violent or those who have committed morally perverse acts. "Sometimes, it's only when we have reached the lowest moment that we are able to move to the other extreme," comments Sholom Lipskar. "Our tradition teaches that a basic reason why Jews are spread out all over the world, in the Diaspora, is to better elevate the sparks of holiness that exist everywhere."

Recidivism is another source of frustration to those engaged in prison outreach work. Sometimes the many hours of long-distance commuting and personal guidance seem fruitless.

Rabbi Lipskar is more philosophical. "I believe that for an individual to experience even a few moments of decency and sanity in his or her life is better than to have experienced none at all. The few moments that we are able to influence someone may linger for a long time. A day may come when what we have said or taught surfaces in his conscience, to remind him what he's doing. So what he experienced with us may not have been a wasted experience."

A final obstacle toward effective prison outreach for the Lubavitchers is what Aleph's director calls "the very judgmental, condescending attitude of the American Jewish community to our program." He recounts a recent episode, in which he spoke with one woman at length about the Aleph Institute: its services for families and children of Jewish convicts, and all the ancillary issues involved. To his delight, she indicated her interest in volunteering and invited him to call the next time he returned to New York City. Later however, he learned that she had commented: "What kind of phony rabbi is that? Who the hell cares about Jews in prison? Why doesn't he worry about children or something!"

Somewhat ruefully, he responds, "That's the general attitude in our society: that they deserve it, that we don't want to know about them, and that we're not responsible for them. With so many more Jews going to prison for committing crimes on Wall Street and in government, there are few communities now where people are not touched by someone who is going to prison. We can't bury our heads in the sand anymore."

Rabbi Lipskar recently had occasion to make this point quite dramatically. Invited by a south Florida B'nai B'rith lodge to speak on "Jews in Prison," he decided to try something more forceful than his usual Hasidic discourse. By chance, his speech coincided with a two-week Torah furlough for federal inmates that Aleph was sponsoring in Miami Beach. Without informing B'nai B'rith's members, he brought the twenty-odd prisoners to the lodge just as the preliminary social hour was beginning. Wearing regular clothing, they quickly dispersed among the entering lodge members and mixed easily before taking seats as the talk began.

He cited Maimonides, the Talmud, and other classic sources, then spoke from personal experience about the importance of helping their "fellow Jews in prison." The audience nodded in polite agreement with his compassionate remarks, but their faces revealed little conviction or interest. "Jewish prisoners are human beings like us," he exclaimed, "and there are some here even in this room."

Suddenly, the B'nai B'rith lodge members looked up sharply. What was he talking about?

"Will all those who are currently serving time in prison please stand up?" he asked.

Two dozen men rose to their feet, as audible gasps were heard all around them.

"The shock in the room was overwhelming," recalls Sholom Lipskar. "Suddenly the nice-looking young man sitting next to them was actually a convict. It was quite an awakening for them."

In their outreach work with Jewish prisoners, the Lubavitchers have been surprisingly successful in transmitting Hasidic precepts to change people's lives. They have also been successful with quite another group of contemporary Jews: professionals, intellectuals, scientists and artists.

VI

THE CREATIVE FLAME

What is the way that will lead to the love and fear of God? When a person contemplates His great and wondrous works and creatures, and from them obtains a glimpse of His wisdom, which is incomparable and infinite, he will straightaway love Him, praise Him, glorify Him, and long with an exceeding longing to know His great name.

—Maimonides

THE LUBAVITCHERS BELIEVE THAT IN ALL CREATIVE FIELDS— from academia to the arts and sciences—traditional Judaism as best represented by Hasidism is a tremendous source of inspiration and guidance.

Not only on the college campus, many Jewish professionals in such fields as psychiatry, psychotherapy, and counseling are discovering insights in Hasidism. Most of them are not Hasidim themselves though many maintain a strong Jewish identity. They are drawn to the intellectual sophistication that seems to dominate Chabad philosophy, especially as it is energetically advanced by the present Lubavitcher Rebbe. New York City psychiatrist Sholom Zev Applebaum is perhaps representative of these American Jews today.

A small, bearded man with a gentle manner, Dr. Applebaum recalls, "My first contact with the Rebbe started with a very deep involvement in trying to run a low-cost mental-health program during the late 1960s. I was having a lot of stress coping with the bureaucratic regulations and the government officials who seemed to be deliberately making things very difficult for us. It was then that I met the local Lubavitcher emissary, operating out of a somewhat run-down old Jewish neighborhood. We were all trying to work with drug cases. It was the Age of Aquarius gone sour.

"Lubavitcher staff would call on me when more than just pastoral counseling was needed, and we got along well together. It was probably because I had always believed that a bond between psychiatry and religion could exist. I felt sure that science alone was inadequate, especially scientism: making a religion out of science. After my early Jewish training as a youngster, I knew that I wanted to bring spirituality into my work in psychiatry. I clearly saw that the psychoanalytic and medical approaches to the mind were too narrow.

"I didn't know much about the Lubavitchers then, Frankly, I had met other kinds of Hasidim who weren't very welcoming. I might not have gone to the Lubavitcher Rebbe quite so soon if I hadn't been in this difficulty. I wanted some advice, some validation from on high, really—advice that might help my mental-health program survive in spite of the odds.

"It was four o'clock in the morning when I went to see the Rebbe back in 1970. Speaking in English, he spent more than an hour with me there in his little study. He held a long discussion with me—putting aside my particular problem—on how belief in God relates to effective psychological and psychiatric treatment. I was amazed that he tuned into something that had been a very deep concern of mine. As far as I knew, he knew nothing about my own background.

"Then he identified the dominant Freudian approach as being intellectually bankrupt and pointed out that psychiatry needs a different, more complete, conception of the human soul. He even addressed specific aspects of current psychiatric treatment, and he suggested something that I had never even heard before: the importance of taking a 'religious case history.' That is, just as there are cultural and sexual factors in any psychological disorder, he encouraged me to find out about my patients' religious beliefs and attitudes, as well as their external religious behavior like synagogue or church attendance.

"He emphasized that our metaphysical outlook and personal philosophy—the kind of religion we believe in—intimately affects how we experience life, with its inevitable ups and downs and stress. It was a profound insight, and couldn't have been more relevant had my own clinical supervisor suggested it. In fact, the Rebbe's comment cut much deeper than anything I had been told in psychiatric supervision. Next, the Rebbe talked about the importance of experiencing meaning in our lives, and he suggested that I read the writings of the Austrian psychiatrist Dr. Viktor Frankl, a Holocaust survivor and founder of logotherapy.

"Finally, the Rebbe addressed my specific problem in trying to maintain my mental-health clinic. I thought that he had almost forgotten it. He told me to amass more community support—staff members of agencies, local government officials—by alerting them to what my clinic was doing, and then to rally them behind my group. I followed his advice, and though I eventually shut down the clinic, his suggestion helped me to keep it going longer than it would have otherwise. Since then, I've had several direct contacts with the Rebbe and also written to him over the years. He continues to be an immensely inspiring figure for me."

Irene Javors is another psychotherapist who has been favorably touched by Lubavitch. Directing the Artists Therapy Service in the fashionable Chelsea section of Manhattan, she specializes in helping artists to overcome creative blocks and has published numerous articles on the creative process. Javors has studied Eastern philosophy since the 1960s and has recently developed a strong interest in Jewish mysticism. Though by no means uncritical of all of Chabad's doctrines, she finds particularly valuable its approach to emotional health, creativity, and art as a spiritual endeavor.

"As a therapist, I like the way the Lubavitchers try to put our personal problems in life into a larger perspective than just what is happening at the moment. The secular traditions that we live in, especially psychotherapy, tend to get us bogged down in the problem rather than its solution. It seems to me that the Hasidic emphasis on finding the positive in everything we experience is a very healthful outlook. I also value their idea that we are given gifts by God in our life, that just being alive is an incalculable gift. The Hasidic notion that everything is holy too seems to me a very healing view, that everything we do can be holy. That's the one branch of Judaism that really talks about the divinity in everyday life.

"I also see art and art expression as a means to distance ourselves from our ego, to get it out of the way, so we can allow the higher part of us—connected to the divine—to shine through when we do creative work. When we are involved in artistic activity, we definitely are drawing upon our spirituality. This is because in order for us to transcend our individual ego, we must gain a higher perspective, and that's a step toward spiritual development. I view art as a spiritual activity as a very important concept, and I admire the Lubavitchers' recognition of this fact."

The interest that therapists such as Javors have in Chabad's approach to aesthetic creation is not accidental. In recent years, the Rebbe has specifically encouraged Jewish artists, including those among his Hasidim, to develop their talents. This attitude represents an innovation for Hasidism, for while its adherents have long extolled music as a pathway to the divine, they have characteristically said little about art until the leadership of the present Lubavitcher Rebbe.

In a letter to Russian-born Hendel Lieberman—known as the "father of Hasidic art" for his impressionistic paintings of Old World Jewish life, the Rebbe described his view: "The genius of the artist lies in his ability to detach himself from his subject's external form. Looking beyond it, he must try to glimpse its inner content and capture this in his art form, revealing to others what they had not previously noticed, obscured as it had been by external trivia. The artist thereby reveals in his art the essence and inner being of his subject. Others can now view it in a new, truer light, realizing how mistaken their previous impressions were." He went on to suggest that this situation parallels the purpose of human existence: to pierce the material veneer that conceals the presence of God in the universe.

To the sculptor Jacques Lipchitz, who grew close to Lubavitch in his later years, the Rebbe wrote in a similar vein. Commenting on the lofty purpose of art, the Rebbe did not need to make explicit for Lipchitz the prohibition of Jewish law concerning idolatrous images. "Those divinely gifted with artistic talent—in painting or in sculpture—have the privilege of being able to convert inanimate objects (brush and paints, wood or stone) into 'live' form. On a deeper level, it is an ability to transform, in a sense, material to spiritual. This is true even if the subject is still life, and certainly if the artwork depicts living beings and people. To utilize the art medium to foster ideals, especially those reflecting Jewish religious study and observance, is to raise artistic talent to its highest level."

Among other artists personally inspired by the Rebbe is the celebrated Israeli Baruch Nachshon of Hebron. "The Creator can be served in many ways," he was advised. "We are each given our destined field of activity—whether in the natural sciences, crafts, or the arts—in which to fulfill ourselves during our lifetime. Generations have passed, but art has never yet been elevated to its ultimate level of fulfillment from a truly Jewish perspective."

Nachshon felt that these words charged him with a special mission to shape art into a medium for expressing the values of traditional Judaism. In a unique gesture, the Rebbe gave him a one-year grant to support his family while he studied art. Though Nachshon had painted since childhood, he had received no formal art education. The grant enabled him to attend art courses and study great art collections in the United States. In this manner, Nachshon developed an independent style. Eventually he returned to Israel and Hebron to raise a large family as committed Hasidim. His surrealist paintings depict sublimely mystical Jewish themes with strongly evocative symbolism.

In the United States, Lubavitch has supported the establishment of a Chasidic Art Institute (CHAI) in Crown Heights. Directed by Elye Gross and Soviet émigré Vladimir Markowitz, CHAI runs a gallery near Chabad headquarters and a traveling exhibition that has visited galleries in over twenty major cities across the country. Several years ago, an exhibition at the Brooklyn Museum received considerable press coverage and featured the paintings of Hendel Lieberman and four younger Hasidic artists of Crown Heights.

Not all Jewish artists drawn to Chabad teachings are interested in becoming Hasidim. More typical are those like native midwesterner Paul Palnik, who values his exposure to Hasidic philosophy through Lubavitch's rabbinic emissaries. Palnik lives near the local emissary in Columbus, Ohio, and observes, "I find that Chabad directly deals with my getting in touch with my innermost, creative self—which, in my view, is connected to the Creator. The whole Lubavitch movement is clearly about getting close to God, and my fascination as an artist is getting close to my Creator, so I can be a better creative personality."

When asked how his attraction for Hasidic belief affects his work,

Palnik—who has illustrated Chabad posters and periodicals for many years—replies. "I remember reading the old tale about Reb Zusya, who had a visionary experience in which he ascended to heaven. Upon returning, he remarked, 'When I reached paradise and thought my time on earth was over, the angels didn't ask, "Why weren't you like Moses?" Rather, they asked, "Why weren't you like Zusya?" ' This beautiful Hasidic parable sustained me when I wasn't yet earning a living as an artist, or when times were tough. It helped support me psychologically and spiritually.

"I haven't found this message in other branches of Judaism as strongly and as clearly as I've heard it in Hasidism. I've studied Eastern religions, humanistic psychology, and Western philosophy. In none of them have I heard this message expressed so eloquently and with such clarity as in Hasidism, especially that of Chabad: 'Be who you are, and fulfill yourself creatively in the most comprehensive way.' "

Though Lubavitch has been increasingly successful in its efforts to transmit Hasidic values to many Jewish intellectuals, for the scientific community there is a particular problem. Hasidim accept on faith every word of the Bible as true, and this deeply held belief is central to their entire way of life and is not a subject for debate. It poses few problems in most of their outreach work, for abstruse questions of cosmology and paleontology scarcely affect decisions about family relations, livelihood, or health matters. But issues such as the age of the earth and the validity of evolutionary theory are very much the concern of today's scientists, most of whom remain skeptical about biblical literalism.

Under the influence of the present Rebbe, Lubavitch has readily embraced the use of high technology in their far-flung emissary, welfare, and publishing endeavors. For example, they were among the first religious groups in the United States to use satellite and cable television in broadcasting worldwide the Rebbe's discourses, and have adopted almost an ardent high-tech professionalism in their organizational activities.

Long Island emissary Rabbi Tuvya Teldon, who frequently offers workshops to his colleagues on computer technology and its applications in Jewish outreach, has developed a special computer software program for Chabad Houses. He observed that the Baal Shem Tov, founder of Hasidism, teaches us that everything on earth is meant to be elevated and serve God. For example, the Talmudic sages commented that when gold was used to adorn the Holy Temple furnishings, the gold was fulfilling its purpose for existing in our world. Therefore, we can use the same analogy for high technology like computers or fax machines. Our Rebbe stresses that not only is there nothing wrong with using such technology, but that the reason that God is giving people so many ideas on this subject is to make technology a holy instrument, to carry His word throughout the world."

Some Lubavitcher activists have begun seeking common ground on which they and Jewish scientists can both stand, and perhaps even meet. In the forefront of such endeavours is Professor Herman Branover of Ben-Gurion University, who has founded an international and interdisciplinary journal dedicated to contemporary science from a traditional Jewish perspective. Entitled *B'Or Ha'-Torah (In The Light of the Torah)*, it has featured articles from prominent academics and researchers in fields ranging from mathematics and physics to psychology and education.

In December 1987, Professor Branover helped to organize the First International B'Or Ha'Torah Conference, subtitled "Absolute Standards in a World of Relativity." In his opening speech, he sought to prove that committed Orthodox Jews can be skillful scientific theorists and empiricists.

Though the participants at the conference differed widely in their particular topics of interest, they clearly shared a consensus that traditional Judaism complements—and sometimes even bolsters—their scientific commitment. For example, several doctorate-level scholars highlighted the striking parallels between Jewish mysticism and contemporary disciplines such as mathematics and quantum physics concerning the very nature of reality. Professor Avraham Hasofer of New South Wales University commented, "It is not necessary to go to Eastern mysticism to find these parallels. They are right here at home in Judaism. The fact that there is such tremendous efficiency of mathematics in the world is the most cogent and indestructible proof of the power, might, and continuous appearance of God in every aspect of physical creation."

Carnegie Mellon's Dr. Zvi Saks, a researcher in the field of artificial intelligence shared the same outlook. "Mathematics for me was always a spiritual area, and I always wondered what potential application there might be for my complex and abstract doctoral thesis, which had no known relation with the physical world. When I began studying Torah, it really amazed me to discover that the creation of the world by God as described in Hasidism was the actual application of the mathematical work that I did."

Several theorists emphasized their intense opposition as observant Jews, not to science, but to *scientism:* the belief that logic and its material expression in empiricism are the only valid ways to know the universe. Speakers like Professor Paul Rosenbloom of Columbia University and physicist Avi Rabinowitz of Ben-Gurion University decisively rejected this approach as not only contrary to fundamental Jewish belief, but scientifically obsolete as well. In their view, science is a strictly human invention and hence a reflection of quite limited perceptions of the cosmos. While science was once venerated as the be-all of human achievement, its own contemporary underpinnings in subatomic physics reject scientific method as the means to grasp ultimate truth.

"Is modern science converging to Torah?" asked Dr. Rabinowitz before an attentive audience. "Prior to quantum physics about sixty years ago, the universe was seen as a deterministic machine with man an insignificant part within it, a cog which arose absolutely by chance and which is itself a machine without a soul, without free will, without even a true consciousness.

"Today, however, quantum physics has opened the door to free will, to the possibility that humans and their consciousness are not mere cogs but necessary to the existence of the universe. The great mathematician Gödel, who revolutionized all of mathematics, has shown how mathematics indicates the possibility that there exists an absolute truth which can be directly intuited rather than analyzed by the human mind. Other areas of science have opened up other doors. It is certainly true that the intellectual climate today is much more favorable to Torah than it was two hundred years ago. Hopefully, all will eventually realize that nature and Torah originate with God."

In Lubavitcher eyes perhaps the most renowned speaker was Herman Branover. An internationally respected researcher in magnetohydrodynamics who has been a recipient of U.S. Navy and Star Wars research grants, Dr. Branover is a former Soviet refusenik. While still living in the U.S.S.R., he became increasingly drawn to his Jewish heritage. Through clandestine encounters with Chabad's extensive underground network of which he became a member by the time he left Moscow in 1972, and later, through numerous personal meetings with the Rebbe in New York City, Dr. Branover became an ardent Hasid. In the past eighteen years, he has struggled to distribute Jewish books and study materials secretly in his former homeland. He and his Chabad colleagues in Israel, heading a special organization of observant Soviet Jews (its Hebrew acronym SHAMIR), had translated into contemporary Russian more than 140 major Jewish texts, which found their way into the Soviet Union. With a full beard, sporty beret, and ready smile, he resembles a bohemian artist more than a topflight scientist. In his moving autobiography, *The Return,* Dr. Branover not only chronicles his odyssey in becoming an observant Jew while remaining true to his scientific love of physics, but stresses his faith in the Torah as the source of all knowledge.

"Science can be very successful in practical applications—in building different machines, tools, and facilities," he stated during an interview, "but it can never even *approach* the fundamentals of which Torah speaks. Science is a *craft,* like the craft of a tailor or a shoemaker— much more sophisticated and complicated, but basically the same. Just as one cannot say that the achievements of a tailor are contradictory to Torah, neither are the works of a physicist or a biologist."

In a frequently reprinted open letter that the Rebbe wrote in 1962, he assured a troubled Orthodox Jewish man: "Basically, the 'problem' has its roots in a misconception of the scientific method, or simply, what science is. We must distinguish between empirical or experimental science dealing with observable phenomena, and speculative 'science,' dealing with phenomena that are sometimes unknown or that cannot be duplicated in the laboratory."

In the same letter, rejecting the notion that science has rendered the Genesis account of Creation outmoded, the Rebbe observed: "Scientists know very little of the atoms in their original, pristine state. In advancing their theories, such scientists blithely disregard factors universally admitted: that, in the initial period of the 'birth of the universe,' a host of cataclysmic factors were totally different from those existing in the present state of the universe."

Despite the currently strong consensus in the scientific community, he also challenged the theory of evolution. "The discovery of fossils is *by no means* conclusive evidence of the great antiquity of the earth." Outlining three reasons for accepting the biblical account of Creation, he commented: "In view of the unknown conditions which existed in 'prehistoric' times—such as conditions of atmospheric pressures, temperatures, radioactivity, and unknown catalyzers, we cannot exclude the possibility that dinosaurs existed several thousand years ago and became fossilized under terrific natural cataclysms in the course of a few rather than in millions of years. This is because we have no conceivable measurements or criteria of calculations under those unknown conditions."

During the 1950s, the Rebbe often met in Crown Heights with groups of college students interested in learning more about Hasidism. On one occasion, when questioned about the Baal Shem Tov's importance, the Rebbe replied: We can understand what he did for Jews at the time, by noticing the relationship of an electric powerhouse with a switch that is connected to it by a wire. "In order to connect ourselves with the powerhouse, we must first find the right switch, or push the correct button. The soul of every Jew is connected with the powerhouse, but in order that we can enjoy its great benefits, we must find the correct switch and push the proper button. It was the Baal Shem Tov's merit to have discovered the right switch to every Jew, so that through their connection to the powerhouse, their lives were transformed from despair to joy. Similarly, in your own work of strengthening Judaism, you must try to find the powerhouse in the soul of every Jew."

In 1969, when the daring lunar landing of the U.S. Apollo astronauts captured world attention, the Rebbe likewise offered an evocative technological analogy for his Sabbath audience. "The imagination of the entire world has been excited by the Apollo flights to the moon. Around the globe, their preparation and progress have been followed with keen interest: the rigorous training of the astronauts, the maneuvers of the spacecraft, the checks and counterchecks of every system. We know what and when the astronauts are going to eat, when they are going to sleep and are permitted to exercise. Everyone understands the respective roles of the astronauts and the Ground Control directors.

"No one dreams of asking, 'Why are the astronauts under the direction of the Ground Control?' No one questions the need for detailed plans about what to eat and when to eat and sleep. What would the world say about an astronaut who jeopardizes the mission and the lives of those on board just because he decides that he is a mature adult who knows better than mission control? Everyone agrees that the success of the Apollo flights depend on mutual responsibility and submission to strict discipline.

"Each of us, as Jews, has also has been sent on a mission, here on earth, for seventy or eighty years of our life. At the 'launch,' we are instructed about the timetables and activities of our mission. We are told what to eat and what not to eat, what to study, how to speak, how to behave ourselves with respect to our companions and with respect to the 'Mission Director,' and in general, are given a carefully worked-out program designed specifically to help us complete our mission successfully."

Carrying the analogy even further, the Rebbe rejected the argument that because Jews in Western nations enjoy a democratic way of life, they are free to do as they wish. "The astronauts also live in a democratic society, yet every single act they perform, even the most trivial, must be carried out in agreement with instructions and plans worked out by a higher authority. If these instructions are followed, the mission has a probability of success. But if the instructions are disregarded or disobeyed, the very mission—and even human lives—are endangered. Similarly, when Jews accept the discipline of the 'Higher Authority' and obey our Torah-given 'flight plan,' we are best able to fulfill our own mission, and to help our companions achieve theirs."

The Lubavitchers are confident that Hasidism will have a growing appeal for all those seeking creative inspiration in their lives. Perhaps nowhere is Lubavitch's Torah commitment more apparent than in its energetic Menorah campaigns during Chanukah season. In such involvement, the Lubavitchers are directly challenging an almost inviolate consensus about the place of religious expression in American public life.

VII

BATTLING FOR LIGHT

The Baal Shem Tov was once traveling, and needed a wagon driver to take him to a distant village. The journey was to go through a lonely, deserted stretch of countryside. After negotiating with an available driver, the Besht climbed into the back of the wagon, and it slowly made its way from the marketplace. As they passed directly under the village church, the Baal Shem Tov noticed that the wagoneer did not cross himself. "Stop!" the Besht suddenly shouted. "Let me out right now!" Surprised, the wagon driver did so, and quickly left the village. As the Besht disembarked, he turned to his astonished disciples. "As you know, to ride with a stranger alone through these plains is always dangerous," he explained, "and I saw that the wagoneer made no gesture of respect as we passed the church. One who is not afraid of God is not afraid of man either. I immediately took no chance to journey with him any further.

—Hasidic tale

AS NEVER BEFORE IN JEWISH HISTORY, CHANUKAH MENORAHS have been appearing in public places all over the world. From New York City's Fifth Avenue to Los Angeles, from Caracas to Melbourne, Paris to Hong Kong, the huge menorahs tower over the throngs assembled to participate in the Festival of Lights. Beside each menorah stand local Chabad emissaries, carrying out the Rebbe's word to commemorate as publicly and visibly as possible the celebrated events of the sacred eight days. Each passing year brings the Lubavitchers greater success in their effort to heighten awareness of this joyous occasion. These celebrations, frequently involving public officials, have become almost a symbol of Lubavitch's unique—and at times controversial—worldwide Jewish outreach.

The menorah campaign began some fifteen years ago, in San Francisco, during the heyday of America's counterculture. It was a time of mass gatherings, particularly demonstrations against U.S. military involvement in Vietnam. The hippie "be-ins" were still a fresh memory, and may have inspired rock megapromoter Bill Graham to organize publicity for the new public Chanukah celebration led by local Chabad emissaries. The event generated so much media attention and popular interest that other Lubavitcher emissaries around the country and abroad quickly followed suit. Soon, the Lubavitch Youth Organization in New York City alone, were sending out twenty regular "mitzvah mobiles" carrying ten-foot-high menorahs lit with flares. In 1978, Chabad emissaries proudly gained President Jimmy Carter's participation in a menorah-lighting ceremony on the White House lawn, and since then, there have been few Jewish communities anywhere in the world without the presence of a Lubavitch-sponsored menorah and Chanukah celebration.

Like virtually all of Chabad's far-flung activities, the menorah campaign emanates from the Rebbe's conviction that enhanced Jewish self-identity and observance are important keys to world peace and harmony. He has helped in many ways (some highlighted in this book) to promulgate this dream, and among the most crucial has been the public emphasizing of the special days of the Jewish calendar, reflecting the Hasidic teaching that we are not merely to commemorate these days as sacred historical events but to relive them as subjectively as possible.

From the Passover precept that each Jew "must see himself as if he were personally liberated from Egypt," Hasidim find personal direction and inspiration in the entire calendar. Because they regard everything within the Torah as a guide to contemporary life, even the order of the festivals and special days is deemed meaningful and instructive.

So too with Chanukah. The festival celebrates the recapture by the Maccabees in 165 B.C.E. of the Holy Temple in Jerusalem from the Syrian Greeks. When preparing to rededicate the Temple the Maccabees could find only one day's supply of the sacred oil used to light the Temple menorah, for the Greeks had deliberately defiled all the other oil. Nevertheless the oil miraculously lasted for eight days, until a new supply was prepared. The menorah was then rekindled with pure and consecrated oil, the visible symbol of the purity of the Jewish way of life. The next year, the Festival of Lights was established for perpetual celebration. On each of the eight days, one extra candle is lit so that their glow, if possible, is clearly visible outside. Chanukah has long been associated with customs such as eating latkes, giving presents to children, and uttering special prayers.

To the Lubavitchers, Chanukah offers a great deal of symbolic significance. Besides representing the triumph of religious liberty over the forces of despotism, it signifies the ability of the Jewish people to survive—often against all odds—persecution and oppression. "This chapter of our history has repeated itself frequently," the Lubavitcher Rebbe has commented. "We as Jews have always been outnumbered. Many tyrants have attempted to destroy us because of our faith. Sometimes, they aimed their poisoned arrows at our bodies, sometimes at our souls. In such times of distress, we must always be like that faithful band and remember that there is always a drop of 'pure olive oil' hidden deep in the heart of every Jew, which, if kindled, bursts into a big flame. This drop of 'pure olive oil' is the 'Perpetual Light' that *must and will* pierce the darkness of our present night, until everyone of us will behold the fulfillment of the prophetic promise of redemption."

The Rebbe has frequently spoken about the significance of Chanukah's specific rituals. He has observed that the lights, symbolizing the brilliance of Jewish study and observance, must be kindled after dark, suggesting that Jews today should not feel discouraged by the surrounding spiritual darkness, for even a small bit of godliness can exert tremendous influence. That Chanukah lights must be placed so that they can be seen outside, teaches that Jews must not be content to illumine their own homes with spirituality but should radiate it outwards. Finally, the candles are lit in a growing number each night, encouraging us to make an increasing effort to spread the light of Judaism.

Because the Lubavitchers fervently believe that the Torah is timeless, they are convinced that the Festival of Lights remains powerfully capable of stirring and uplifting the Jewish people, even in this high-tech age. Though hundreds and even thousands of people have participated in public menorah celebrations across the United States and elsewhere, Chabad emissaries avoid head counting as the chief criterion of their success. On a more intangible and perhaps more important level, they feel that these highly visible displays are touching something deep and long suppressed within the contemporary Jewish soul. In their view, they are simultaneously sharing Chanukah's universal features—its celebration of religious liberty—with non-Jews in a joyful and uplifting way. The emissaries see the menorah campaign's successful high visibility as yet another example of the Rebbe's foresight and wisdom: his ability to take Torah precepts and make them come alive to benefit the whole world. Underlying all the programs he leads, they emphasize, is the Hasidic view that one Jewish action or observance leads to another. The crucial thing is to begin somewhere.

Chabad's chief American spokesperson, Rabbi Yehuda Krinsky, comments, "We are very much involved with grass-roots Jews around the country. Invariably, we have found that when there is a public menorah and a ceremony, with the customary party afterward, people come. We hear Jewish people talking amongst themselves, and what is most apparent to us, is their pride: men, women, and especially children. Before we began these menorahs, Jews would see that only Christians seemed to celebrate their holiday publicly and that Jews were somehow shy. Well, Jews are feeling more pride now. Perhaps, seeing the public menorahs makes them want to light a menorah in their own home, or do other things to become more observant. They wonder why have we been covering up our religion and not doing the things we should be doing."

But not all American Jews have been gratified by the Lubavitchers' public menorah displays. In particular, the heads of the major non-Orthodox Jewish organizations have come to view these displays as wholly inappropriate, representing an unacceptable—potentially even dangerous—breach in the wall they have long believed should separate religion and state. These individuals regard the menorah campaign, however well-intentioned, as a direct challenge and threat to the mainstream Jewish consensus supporting this separation.

In several communities, the American Jewish Congress (AJC), the Anti-Defamation League of B'nai B'rith, the Jewish Federation, and the Reform movement's Union of American Hebrew Congregations (UAHC) have joined hands with the American Civil Liberties Union (ACLU) in challenging the constitutionality of conducting menorah-lighting ceremonies, or even merely displaying menorahs, on public land such as city halls or parks. The legal fight that these organizations have initiated has created the unusual and perhaps unprecedented spectacle of an internal Jewish conflict within the U.S. legal system.

During the past few years, about half a dozen test cases have worked their way through the courts. In some cases, local municipalities have been sued by the ACLU, with direct AJC and UAHC backing, for allowing Chabad's menorah display. In other cases, Chabad has had to sue to compel the local municipality to permit a menorah display— frequently next to a Christmas crèche or tree. In the summer of 1989 the U.S. Supreme Court ruled in favor of Chabad in one such case. The Court was clearly divided on the issue however, and no clear consensus seems likely to emerge.

Why are the Lubavitchers pursuing this issue so vigorously? Their fight for the right to erect public menorahs is undoubtedly exacting considerable cost in time, money, and human resources. It may also be accentuating a polarization in the American Jewish community. The Lubavitcher Hasidim have moved far beyond their original Brooklyn milieu, and to see them placing eye-catching menorahs in city halls or parks elsewhere is undoubtedly unsettling for some.

These court cases have come at a time when a growing number of social thinkers—among them activist Jews—are now advocating a serious rethinking of the whole question of religion-state separatism.

They start from two separate pronouncements. The first can be found at the beginning of the Declaration of Independence: "We hold these truths to be self-evident, that all men are created equal, that they are endowed by their Creator with certain unalienable Rights, that among these are Life, Liberty, and the pursuit of Happiness."

The second (known as the Establishment Clause), comes from the First Amendment to the Constitution: "Congress shall make no law respecting an establishment of religion, or prohibiting the free exercise thereof."

These words indicate that their authors believed that the construction of something enduring requires familiarity with metaphysical and moral notions, and a theological perspective related to the public world. Of course, the authors of the Constitution were not consciously thinking of theology in the way it might be taught in a seminary or biblical study group. Nevertheless, their assumptions indicated a fundamental belief among those who drafted the Constitution. These concepts had been vigorously debated for several centuries, and were already "second nature." They were shared by the American colonists to the extent that they would agree to accept what the framers had rendered as true and practical.

For nearly two hundred years, the American courts sustained a general consensus that the Constitution prohibits favoring any one religion while respecting the rights of all religions to be practiced freely. In the 1960s, the Warren Court began to alter that consensus dramatically in favor of the view that no religion at all should occupy a place in the public sphere, that there must be a high "wall of separation" between church and state.

Yet, the words "separation of church and state" do not appear in the text of the First Amendment. Both the words and the idea behind them originated with Thomas Jefferson, though he did not develop them into a complete legal theory. The Warren Court did this through its "purpose and effect" approach in the 1960s.

An obvious turning point came in 1962, when the Supreme Court banned by majority vote the Regents Prayer from American public schools. This prayer, which in many schools was read by students together with their teachers, declares: "Almighty God, we acknowledge our dependence upon Thee, and we beg Thy blessings upon us, our parents, our teachers, and our country."

The Warren Court's reasoning was that an act of Congress, or of any state legislature, must have both a secular purpose and a secular effect to remain true to the First Amendment's Establishment Clause. Hence, a state law mandating a moment of silence for public school children is forbidden, as its purpose is to encourage reverence toward, or at least thought about, God. Since that purpose is *not* secular, the law is unconstitutional.

Another example. Suppose a state assigns public school teachers to spend some time in a parochial school, teaching secular subjects like mathematics or earth science. The legislature's purpose is the complete education of young citizens, with special reference to those who are not enrolled in public schools. This is a secular purpose and is therefore permissible. But one effect of the law will be to assist the religious group that administers the schools being aided. That effect is *not* secular, and consequently, this law is judged unconstitutional.

The Warren Court's rulings antagonized many religious groups, who have vigorously sought a total reversal. The subsequent Burger Court, in contrast, managed to effect a slow transition away from the perceived rigidities of the Warren Court's "high wall" outlook towards a looser, "no excessive entanglements" perspective. It conceded that some "entanglement" of religion with politics is inevitable and that the original Establishment Clause related to "excessive" governmental entanglement as perhaps exemplified by the seventeenth-century Salem witch-hunt trials. Since Chief Justice Burger's retirement, the trend away from the Warren Court's strict "purpose and effect" has continued.

Unlike most Roman Catholics and members of Protestant denominations, American Jews were generally pleased with the Warren Court's stance, for they had felt most secure living in as secular an American milieu as possible. This attitude is deeply rooted in Jewish historical experience, since most Jews came to the United States fleeing pogroms and persecution in czarist Russia and other church-allied authoritarian regimes. Such groups as the American Jewish Congress and the Anti-Defamation League of B'nai B'rith were organized early in this century to combat pervasive anti-Semitism in housing, employment, and education. For decades, such organizations valiantly won small victory after small victory, until open discrimination against Jews had been substantially eradicated. It has not been an easy fight, and it is still not over. It has thus become a fundamental, virtually unquestioned, axiom that whenever possible, American Jews had to foster secularism, lest the doorway be opened for prejudice and discrimination.

Through well into the 1950s and 1960s, nearly all American Jews except for the Lubavitchers and some other Orthodox groups subscribed to this position. For example, American Jewish Congress directors Arthur Hertzberg and Leo Pfeffer have publicly argued that without a strict separationism, it becomes increasingly difficult to sustain a free society in which Jews can flourish.

Both Hertzberg and Pfeffer regard sustaining a free society and preserving Judaism as complementary processes, dependent upon this separation. To this day, most American Jews similarly regard religion and public life as appropriately distinct and to be demarcated by a "wall of separation." Their view is that religious belief ought to be a private matter and that democracy benefits from the separation of religion and public life; when the two are demarcated, potential fanaticism cannot constrict individual freedom. Religion also benefits, they insist, because the separation ensures that religion remains free. In short, this outlook says: secularism equals security.

Interestingly, a recent survey showed that the vast majority of Reform and Conservative rabbis shared this position, believing that government should provide no support to religion. On other topics where separation is a contemporary issue—for example, opening a high school sporting event with a prayer, or allowing religious groups equal access to public school classroom space, or mandating moments of silence in public schools, again Reform-Conservative rabbinical opinion takes a hard separationist line. Such a stance departs from other clergy's views and deviates dramatically from the general public's perspective.

Perhaps even more telling is that nearly half of the rabbis surveyed believed that the relative presence or absence of a religious citizenry "makes no difference" for democracy to work well. The comparable percentages for ministers and priests were below 17 percent. Indeed, significant minorities of Christian clergy consider religion to be "absolutely essential" in maintaining a democratic society.

It is hardly surprising that the Lubavitch menorah campaign has therefore evoked such heated opposition among some American Jews. The campaign runs directly counter to an entire array of beliefs concerning the proper place of religion within society. To be sure, it is not without some justification that those advocating this outlook can argue—simply on pragmatic grounds—that it has been highly effective. American Jews have probably enjoyed greater security than their co-religionists anywhere on earth. They have been able to enter the highest levels of government and commerce, medicine and law, science and the arts. Synagogues and Jewish community centers have sprouted throughout the United States, and can now be found even in the most affluent suburbs.

• • •

From the perspective of the Lubavitchers, though, all has not been rosy for American Jews; despite their vital and praiseworthy support for Israel, assimilation has been rampant. The figures are fairly well known. Jewish intermarriage is close to fifty percent; in some communities, it approaches two-thirds. Fewer than half of Jewish boys are bar mitzvahed anymore: what even most wholly nonobservant families only one generation ago considered an absolute necessity for maintaining Jewish identity. Synagogue membership has steadily dropped during the past decades, as has the proportion of Jews providing donations to Jewish causes.

Surveys consistently show that Jews are the most secularized major religious group in the United States. According to a recent Gallup poll, only 44 percent of Jews are synagogue members. By contrast, 19 percent of Catholics and 20 percent of Protestants are nonchurchgoers. Eighty percent of Jews had not attended services of worship within the previous seven days, as contrasted with 51 percent of Catholics and 59 percent of Protestants. On other measures, such as questions like: "Do you believe in an afterlife?" Or even, "Do you believe in God?" Jews consistently score as the most secular too. There is essentially only one anomaly in this consistent picture of American Jewry's hypersecularism: an unswerving support for Israel.

Lubavitch attributes this state of affairs to the policy that religious expression must be totally walled off from public life. In the long run, the Lubavitchers insist, this outlook, however well-intentioned, will continue to tear apart the very fabric of Jewish existence in this country. They also contend that religious practice among all peoples is a vital element for worldwide harmony.

The Lubavitcher Rebbe became increasingly outspoken on this issue shortly after the Supreme Court decision of 1962 outlawed prayer in the nation's public schools. One might think that because all Hasidic children attend private Hebrew schools, he would have little personal interest in combating this ruling. But quite the reverse was the case. In an extremely strong manner, he eventually urged legislators to mandate a moment of silence; consistent with the view of Maimonides, the Rebbe has always viewed the sphere of Jewish responsibility as rightfully embracing the entire world. "It is vital to realize that this issue concerns a vast number of children in the public schools who receive no other religious training or instruction in the morning, the majority of them not even in the afternoon, and many of them not even in Sunday school. The overwhelming proportion of schoolchildren today receive no religious instruction at all."

Arguing that a moment of silence is permissible and worthy for Jews as well as non-Jews, the Rebbe has stated: "Precisely in the case of a great number of public schoolchildren and their parents, it seems probable, sad to say, that many days, weeks, and even months might pass without their giving a single thought to God in some personal way—that is, neither love nor reverence for God. Therefore, a moment of silence allows an opportunity for them to acknowledge their dependence upon God: that the welfare of this country and its parents, children, and teachers depends on God's benevolence. A moment of silence offers in many cases the only opportunity for children to make some personal 'contact' with God every day."

For several decades, the Lubavitcher Rebbe has also emphasized the importance of federal aid to the secular departments of parochial schools of all faiths. His strongest words, though, have been directed at Jews who have consistently opposed such assistance. "The clear majority of Jewish antagonists to parochial schools are philosophically opposed to the very *idea* of parochial schools. Many of these individuals have the chief voice in how Jewish Federation funds are distributed, and resist support of Hebrew day schools or rabbinic academies, either by giving them miserable token funds, or by totally denying them any allocation. This painful subject requires no elaboration."

The Jewish organizations who are vigorously opposing the public menorahs are convinced that their stance is best for America as a whole, and for Jews in particular. Their position entails steadfastly opposing all religious symbols or practices in public places. As noted earlier in this chapter, it is not a new stance; for many decades, there has been an overriding Jewish consensus to help erect and defend a high wall separating religion from public life. The consensus is more tightly held by American Jews than the other major religious groups, certainly in part because of Jewish historical experience as a persecuted minority. It is a measure of the allegiance that some Jews feel toward the consensus that leads them to denounce those who openly challenge it—like the Lubavitchers—as "extremists," "fundamentalists," or even as "un-Jewish," which does little to bring about an examination of this issue in a rational manner, and does much that is detrimental.

The Lubavitch argument rests on the view that the framers of the Constitution never intended to erect a "wall of separation." Although the founders were against favoring any particular religion, they were not against aiding all religions, or all religion, equally. In this sense, the "establishment of religion" clause is being misinterpreted by those opposing crèches and menorahs. Those who reflexively cling to separationism show a deep lack of appreciation for the origins of American democracy and the close link between the historical struggles for political and religious liberty.

As the late philosopher Will Herberg argued, "Neither in the minds of the founding fathers nor in the thinking of the American people through the nineteenth and into the twentieth century did the doctrine of the First Amendment ever imply an ironclad ban forbidding the government to take account of religion or to support its various activities."

Of course, it is true that the framers were thinking of propertied white males when they wrote in the Declaration that "all men are created with certain unalienable rights." But it may be argued that the principles they perceived were more valid than their own comprehension of them. For "all" did not refer to citizens in a nation state; it was more universal than that. Indeed, the United States of America did not yet exist as a nation state when that sentence was composed. The Founders were not describing those who were subjects of the government, and certainly not subjects of the British Crown.

They were addressing, in the language of their day, those matters which for centuries had been discussed theologically. As Professor Max L. Stackhouse of Andover Newton Theological School has cogently observed, the founders specifically believed that: "All people are under God, created by God, children of God, made in God's image. Human dignity is conferred by God. It is not established by governments, nor by agreements among the people, nor by the 'spirit of the times.' Were this the case, governments could repeal human rights as easily as grant them, people could redraft their contracts ignoring such rights, or swallow them into 'new' spirits of 'new' times as the Zeitgeist changed."

As Stackhouse and other political philosophers today insist, it is on the basis of this worldview that Americans have fought in this century against a variety of tyrannies. It is on this basis too that we "presume . . . to defend movements and leaders . . . who will enhance human rights" around the globe. "We may argue over who it is that is most likely to aid or threaten" such rights, "but we have a common standard by which to asses the merits of our agreements. This is the 'all' that generated the United Nations Declaration on Human Rights after a twentieth-century barbarism denied that all were equally under God and claimed that 'natural' differences are more important."

It is not being argued here, of course, that the Lubavitcher Rebbe and his followers searched for justification in American constitutional law before undertaking their public menorah campaign, which is still ongoing. Instead, they did it out of a particular clear vision—emanating from the Torah and Chabad Hasidism—of the vital role that Judaism must carry out in the world. Yet they recognize that their outlook is inherent, in part, in the Founding Fathers' worldview.

In a recent legal brief, Chabad attorneys aptly quoted the late Supreme Court Justice Arthur Goldberg in a court decision from 1963. "It is said, and I agree," insisted Goldberg, "that the attitude of government toward religion must be one of neutrality. But untutored devotion to the concept of neutrality can lead to invocation or approval of results which partake not simply of that non-interference and non-involvement with the religions which the Constitution commands, but of a brooding and pervasive devotion to the secular and a passive, or even active, hostility to the religious. Such results are not compelled by the Constitution, but, it seems to me, are prohibited by it."

Much has intervened to make Goldberg's argument more compelling, especially the growing conviction of many Americans of varied denominations and backgrounds that it is necessary to reassert the link between public morality and religious belief. It is a position that may certainly be criticized in a pluralistic society like ours. But to attack as "extremists" those who favor a greater role for religion in public life is simplistic. Though Goldberg's outlook does not yet command the support of the Jewish "establishment" organizations, which still remain fettered to the old doctrine of separatism, it is garnering greater intellectual force and weight in the mainstream.

Granted that such a view is constitutionally valid, is it not potentially dangerous for American Jews—a tiny minority—to favor greater accommodation to religion in public life? If crèches and menorahs are permitted in the public square, what forms of religious expression will next be approved? Are not Jews in the United States more secure if religion is walled off from the state as completely as possible? It is no historical accident that collective memories of pariah status and persecution—the Crusades, the Inquisition, and countless pogroms—are still indelibly stamped onto the Western Jewish psyche.

Yet it is precisely on such pragmatic grounds that a variety of social critics now challenge the prevailing Jewish consensus on separationism. From a self-consciously Jewish standpoint, figures like Murray Friedman, Milton Himmelfarb, Irving Kristol, and the late Will Herberg and Seymour Siegel have contended that an American political culture devoid of religious beliefs and institutions itself poses a danger to the position and security of American Jews. In their view, the very basis of our democratic way of life has emanated from Judeo-Christian morality, and for Jews to seek a severance from this tradition is both foolish and dangerous.

For example, following the Supreme Court ruling that banned the Regents Prayer and Bible reading in the public schools (a decision most American Jews applauded), Will Herberg wrote: "Within the meaning of our political tradition and practice, the promotion of religion has been, and continues to be, a part of the very legitimate 'secular' purpose of the state. Whatever the 'neutrality' of the state in matters of religion may be, it cannot be a neutrality between religion and no-religion, any more than . . . it could be a neutrality between morality and non-morality . . . [both religion and morality being] as necessary to 'good government' as 'national prosperity.' The traditional symbols of the divine presence in our public life ought not to be tampered with."

In other words, a public square empty of all religious sentiment may prove far more hazardous to Jews than one proudly filled with displays of Christian and Jewish religious symbolism.

The Lubavitcher Rebbe has confronted this utilitarian, "Jewish safety" argument head-on. Anti-Semitism increases, he has often argued, when Jews seek to assimilate and abandon their heritage, for such behavior breeds suspicion rather than admiration. "An old, long-discredited assimilationist slogan declared: 'Be a Jew at home but a person outside.' It did not take long to become apparent that one who is ashamed of his Jewishness in the street soon becomes weak in his Jewishness at home. A diluted version of this same approach still plagues some of our people today. They feel that here in the United States, we resemble a 'lone sheep' and we should therefore 'keep quiet' and not be too blatant about our Jewishness. But in view of what happened in Europe and elsewhere in this century, anyone who still clings to this belief is seriously out of touch with reality."

Finally, critics of the separationist consensus assert that though support for the wall may once have made some sense, it no longer does: historical changes in American life necessitate that Jews reconsider their reflexive allegiance to separationism. As Herberg observed, "The American Jew must have sufficient confidence in the capacity of democracy to preserve its pluralistic character without any absolute wall of separation between religion and public life."

Jews are now full members of American society, and consequently must accept the burden of determining how best to preserve their own integrity while also sustaining a free society in which religious beliefs in public life may exert an important, constructive influence. Otherwise, this consensus may ensure for Judaism in American public life a very real form of suicide.

The Lubavitchers also argue that making sheer physical safety the raison d'être for Jewish existence is neither inspiring nor compelling, not even very convincing in historical terms. If physical survival had been the paramount value of Jews, it would have been far, far simpler for our ancestors to convert to the dominant religions a very long time ago.

American Jews now enjoy greater freedom and material prosperity than their forebears could possibly have imagined just a few generations ago, indeed, perhaps since the beginning of the Diaspora. For the

Lubavitcher Rebbe, these benefits—blessings, he might say—are neither accidental nor to be taken lightly. They carry an immense responsibility and tremendous opportunity for spreading the light of Judaism to the entire world. Not to recognize this situation is an evasion of the Jewish historical experience itself, its very essence.

It is precisely for this reason that the Lubavitchers are pressing so vigorously for the presence of menorahs in public during Chanukah: to revive Jewish pride and religious activity, and ultimately to help bring about a world of harmony and peace long envisioned by the prophets. It is a vision that the Lubavitchers seem fully prepared to defend, not simply for Jews, but for all Americans, and indeed, the whole of civilization.

Another social issue that the Rebbe has forcefully addressed has been the preservation of Crown Heights as a thriving Jewish community. Not only has the Rebbe's stance directly affected the daily lives of some twenty thousand adherents in Brooklyn, it also has wide implications for Jewish neighborhoods throughout the United States and abroad.

The story begins in 1940, when Chabad Hasidim settled their sixth Rebbe—Rabbi Yosef Yitzchak Schneersohn—in the central Brooklyn area known as Crown Heights. Having barely escaped after nightmarish months in Nazi-occupied Poland, and with two daughters and their husbands still trapped in Europe, Rabbi Schneersohn was probably not inclined to be critical of the neighborhood his followers had chosen. And at least physically, the setting must have appealed to him. The spacious, three-story structure situated at the corner of tree-lined Eastern Parkway and Kingston Avenue had previously belonged to a Jewish physician and possessed a pleasant urban ambience.

At the time, Crown Heights was a solidly middle-class neighborhood composed largely of Irish and nonreligious Jewish families living quietly in detached houses, row-houses, or scattered apartment buildings. As a highly visible indicator of their newfound affluence, local Jewish residents twelve years before had established the Brooklyn Jewish Center. It was an imposing Conservative synagogue occupying nearly an entire city block on Eastern Parkway. However, virtually no Hasidim inhabited the immediate area; almost none were affluent enough to afford homes or even apartments in Crown Heights. Yet many religious Jews were only a short bus ride or a brisk, twenty-minute Sabbath walk away from their homes in Brownsville, known for decades as the "Jerusalem of North America." Thus, Rabbi Yosef Schneersohn felt certain that there would be enough Hasidic supporters nearby to help him create a viable Orthodox community, and he was right.

During the 1940s, from his headquarters-home on Eastern Parkway, the sixth Lubavitcher Rebbe attracted a cohesive local following of perhaps several dozen such individuals. Nearly all were Eastern European immigrants like himself, but they were not actually Lubavitchers and tended to be clean-shaven and more moderate in their Orthodoxy. Indeed, true Hasidim were so rare, even in New York City, that Chabad's bearded yeshiva students often provoked incredulous stares when they rode the subways. But several years after World War II ended, sizable numbers of Holocaust survivors from Central and Eastern Europe began arriving in Brooklyn and the city's other boroughs. In this way, a growing number of Hasidim, representing a variety of groups including the Lubavitchers, settled in Crown Heights. Undoubtedly, Rabbi Yosef Schneersohn's sheer inspirational presence, as well as the Chabad institutions he had locally organized, drew many religious Jews to the area.

As a result, a perhaps historically unprecedented but unmistakable demographic pattern started to emerge. It began shortly before Rabbi Schneersohn's death in 1950 and continued unabated through the early leadership years of his successor, Rabbi Menachem Schneerson. In effect, the influx of Orthodox Jewish immigrants into Crown Heights hastened the exodus of their more assimilated, affluent brethren. Most likely it would have happened anyway, but at a slower pace. Suburbanization was the trend throughout the United States, and in that postwar economic boom, cheap land and tract houses were enticing urban dwellers of many ethnic groups, not only Jews. By the late 1950s, falling property values in Crown Heights enabled significant numbers of modest-income Lubavitchers to move into the neighborhood. Some could now afford to own homes for the first time, although the majority were renters. To nearly all of their Rebbe's followers, contentedly living close to him, it seemed that Crown Heights was becoming a wonderful place to live as observant Jews.

But other social forces were at work and came to a head in 1964, a year which saw a huge outbreak of crime in the middle-class neighborhoods of New York City and other major metropolitan centers. Many citizens began to fear walking in the street after dark for the first time in their lives. The Republican presidential candidate, Barry Goldwater, raised the national campaign issue of "crime in the streets" against Democrat Lyndon Johnson, but to little avail. Four years later, Richard Nixon employed it far more effectively as the Republican standard-bearer, running on an explicit platform of "law and order."

In Crown Heights, a series of apparently random and brutal crimes quickly escalated local fear. A blind newsstand dealer was nearly beaten to death; a group of yeshiva boys was attacked by a teenage gang; a rabbi's wife was dragged at knife-point out of her apartment and slashed in an attempted rape. In response to these incidents, some 120 Lubavitcher volunteers organized a citizens' patrol that they named the "Maccabees." "Hasidic Jews Use Patrols to Balk Attacks" ran the front-page *New York Times* headline. Though the Rebbe may have given his tacit support to the activity, he was not personally involved.

Whether the four-car Hasidic patrol was fueled by emotions of vigilantism or racism—as the media widely implied—the Maccabees were not very effective. Three days after they had organized in Crown Heights, a female schoolteacher was raped and murdered in her apartment building's self-service elevator. The next day, additional hundreds of Lubavitchers volunteered for the Maccabees, and within weeks the patrol had publicly gained the vigorous support and participation of local black church leaders.

Nevertheless, violent crime continued to increase sharply in Crown Heights. In 1965, when Lubavitch educators began planning the site of their large new yeshiva, they decided to build it many miles away on Ocean Parkway. They doubted whether there would even be a Jewish community left in the area before very long. Indeed, by the time their building was completed in 1966, thousands of Jews, as well as other white ethnic groups, were fleeing Crown Heights. This was in great measure the result of blockbusting, engineered by unscrupulous realtors, who employed racial fears to manipulate homeowners into selling their property as cheaply as possible.

"To a large extent, the tactic worked," recalls one Hasidic resident, "Everyone except for the Lubavitchers started moving out in 1966, '67 and '68. It was like a stampede. First nonreligious Jews and non-Jews left. Then in 1968 the Bobover Hasidim suddenly decided to resettle in Borough Park, several miles away. Hundreds of families left in less than three months. And people started wondering aloud: 'Are the Lubavitchers going to move out, too?' "

If Rabbi Menachem Schneerson had had his way, none of Crown Height's Jews would have left. He privately urged the Bobover Rebbe to stay: if necessary, Rabbi Schneerson insisted, he would personally help their entire community to find safe local quarters. But the Bobover Rebbe and all his followers moved out of the area. The Lubavitcher Rebbe sought to persuade Jewish residents and synagogue heads to remain in Crown Heights on many other occasions, but few were willing to listen to him.

Even his own adherents seemed ready to move. They began to hold weddings in other, safer, sections of New York City. At one public celebration in 1968, the Rebbe remonstrated: "Why don't you hold your marriage canopy here, the holy place where our previous Rebbe lived? Besides that, I want to hear your marriage vows and personally answer, 'Amen!'"

Finally, during a Passover celebration in 1969, the Rebbe spoke strongly before a gathering of three thousand followers. His speech is credited among the Lubavitchers as reversing the abandonment of Crown Heights as a Jewish community, and they also regard it as having wider implications, still relevant today. The Rebbe addressed the issues of physical safety and fear not from an emotional—or even sociological—approach, but from the vantage of Judaism's teachings.

"In recent times," he declared, "a plague has spread among our brethren—the wholesale migration from Jewish neighborhoods. One result of this phenomenon is the sale of houses in these neighborhoods to non-Jewish people. Even synagogues and places of Torah study are sold. Furthermore, the livelihood of many members of the community becomes undermined or completely destroyed by this precipitous flight. Since this matter concerns tens of thousands of Jews, I feel compelled to express my opinion openly and clearly, and to call attention to at least *some* of the references on the subject in Torah law."

The Rebbe then cited a host of Talmudic and other classic sources prohibiting the sale of Jewish-owned houses when the result has negative consequences for the Jewish community. "Such stringent prohibitions of Torah law would apply if the sale of the house to a non-Jew caused damages to only one person," he observed. "How much more so does it apply when, as in our case, the damage is suffered by *all* neighborhood residents! To make matters worse, neighborhood flight in any one area has a 'ripple effect,' sending harmful shock-waves to the Jewish residents of other neighborhoods, other cities, other states—and even other countries."

Next, the Rebbe cited Torah rulings prohibiting the sale or closing of synagogues unless mitigating circumstances existed. However, he emphasized, to jettison such vital Jewish institutions as synagogues and day schools in order to flee was flatly contrary to the spirit and law of Judaism. "If the Torah commands us to take drastic measures for monetary self-defense and certainly for bodily self-defense," the Lubavitcher leader insisted, "it follows that we are commanded to use every possible legal means to prevent the ejection of Jews from the neighborhoods in which they have lived for so many years."

Finally, the Rebbe argued that those who hastily abandoned cohesive Jewish neighborhoods like Crown Heights were ultimately pursuing a course of spiritual self-damage. "In the old neighborhoods, people had found their own particular circles, had sunk roots into their particular Jewish environment. Each person belonged to an organization devoted in some measure to studying Torah, maintained active synagogue membership and attendance, and supported charitable organizations. In short, in the course of many years, most residents had gradually achieved a personally rewarding environment for themselves, a spiritual 'piece of property,' a *home* in the broadest sense, and their children had in great degree been influenced to follow the familiar, well-trodden path.

"All this is endangered with the move to a new neighborhood. In many instances, this precious 'piece of property' becomes greatly diminished—at least until the family adapts to its environment. The trauma of settling down in a new residence takes time and energy, and does not always meet with success."

The Rebbe did not minimize the issue of physical safety. Indeed, he explicitly mentioned the esclation of violent crime that had occurred in Crown Heights during recent years. Nevertheless, "the practical way to eliminate danger is not precipitous flight, but the mounting of a suitable publicity campaign. A number of Jewish neighborhoods have demonstrated clearly that when residents stand together and declare their irrevocable and resolute determination *not* to leave the area, they can succeed in securing the safety of their neighborhoods."

To this end, the Rebbe recommended that local Lubavitchers form a community council to help Crown Heights survive as a viable Jewish area. He also advised that they create a housing-loan society, so that interested Hasidim could purchase homes with Chabad's active financial assistance. Both suggestions were soon followed, as well as another that adherents lobby municipal officials to obtain better police protection.

Today, Crown Heights is one of the few truly integrated sections of New York City, where black and Jewish homeowners co-exist as next-door neighbors, each determined to maintain the safety and viability of their community as a place for families to live peacefully. The contrast to other sections of Brooklyn could not be more striking: burned-out tenements and boarded-up storefronts dominate the rubble-strewn landscape. But here, as many Lubavitchers proudly insist, the Rebbe's devoted application of Torah principles to contemporary life enabled Crown Heights to remain a thriving Jewish area in a time when fewer and fewer exist any longer in the United States and other Western countries.

"In the case of both public menorahs and the preservation of Crown Heights, the lesson is clear for Jews everywhere," observes Rabbi Faivish Vogel of London. "By following with eagerness the truth of Judaism, without even necessarily knowing in advance where it will lead, we come to beneficial consequences. That understanding and commitment is central to the perspective of our Rebbe and our entire religious movement."

Certainly, this important outlook has dominated Lubavitcher activity not only within the United States but throughout the Jewish world. Perhaps the most vivid demonstration of such commitment has been manifested in the Lubavitcher presence in Israel during its troubled existence as a modern nation.

VIII

THE HOLY LAND

Sojourn in this land, and I will be with you, and will bless you.

—Genesis 26:3

THE AUTUMN SUN GLISTENS ON THE SPIRES AND DOMES OF Jerusalem. Yet the stones of the Old City are cool as crowds of tourists, intermingling with local residents of every nationality, clamber through the narrow, winding streets or stand silently before the Western Wall. Unknown and perhaps ultimately unknowable dramas are enacted here daily, facing the only remaining trace of the ancient Temple of Jerusalem. Mere yards but also worlds away from what seems to be a large bar mitzvah celebration, several beshawled women sit on a gnarled wooden bench conversing in low voices.

Jerusalem is a city of great contrasts as well as tremendous vitality, and only a few miles away, leading Israeli physicist Herman Branover mounts the steps into the new high-tech building known as SATEC. His two-hour drive northward from Ben-Gurion University in Beersheva has taken longer than expected, and as SATEC's research director, he is already running late for today's array of administrative and scientific meetings.

Scarcely glancing around him at the modern industrial park—just off the Tel Aviv–Jerusalem highway—that symbolizes contemporary Israel, Professor Branover has a lot on his mind. Two SATEC research teams, in hydrometallurgy and natural-resource exploration, have marketing presentations scheduled that day.

Before starting the first meeting, Professor Branover hurries to the dining room. Taking a Hebrew prayer book, he joins SATEC's staff members in the afternoon religious services already under way. The observant Soviet-Jewish scientists are participants in an unprecedented residential-work community conceived and guided spiritually by the Lubavitcher Rebbe in New York City.

Less than a year before, the Rebbe had startled his Hasidic followers by announcing during several public discourses at Lubavitcher headquarters at Crown Heights that conditions for Soviet Jewry would soon be improving dramatically. "Changes are coming, and they will be better and better," the Lubavitcher leader had predicted with confidence. "There will be renewed opportunity for Jews to emigrate in large numbers, and we must help our brethren choose Israel as their new home. No one should compel them to go there, for that course is both anti-Jewish and antihuman. Instead, we should help make it attractive enough so that they will voluntarily settle there."

Such remarks seemed unwarrantedly optimistic to Professor Branover and others who were working clandestinely to support Jewish religious freedom within the Soviet Union. In fact, when these Hasidic emissaries relayed the Rebbe's encouraging words to Soviet refuseniks in Moscow the reaction was sheer incredulity. "I was frequently telephoning different Jewish activists," Branover recalls with irony, "and they simply couldn't accept the Rebbe's view. In fact, they bitterly complained that the repression around them was becoming worse and worse. One worried activist told me, 'The KGB car is parked downstairs right now.' A second man said, frightened, 'My wife has just been interrogated.' And I was telling them, 'No, the Rebbe has said, "It's going to keep getting better and better." ' I didn't know on what basis the Rebbe was saying this. Not even the top Sovietologists had any inkling of the changes that were coming."

Though the Rebbe was intimating that increased Soviet-Jewish emigration would soon take place, Branover doubted whether very many of these thousands, or even hundreds, would choose Israel as their new home. He knew full well that the majority of such émigrés would be professionals in highly technical fields such as engineering and medical research. Israel, a country of fewer than five million people, was ill-equipped to absorb so many scientists in a manner appropriate to their expertise. So why would they opt for life there, when Western countries craved and amply rewarded well-trained researchers?

The Rebbe, it seems, had the same question in mind. In a private meeting at Lubavitcher headquarters, a plan was developed whereby Soviet-Jewish émigrés in Israel would live together, work together, and practice Judaism together. They would pool their rich technological skills to create a viable and self-sustaining new community. "We were directed to establish a neighborhood in Jerusalem immediately, to serve as a 'shop window' to outsiders and to be publicized as completely as possible," Branover recollects. "In that way, Soviet Jews would be attracted to Israel, knowing that they would have good apartments waiting for them, and would not have to deal with a formidable bureaucracy as soon as they got off the plane. And importantly, too, we were directed to get involved in finding them relevant jobs."

For many decades, the Rebbe had possessed the reputation of being an indefatigable leader who set almost impossibly high goals for his emissaries and followers. With admiration rather than dismay, the common refrain among his worldwide adherents is, "No matter what we do to help spread Judaism, he is never satisfied." But now, the Rebbe seemed to be exceeding even his own matchless zeal in urging that a pilot housing project for at least fifty Soviet émigré families—coupled with a high-tech research facility—be built and completed within *months*. There was not a moment to waste, he insisted. Before long, Soviet Jews would be allowed to emigrate en masse, and Israel had to be ready to attract them. "I want you to give this project so much thought and attention," he told a stunned Branover, "that you will even dream about it at night."

Herman Branover is a great dreamer and an idealist committed to the cause of Soviet Jewry. Together with his Chabad colleagues he swiftly secured the enthusiastic backing of Israeli officials of diverse political stands, as well as generous support from American and Australian philanthropists Ronald Perelman and Yosef Gutnick. Within less than six months, the Rebbe's vision had become reality. Fifty-two newly emigrated Soviet-Jewish families were living comfortably in the Ramot section of Jerusalem and some two dozen scientists were engaged in research work for SATEC. As Jerusalem's longtime mayor Teddy Kollek remarked, "Only the Lubavitcher Rebbe could have accomplished this!"

Today's meetings have gone smoothly, and Branover is delighted to learn that SATEC's project in natural-resource exploration may be operational quite soon. Led by the former chairperson of Moscow University's geology department, a small research team will be utilizing complex, computer-generated mathematical models to pinpoint possible sites for oil drilling. Because few potential oil wells prove viable, and each costs millions of dollars to explore, this new method may represent a tremendous industrial boon. It may also bring much-needed cash into SATEC's coffers.

Their scientific work over for the day, interested SATEC staff members are ready for formal Jewish study before returning home and opening their Russian-Hebrew Bibles, which SHAMIR produced and published several years ago. These materials, distributed through the network of more than 180 Chabad Houses across Israel, have become a vital resource for thousands of former Soviet Jews who were denied the right to learn Hebrew and all access to their tradition. Next, they briefly review the Lubavitcher Rebbe's latest Hasidic discourse, as Branover explains several Talmudic references in response to questions.

"Only about forty percent of our staff are religiously observant," Branover admits. "The rest are not *yet* religious, as I like to think of it. And not all who work at SATEC live in the apartments at Ramot, which has a religious atmosphere. We don't force them to participate in our afternoon prayers or the after-work Torah class, or anything else connected with Judaism. But some are looking and participate when they feel a desire to do so."

As Herman Branover drives back toward Beersheva that evening, the desert landscape seems serene. He is optimistic about the future.

"We have two hundred more apartments in the planning stage now," Professor Branover announces, "and long lists of Soviet Jews, some of whom have not yet left the country, waiting to join us. We know of many examples of émigrés who were planning to settle in America or Europe suddenly changing their minds. When they heard about this program, they decided to move to Israel instead."

• • •

While religiously observant Russian-Jewish scientists certainly represent a new element in Israeli society, Russian Hasidim have lived continuously within the Holy Land for more than two centuries.

When the first massive wave of pogroms within Russia took place in 1880, the settlers' ranks were swelled by the arrival of new Hasidic immigrants in both Jerusalem and Hebron. Though neither community comprised more than a few hundred Hasidim, the number of Lubavitch émigrés soon grew large enough to support two yeshivas in Hebron. The first yeshiva, authorized by the fifth Lubavitcher Rebbe, was opened in 1904 and the second, much larger, in 1911. The latter, known as Torat Emet, immediately gained worldwide stature as a major Lubavitcher seminary, and attracted leading rabbinic students from Eastern Europe. But when World War I broke out three years later, the Turkish government—at war with Russia—forced all the Russian-born Lubavitchers out of the country. After the war, most returned to Jerusalem rather than Hebron, which was rapidly undergoing modernization in religious education and outlook.

In 1929, the sixth Lubavitcher Rebbe became the group's first leader to set foot in the Holy Land. Denied access to the sacred graves of his ancestors by the Soviet government, which had exiled him after imprisonment and near-execution, Rabbi Yosef Schneersohn decided to make the unprecedented visit before embarking on a visit to the United States. The whirlwind two-week trip was exhilarating both for him and his followers, who flocked around their spiritual leader wherever he went. Aside from conferring with leading rabbis, he spent most of his time making pilgrimages to holy burial sites, such as the Cave of Machpelah, the tomb of Rachel, and the resting places of Rabbi Akiba, Shimon ben Yochai, Maimonides, Isaac Luria, and other great mystics and sages.

Later on the trip, the sixth Lubavitcher Rebbe met with yeshiva students and their teachers in Jerusalem. In an especially moving ceremony, he declared, "Obstacles affect everyone, not only those in Russia, but everywhere in the world, for the entire globe is in exile. There are always tests and obstacles that one has to overcome." Before leaving the fervent gathering, he offered in conclusion, "I am traveling away, but we are not really parting. Distance is not a factor, so we are not really separating. Each one of you should be as ten thousand to radiate the light of holiness."

But such joyful moments for religious Jews in the Holy Land were destined to be short-lived indeed. Less than two weeks after the sixth Rebbe's inspiring visit, Arabs rioting in Hebron massacred more than sixty Jews and wounded hundreds. Among those killed was a loyal Lubavitcher whose son now lives in Crown Heights. Over the next ten years, Hasidic immigration to the Holy Land slowed to a trickle. One cause lay in British policy, which set strict immigration quotas in order to limit Jewish settlement. The other lay in Stalin's growing consolidation of his power in the Soviet Union and his refusal to allow virtually any Jews to escape his control.

Only an hour's drive west of Jerusalem the Mediterranean coastline offers a very different landscape and climate. Southeast of Tel Aviv, near Lod Airport, the air is hot and muggy on an unseasonably warm autumn morning, as thousands of schoolchildren and vocational students at Kfar Chabad settle down to their scheduled classroom activities.

Kfar Chabad is the nation's largest independent agricultural collective. Comprised of seven hundred large Hasidic families, this community—inhabited permanently only by Lubavitchers—is particularly known for its vocational and technical schools. Established with separate classrooms and dormitories for boys and girls, these schools provide rigorous vocational training coupled with intensive religious study. Generally, boys specialize in printing, mechanics, carpentry, or agricultural work, and girls focus mainly on careers in education. Few of the youngsters, who arrive at Kfar Chabad each fall from all over Israel, are themselves Hasidim.

Besides housing Lubavitch's major rabbinic seminary, Kfar Chabad attracts thousands of schoolchildren who annually visit its *shmura* (hand-baked matzo) factory before Passover. Each fall, second-graders in the Tel Aviv area also attend festivities that mark the start of formal Bible study, both in Israel's secular and religious schools.

In a country where the majority of Jews lead surprisingly secular lives, the Lubavitchers regard outreach as crucial to Judaism's world-wide revitalization. Their settlement in Israel has been a deliberate effort to reverse the modern trend toward Jewish assimilation. Though he carefully eschews any messianic implications in the founding of the official State of Israel, the present Rebbe—and his predecessor—have emphasized the importance that this Holy Land nation has for all Jews, and indeed for all humanity. In their view, not only is such a large concentration of world Jewry significant for its sheer size, but its sus-tained presence in the Holy Land signifies tremendous religious respon-sibility and opportunity.

If today the Israeli population is steadily becoming more religious in daily attitude and practice, the Lubavitchers may justifiably claim much credit for this trend. With dozens of active Chabad Houses criss-crossing the small country, their rabbinic emissaries and teachers feel a growing optimism that the secularist-socialist vision of many of Is-rael's founders, such as David Ben-Gurion, Golda Meir, and Chaim Weizmann, is being replaced by one favorable to traditional Jewish practice.

Between 1946 and 1949, many émigré Lubavitcher lived as refu-gees in Allied-run Displaced Persons (DP) camps in Austria, France, and Germany. At first, in their correspondence with the sixth Luba-vitcher Rebbe in New York City, most wrote of their wish to go to the United States and be close to their spiritual leader.

These ardent followers were surprised—and, initially, dismayed—to learn that their Rebbe emphatically discouraged such expectations. Because of both immigration barriers and economic factors, Rabbi Yosef Schneersohn urged them to consider settling elsewhere. This was not easy advice to accept. But as loyal Hasidim, the refugees heeded the Rebbe's guidance and, eventually, chose other homelands. Some settled in England or France; others in Italy or Canada, a few even went to Australia.

The largest number of Lubavitcher refugees to leave war-torn Europe were advised by the Rebbe to relocate in the new State of Israel, and of these, seventy-four families agreed to form an agricultural collec-tive south of Tel Aviv, at his request. Free cultivable land would be provided by the Israeli government. The vision of a cohesive Hasidic community was welcome after their harrowing underground Soviet existence. But when the prospective pioneers anxiously arrived in the Promised Land during the spring of 1948, conditions were far from favorable.

Kfar Chabad was a bleak village whose Arab residents had fled during the Israeli War of Independence. It comprised a few dozen dilapidated houses and little else. "Each family took a broken house and tried to fix it up a little," recalls Rabbi Sholom Levine, now director of Lubavitch's main library in Crown Heights, who arrived with his parents as part of Kfar Chabad's founding settlers. "The houses were big, with empty rooms. So each was divided into several smaller apartments, for different families. You had maybe a few chickens in each yard, and most families tried to do at least some part-time agricultural work. But it was very, very hard."

For the first four years, the community had no running water or electricity. "We used candles," says Sholom Levine, "and had only outside communal bathrooms that six or seven different families shared. It was not what people had hoped for."

In those early years, Kfar Chabad's residents often wrote imploringly to the Rebbe. Some families still dreamed of living near Lubavitcher headquarters in the United States; others hoped that they could at least join their fellow Hasidim in more hospitable surroundings in Jerusalem or Tel Aviv. Some considered dividing Kfar Chabad into two separate communities, in order to improve the supply of arable land for each struggling family. But in a characteristic letter in early 1952, the new Rebbe adamantly opposed such plans:

"Be very careful about changing from one situation to another. Any change can involve a greater crisis . . . and can create a great shock," he warned. "You who left Russia and came to Israel are in a situation where you are all in one place, and therefore have the capability—if only you have unity—to become accustomed to the various changes that have taken place in your lives. There's no need to make a new change. I feel certain that if you divide into separate places—even just two—this will create several different groups, and the smallness of your numbers will mean that you will become influenced adversely by your environment, both materially and spiritually."

At the same time the Rebbe directed many of its rabbinic inhabitants to conduct Hasidic outreach across the length and breadth of

Israel. As hundreds of thousands of Sephardic Jews poured out of Iran, Morocco, Turkey, Yemen, and other Middle Eastern countries, the Rebbe felt it imperative that their age-old allegiance to Judaism be retained and even strengthened upon entering the modern, secular State of Israel. Seeking to overcome Eastern European Ashkenazi prejudices against the dark-skinned and often poorly educated Sephardim, he urged Lubavitch emissaries to help these new immigrants as much as possible. "The Rebbe would tell us that we need them more than they need us," recalls one Chabad educator active in that period. "He told us that Hasidism had to be carried now to Jews in the Sephardic world for its true and complete impact to be realized."

Meanwhile, in 1953, living conditions in Kfar Chabad improved significantly when it finally entered the age of electricity. The momentous event occurred just a few days after the annual Lubavitch holiday of the nineteenth Kislev, commemorating the release from czarist prison of their movement's founder, Rabbi Schneur Zalman of Liady. "It is with pleasure that I received the news that the electrical illumination of Kfar Chabad has been set up and working properly," the Rebbe wrote to its rabbinic chief. "It is an old Jewish custom to find lessons in everything that happens. As the Torah says, 'Who is wise? One who learns from everyone.' The Baal Shem Tov added, 'one who learns, too, from every happening, every detail.'

"On the day of his liberation, Rabbi Schneur Zalman began to spread the light of Hasidism without any hindrances or obstacles. This is the essence of Hasidism: to draw down the highest reaches of God to the lowest levels of our existence. One could say that electricity is one of those powers that are hidden in nature and cannot be grasped through the five senses. It is only through its effects that its existence is known. The light of this hidden power pushes away the darkness. So, too, the hidden aspects of Torah are revealed through Hasidism and the Hasidic way of life. They push away the darkness of our material world."

Over the next few years, Kfar Chabad slowly expanded and prospered. A few months after electricity was introduced, the first of several vocational institutes for boys was opened, at the Rebbe's request and with the help of a most generous benefactor, Emma Lazaroff-Schaver. It combined a half day of Torah study with a half day of technical training. Accredited by the Israeli education ministry and soon offering diplomas in agriculture, carpentry, and printing, the program seemed from its inception to hold a special appeal for Sephardic boys trying to maintain Jewish observance while bettering themselves economically. Kfar Chabad's agricultural system also began to expand into breeding turkeys and geese, even establishing an export trade of goose livers for pâté in France. In 1955, the settlement's educators opened "Gan-Israel" (Garden of Israel) summer camps, providing holiday accommodations for thousands of Ashkenazi and Sephardic children around the country.

During this period, the Lubavitchers in Israel had a powerful ally behind the scenes in President Zalman Shazar, the son of Lubavitcher Hasidim in czarist Russia, who was originally named Schneur Zalman Rubashov, after the movement's founder. As a youth, he became an ardent Labor Zionist, and after immigrating to the Holy Land in the 1930s he rose to prominence in the dominant leftist Mapai party. But shortly after the founding of Israel in 1948, he began to feel religious stirrings, and became an admirer and friend of the late Lubavitcher Rebbe and Rabbi Menachem Schneerson. Whenever Shazar came to the United States on political goodwill or fund-raising tours, he always visited Lubavitch headquarters in Crown Heights and spent hours in private discussions with the Rebbe.

As Shazar became more religious in his personal life, he questioned the value of his serving as Israel's President, a largely symbolic post, but with the encouragement of the Rebbe he decided to keep his position. Until his death in 1979 Shazar remained an energetic supporter of Chabad activities throughout Israel. To many senior Lubavitcher figures, Shazar's personal transformation was of great symbolic importance. The Israeli President's transformation from being an antireligious Labor Zionist to being a strong Hasidic sympathizer epitomized the Rebbe's influence.

Kfar Chabad had its share of tragedy during its early years. In 1956, Arab terrorists attacked the settlement without warning one afternoon and, invading the synagogue where services were being held, began firing machine guns, killing five students and a teacher, and wounding many others. "I can still see myself as a boy carrying the bloodstained prayer books from the synagogue the next morning," recalls Sholom Levine. "I think they buried the prayer books with the six men who died."

The next day, the Rebbe sent a telegram of condolence and support for the Kfar Chabad community: "It is my strong hope that with the help of God, who guards with a watchful eye and watches over with divine providence, you will overcome every hindrance and will strengthen yourself and expand both qualitatively and quantitatively. May you have no doubts or misgivings, and spread the wellsprings of Hasidism and Torah and of our holy leaders, so that they should bring kindness and mercy from our Father in heaven, and bring the true and complete redemption . . . very speedily."

When the Sinai War broke out in the fall of 1956, many of Kfar Chabad's young men waived their religious exemption as ordained rabbis and joined the army, seeing combat in the Mitla Pass and elsewhere. Over the next few years, the community opened its teachers' seminary for women, followed by the Beth Rivkah Girls High School and Girls Vocational Schools. In response to the Rebbe's encouragement, Kfar Chabad also established a new group of modern printing schools, dedicated in a moving ceremony to the memory of the five massacred students. Then, in 1959, the Rebbe finally gave the go-ahead for a Lubavitcher settlement for women, Kfar Chabad Bet. Ten years later, the Lubavitcher community of Nachalat Har Chabad was founded to accommodate the new wave of Russian Lubavitchers emigrating to Israel. Many of them had waited since the end of the second World War, to leave the Soviet Union and live freely as Jews in the Holy Land.

One of those who has been a beacon to Israelis of all backgrounds and political persuasions is Shifra Golombevitz. Director of Chabad's war-orphan program and a resident of Kfar Chabad, she organized the annual group bar-mitzvah ceremony that meant so much to those boys whose fathers died defending Israel from its enemies.

The daughter of Rotterdam's chief rabbi, Shifra was twenty years old when, in 1963, she met Lubavitcher David Golombevitz while both were serving their mandatory tours of duty in the Israeli Army. They married, and settled in David's home community of Kfar Chabad, where he enrolled to become a Hasidic rabbi. In early 1967 Shifra became pregnant, and the young couple began planning their family life. Then, the frightening political events of that spring suddenly unfolded.

With strong Soviet encouragement, Egyptian President Nasser demanded that the United Nations withdraw its entire peacekeeping force from the Sinai Desert. The UN capitulated to Nasser's demand and evacuated the area on May 19. Palestinian Liberation Organization soldiers then took over the position.

While Arab and Israeli forces raced to mobilize, Egyptian troops seized the Straits of Tiran, denying Israeli ships access to the port of Eilat. Israel's Foreign Minister, Abba Eban, hastily embarked on a tour of Western capitals for meetings with President Charles de Gaulle, Prime Minister Harold Wilson, and President Lyndon Johnson, but none was willing to act decisively to end the blockade. By late May an Egyptian army of soldiers and tanks had massed on the Sinai border, and Palestinian forces in the Gaza Strip began shelling an Israeli settlement. On May 30, King Hussein of Jordan flew to Cairo to sign a military agreement with President Nasser, and returned home with two guests on his plane: the heads of the PLO and the Joint Arab Command.

It was a time of anguish for Jews throughout the world. The Rebbe's speech in Yiddish to participants in a Jewish holiday parade in Crown Heights was broadcast frequently over Israeli national radio in the days that followed: "Our brothers and sisters in the Holy Land are now in such a situation that the Almighty is protecting them, and sending His blessings and salvation in a much larger measure, in order that they should come out of this situation successfully. There lies upon you and us a special duty and privilege to help them. You, through your learning an extra portion of Torah, to fulfill another mitzvah and another mitzvah. . . . And also to follow the command that you shall love your neighbor as yourself, which means to influence relatives and friends and family that they should utilize all their possibilities to spread Torah and mitzvahs.

"As the Torah portion this week declares, the Jews in the Holy Land shall dwell there safely, and the Almighty shall make it successful that there will be peace in the Holy Land. God will be our God, of all the Jewish people, wherever they are. Every one of you, and all of you together, and all of us together, will be God's people. He will take us out with his full, open, and holy and broad hand from all difficulties. He will bring peace and safety to all . . . and will lead every Jew with an upright stature and upraised head to the true and complete redemption . . . and He will take us out of exile, and will, to the whole world, speedily bring the Kingdom of God Almighty."

At the same time, the Rebbe initiated a worldwide spiritual "campaign" encouraging greater ritual observance as a means to help defend Israel from on high. He instructed his far-flung rabbinic emissaries to foster the donning of phylacteries *(tefillin)* throughout Israel and the Diaspora. The efficacy of this effort, of course, cannot possibly be judged by means of rational analysis. But its scope and intensity clearly signified the Lubavitcher Rebbe's extent of global influence, as thousands of Hasidic rabbis, advanced seminary students, and even young teenagers, went out into the streets of five continents to promulgate the Rebbe's message to the Jewish people.

When Israeli forces led by Defense Minister Moshe Dayan seized the initiative on June 5, many Lubavitchers were among those fighting for their nation's survival. In a representative account during that frightening and then exhilarating week, London's *Jewish Chronicle* reported of a desert battle, "Among the tank men is a Chabad Hasid who, until his mobilization, was studying in the yeshiva at Kfar Chabad. . . . His job is to load the guns on the tank with ammunition. His tefillin bag lies close to his ammunition supplies."

That particular soldier survived the war to return to Kfar Chabad and continue rabbinic study. But not all his friends and neighbors were so fortunate. Seminary student David Golombevitz served on Israel's southern front at the Suez Canal where he was killed by a shell in the new "war of attrition" launched by Arab forces.

Though Israel's government provided vigorous financial help to those families who suffered losses during the Six Day War of 1967, the Lubavitcher Rebbe wanted to minister to their spiritual needs. Understandably enough, the Israeli Ministry of Defense was initially reluctant to supply Chabad Hasidim with the names and addresses of all families who had been bereaved during the war, but it eventually agreed to do so. With generous philanthropic donations raised largely by Lubavitcher communities abroad, Shifra Golombevitz became head of the new program: sponsoring social occasions throughout the year for war widows and orphans, providing holiday clothes, supplies, and toys, and extending special logistical and financial assistance for bar mitzvahs and weddings.

The ceremony which takes place each summer at Kfar Chabad for all those who were bar mitzvahed during the preceding year, is very moving and is attended by Israel's President and its leading political-military figures. "I have devoted my life," Shifra Golombevitz says, "to promoting the cause that Chabad represents: love and concern for all Jews whoever and wherever they may be."

It is a bitter irony to most Lubavitchers—whether they are serving as activist emissaries or living in their local communities—that the secular public often confuses them with the anti-Israel Neturei Karta brigade ("Guardians of the City"), affiliates of the Satmar group, which originated in nineteenth-century Hungary and is based in New York City and Jerusalem. The Satmars have gained notoriety for their well-publicized spectacles—often seen on television—of burning the Israeli flag, or their denunciations of Israel in advertisements in *The New York Times*.

Ever since the Six Day War of 1967 the Lubavitcher Rebbe has taken a firm position with regard to Israel's security: categorically rejecting the idea of giving land to the neighboring Arabs, an issue that arose with the momentous week of lightning victories, when the Israeli Army conquered Jerusalem and the West Bank of the Jordan River, the Golan Heights, the Gaza Strip, and a few other territories.

Jews in Israel and around the globe are divided as to what to do next. Those associated with the political doves of the left have recommended returning some or even all of the conquered territory to its former Arab rulers in an attempt to secure lasting peace. Hawks on the other hand, mostly linked to the political right, have advocated formally annexing these territories.

The Lubavitcher Rebbe, however, has explicitly based his entire position neither on political considerations nor questions of the "sanctity of the Land of Israel," but solely on the basis of Jewish law's overriding concern for the sanctity of human life. The Rebbe's view is firmly rooted in the universally accepted ruling of Jewish law that a

"danger to life" *(pikuach nefesh)* situation supersedes all other considerations.

He quotes the specific directive in the Codes of Jewish Law concerning the situation in which a Jewish border town is besieged by
non-Jews ostensibly seeking "straw and hay." In such an instance, it
has been definitively ruled, Jews are obliged to mobilize immediately
and take up defensive arms, even if this means violating the Sabbath.
Why? Because the possible danger to the Jewish community, as well as
neighboring ones, necessitates breaking even Sabbath law for the
greater duty of self-preservation.

Should there be a question whether the risk does indeed create a
situation of "danger to life," then—as in a case of illness, where a
medical authority is consulted, the relevant authority is vested in military experts. If they decide that there is a danger to life, there can be
no other overriding considerations. As long as any risk exists, political
considerations for goodwill are forbidden by Jewish law.

"With regard to the liberated areas," the Rebbe has observed,
"military experts, Jewish and non-Jewish, agree that in the present
situation, giving up any part of them would create serious security
dangers. No one says that relinquishing any part of them would enhance
the defensibility of the borders. But some military experts are prepared
to take a chance in order not to antagonize the American government
and/or to improve Israel's 'international image.' To follow this line of
reasoning would not only contradict the clear verdict, but also ignore
costly lessons of the past."

The Rebbe points to Israel's conduct before the Yom Kippur War
as a glaring example. Days and hours before the attack, intelligence
experts in Israel pointed to evidence that an Egyptian attack was imminent and advised a preemptive strike that might save many lives and
prevent an invasion of Israel. But the Israeli government rejected this
advice on the grounds that such a step, or even merely a general
mobilization before the Egyptians actually crossed the border, would
brand them as the aggressor and jeopardize Israeli-American relations.

The Rebbe held that this decision was contrary to Jewish law, and
its tragic results confirmed for him the validity of the Torah's position.
Many lives were sacrificed, and the military situation came close to
disaster.

The Rebbe has recognized that some may argue that the case of the border town in the Codes of Jewish Law is not identical to the present situation, because the Land of Israel is not in a state of "being besieged by gentiles"; or that the present surrendering of some areas would not endanger lives. In response, the Rebbe has insisted that such arguments are based on misinformation. "The Arab neighbors are prepared militarily. What is more, they demand these areas as theirs to keep and openly declare that if not surrendered by Israel voluntarily, they will take them by force and eventually everything else."

As further proof of how misinformation and distortion of facts have had tragic results for Israel in the past, the Rebbe offers the example of Sinai's oil wells. "Some warned at the time that it would be a terrible mistake to return them, since oil is a crucial weapon. Without it planes and tanks are put out of action as surely as if they had been attacked. Nevertheless, some rabbis defended the surrender of the oil wells on the basis of 'information' that Israel had ample oil reserves that could last for months. The suggestion that this information should be checked with those who understood the difficulties of storing oil was ignored. Sure enough, before long, the Israeli government found it necessary to ask for urgent oil deliveries from the United States, because the reserves would last only a few days. Moreover, prominent governmental officials publicly admitted that they had made a serious mistake in surrendering the oil wells."

The Rebbe has also noted that since Israel relinquished the Sinai oil wells, its government's own figures reveal payment to Egypt of some $2.5 billion for oil produced by these same wells. Israel has also been obliged to buy oil in the market at exorbitant prices.

In summing up his argument, the Rebbe concludes, "Since the subject matter is purely Halachic (dealing in Jewish legal matters), namely, the question of "danger to life," the sanctity of the territories as biblical land is irrelevant. Irrelevant too are such considerations as political affiliation or philosophy or personal attitudes to the current Israeli government. A rabbi must rule on the matter purely from the objective point of view of Jewish law, without allowing any other factors or opinions, however strongly he may feel about them, to influence his judgment. "It is clear," he said, "that ceding land would be suicidal."

Since the matter pertains to "danger to life," the Rebbe insists, "it is the duty of every Jew—whether lay person or rabbi—to do all that is permitted by the Codes of Jewish Law to help forestall or minimize the military danger to Israel. In a case of 'danger to life,' every possible effort must be made even if one doubts whether the effort will succeed."

Both at the time, and subsequently, the Rebbe opposed Israel's territorial concessions in the Camp David agreement as misguided. After stressing the highly unstable political climate of Arab countries like Egypt, he warned: "With whom can Israel sign a valid peace treaty now? With no one! Those who cry for 'peace' and 'peace now' deliberately choose to ignore such points. . . . They are ready to make concessions which will place the lives of millions of Jews in mortal danger."

Dismissing as naive the relieved greeting that many bestowed upon President Anwar Sadat, the Lubavitcher Rebbe condemned the Camp David agreement with Egypt as illusory and possibly quite temporary: "For all we gave, we received nothing." On Talmudic grounds he regards the issue of Jewish safety as the only relevant one and consequently he has welcomed the establishment of new Jewish settlements along Israel's entire eastern border with Jordan.

Lubavitchers seem understandably quick to stress that the Rebbe's stance has, in his own words, "nothing to do with the sanctity of the Land of Israel," or with the slightest messianic pretensions about the post-Holocaust existence of the State of Israel. In a representative discourse published in 1980, the Rebbe declared that the State of Israel is certainly a worldwide haven for Jews and Judaism, but that it nevertheless has "nothing to do with the Redemption or the Beginnings of the Redemption." Following his lead, Chabad Hasidim emphasize that the Talmudic precept he cites applies equally to the defense of Jewish settlements in the Diaspora, being solely a matter of protecting lives in potential danger.

Israel is a land of diverse nationalities and stark geographic contrasts, and new towns such as Kiryat Gat in the Negev are very different from Jerusalem and Tel Aviv. For millennia, dreamers and mystics have been irresistibly attracted to this stark desert landscape. During the day, the blazing sun permits no compromise between shadow and light. At night, the sky is so full of stars that, in the words of a visiting artist, "You can almost reach up and pull a star down."

One of the mystics drawn to the Negev is Lubavitcher emissary

Rabbi Sholom Ber Wolpo. An Israeli with spectacles and a trim beard, he has a scholarly air. Born in Jerusalem two months before Israel's War of Independence, Wolpo was drawn to the Lubavitch movement while an adolescent and was ordained at the age of twenty-two. Hearing of the new development town of Kiryat Gat, the young rabbi and his American-born wife, Chana, decided to make it their home.

At the time, Kiryat Gat was being settled mostly by poor families from Morocco and Tunisia. Many had been raised to be observant Jews, but in Israel's secular atmosphere, they were rapidly losing their traditions, and it seemed doubtful whether their children would know much about Judaism. It was this situation that Rabbi Wolpo, obtaining the Lubavitcher Rebbe's blessing, sought to prevent. Starting first with an adult education group, he and Chana next opened a kindergarten program in 1971. Their plan was to offer informal preschooling to parents pressed by child-care responsibilities, and persuade them to send their children to the religious classes that the Wolpos hoped to open. By the end of the year more than three hundred children had enrolled in the kindergarten, far more than had been anticipated.

Then, in 1972, a large influx of Soviet Jewish émigrés from the Georgia region arrived in Kiryat Gat. Many of them were familiar with what Lubavitch represented, having been exposed to its teachings in Georgia where there had been a Chabad Hasidic community since the early twentieth century. Consequently, the Georgians needed less inducement than their new Sephardic neighbors to send their children for Hasidic schooling. Before long, Rabbi Wolpo found himself in charge of a rapidly growing educational system. As enrollment climbed, he began employing fellow Lubavitchers from Kfar Chabad and other communities to serve as teachers and administrators. By 1978, he was presiding over an annual enrollment of nearly one thousand schoolchildren, with several hundred additional attending Chabad summer camps and afternoon youth centers. In addition, a rabbinic seminary was already nearing completion.

Communities like Kiryat Gat are swiftly becoming representative of the "new Israel," where political power and influence are shifting from the Eastern European Labor-Zionists who have for generations run the country. But this thirty-year-old Negev settlement has suffered its share of social problems. The local sugar factory is the leading employer, and most residents are far from affluent. Perhaps inevitably, too, the transition that many of its thirty thousand inhabitants have had to make from their sleepy Arab homelands to the complexity of contemporary Israel has not been easy.

Not surprisingly, Kiryat Gat's Chabad House emissaries blame many of these social problems on the abrupt loss of traditional Jewish values that its Sephardic émigrés experienced upon coming to Israel. "When we work with them," observes Sholom Wolpo, "they may not be religious any longer, but they have still their faith in God. When we say, 'Let us teach your child how to pray and learn Torah,' they don't object." Besides offering a free-clothes store, after-school child care for "welfare" mothers, and a youth recreation center, Lubavitchers here have energetically promoted increased ritual observance throughout the Jewish calendar year. During each holiday including Chanukah, Purim, Passover. They make food and religious items available at little or no cost to Kiryat Gat's hard-pressed residents. Dozens of adult-education classes are offered, and a senior citizens' center is being built. Each local seminary student is also entrusted with a specific helping task, such as taking children on outings or visiting nearby kibbutzim to lead Sabbath services.

As a measure of what the Lubavitchers have accomplished, Rabbi Wolpo points to a heavy-set young man dressed in full Hasidic garb, who is chatting amicably with several teenagers at the youth center. "When I first met Shmuel," says Sholom Wolpo, "he was a teenager who hung out at the pool hall the whole day. He was a child of the streets. His father drank, and he didn't even know his mother. He was taking drugs and getting into trouble. So I taught him to put on tefillin, and eventually he came to our school. He got married and had children. He finally began coming to the same pool hall and straightening out teenagers who were as lost as he once was. I thank God that I could reach him before he ended up in prison, or became crazy on drugs. Then, a few months ago, Shmuel came in and said to me, 'Close the door. I want to speak to you.' And suddenly, he handed me fifty shekels.

"Why are you giving me this?" I asked.

" 'Because when I was living in the streets, I once broke into a Lubavitcher kindergarten and stole money from the children's charity boxes. Here is the money back.' "

Rabbi Wolpo and his staff find providing religious education to be an expensive commitment. "We have to give credit to the Israeli government," he explains, "because we are getting some funds from them. But a yeshiva is not like a university. You can't refuse students who aren't really paying their way. It might be costing us five thousand dollars a year per yeshiva student, and the boy's family gives us five hundred."

Rabbi Sholom Wolpo's fund-raising burden has been made somewhat lighter in recent years by the help of sympathetic U.S. governmental officials. Through the Agency for International Development, they have been able to provide half a million dollars to expand Kiryat Gat's high school for girls. The four-story concrete shell now standing in the center of town will be completed in a year.

Rabbi Wolpo takes justifiable pleasure in recounting how North Carolina's conservative Senator Jesse Helms has become a strong supporter of the State of Israel and Lubavitcher projects in Kiryat Gat and elsewhere. But probably most important to Sholom Wolpo is the change he has seen in Jewish self-identity in this Negev development town. "You never know what you can accomplish," he observes. "You speak to someone, you help teach him to perform a single mitzvah. But, 'one mitzvah brings another,' and you can uplift someone's entire life."

One of the most unusual and interesting of the emissaries of Lubavitch with particular responsibilities in Israel and totally dedicated to the service of the Rebbe is Rabbi Yoseph Gutnick.

Born in Sydney and brought up in a completely Lubavitch environment, he completed religious studies in New York, began a career in education and then switched to business. The chairman of a number of Australian and U.S. publicly quoted companies, his outstanding success in gold mining and prospecting in Western Australia has enabled him to become one of the principal figures in Lubavitch, not only in Australia and Israel, but worldwide. He has been instrumental in the setting up of Chabad Houses, Mikvoas and other Jewish institutions in places as far apart as Tasmania and Tibereas. His company is the principal backer of SOLMECS and SATEC, the new hi-tech ventures in energy and electronics now established in Israel.

"The Rebbe didn't influence me to go into business," Rabbi Gutnick says, "but he has been increasingly supportive, especially over the
last few years. There is a nice story that relates to a response once given
by the Rebbe which I apply to my own life. Digging for diamonds at
the edge of the sea is dangerous and, if I am asked if someone should
do it I have to tell them, 'No.' But if they go anyway and do return
unharmed, of course we should make use of the diamonds."

Together with his wife, Sterelle, and their six children, Yossi, as
he is known, continues to live the modest lifestyle typical of the Lubavitch community in Melbourne, with an "open" home for guests and a
total indifference to the more usual trappings of affluence. Their grandparents were among the first couples sent to Australia from Russia by
the previous Lubavitcher Rebbe in the late 1940s. A school was started
on a small scale by Rabbi Zalman Seryebranski, a devout Hasid and a
leading activist among the group. Later the present Rebbe sent Rabbi
Yitzchok Groner as his personal emissary to Australia. Since then, the
school has grown to over one thousand children, and in 1967 a Rabbinical College was added together with a Girls' Seminary.

Due in great part to the efforts of the Rabbi, the 80,000 Jews of
Australia have become one of the most involved Jewish communities in
the world and a source of much pride to all Lubavitchers.

Though Lubavitch activists in Israel have cultivated powerful
American figures as allies, they have, from the earliest days of the state,
carefully avioded direct participation in the election of members of the
Knesset, and have refrained from declaring their preference for any
particular candidate.

There was, however, a noticeable change in the 1988 elections, in
which Lubavitch openly supported the small religious party Agudat
Israel. This was in response to an agressive campaign by anti-Hasidic
religious factions to remove Lubavitch and other Hasidic groups from
those Orthodox institutions recognized and supported by official Israel
government agencies. The Lubavitchers campaigned vigorously and
succeeded in increasing the number of Agudat seats from two to five.
This demonstration of widespread popular support clearly showed the

respect in which Lubavitch was held throughout Israel and was critical for the next stage of the battle between the two major political parties.

The significance of the "extra" Knesset members became evident in the spring of 1990 when they played a key role in preventing the formation of a Peres government committed to negotiations with the PLO, and facilitated the establishment of a narrow "Shamir" government firmly opposed to such policies. In the view of the Rebbe, only such a government would weaken the PLO and other enemies of Israel and would prevent grave danger to the security of all Jews living in Israel and around the world.

The Lubavitchers have also been involved in a long running campaign to amend Israel's Law of Return and its related "Who Is a Jew" controversy.

This issue, increasingly heated in Israel today, dates back over forty years. In the summer of 1950, the Knesset passed the Law of Return, representing Zionist doctrine's most forceful legal expression. As indicated in its title, the law characterized the immigration of Jews as a "return" to their ancient homeland. The law thus accorded every Jew—of any citizenship or nationality—the automatic right to immigrate and legally claim Israeli court enforcement of this right. Specifically exempted by the law were those conducting activity directed against the Jewish people, and those likely to endanger public health or safety. In 1954, an amendment additionally exempted Jews who had been criminals.

All this, of course, sounds reasonable enough, but significantly, and scarcely accidentally, the Law of Return had refrained from defining what it meant by the term "Jew." During the State of Israel's first decade, questions of Jewish identity were therefore decided on a decidedly haphazard, case-by-case basis. But in early 1958, the situation abruptly changed when the country's secular-oriented Minister of the Interior issued a set of explicit instructions to civil service workers: any potential immigrant who in good faith calls himself or herself Jewish must be recorded as such. And if a married couple declares their child Jewish, the child must be automatically recorded as such, even if the mother is a non-Jew (thus violating millennia of Jewish law).

In response to the immediate religious outcry that ensued, the Minister somewhat disingenuously argued that this secular definition of Jewish nationality was *not* to be construed as having any religious significance. The religious parties, however, did not see the matter that way. Resigning in protest from the government, they insisted that even a gradual validation of such secular criteria for Jewish identity would create a nightmarish schism in world Jewry. If only from political motives, Prime Minister Ben-Gurion resolved to clarify the issue. He consulted forty-five eminent rabbinic authorities, secular jurists, and scholars living within Israel and abroad.

Among these was the Lubavitcher Rebbe, who replied, "My opinion is absolutely clear, in conformity with the Torah and the tradition accepted for generations, that in these matters there can be no validity whatsoever to a verbal declaration expressing [one's] desire to register as a Jew. Such a declaration has no power to change the reality. According to the Torah and the tradition of ages which still exists today, a Jew is only a person born of a Jewish mother, or a proselyte who has been converted in conformity with the exact procedure laid down in the authoritative codes of Judaism dating to ancient times. This applies not only to children whose parents or guardians declare their desire to register as Jews, but whoever declares his or her wish to enter the Jewish community. I do not cite sources, since there are clear and detailed rulings on this matter."

Such unequivocal remarks were typical of the correspondence that Ben-Gurion received. Under his direction, the government sought to lay the matter to rest, albeit only temporarily. It canceled the Interior Minister's recent instructions and instead stipulated that the register and identity cards of children of mixed marriages be left blank under the headings of nationality and religion.

Then, in 1970, the Knesset passed a law that specified, in effect, that an individual is legally a Jew as a result of two possible occurrences: "birth to a Jewish mother or by conversion." But this decree hardly resolved the controversy, for the Knesset had not defined what it meant by *conversion*. This literally meant that anyone coming to Israel, with any kind of "conversion" certificate, automatically receives Israeli citizenship and a registration card issued by the Ministry of the Interior stating that the bearer is a Jew.

The religious parties within Israel, as well as many Jews abroad, were enraged. They considered conversion to Judaism a serious matter, and legitimate only if conducted according to traditional Jewish law.

The Lubavitcher Rebbe had known in advance, of course, that the

Knesset was planning to pass this legislation. He had urged that it not even be considered for a vote, and within weeks of its signing into Israeli law, he began to urge rabbis throughout the world to bring about its repeal. Initially, the Lubavitcher leader sought to influence relevant Knesset politicians quietly, diplomatically, and from behind the scenes. When that approach appeared fruitless, and none of the religious leaders within Israel showed the will or strength to fight, the Rebbe began to speak out publicly.

He contended that for the Knesset to grant Israeli citizenship to whomever it chose was a purely political decision. But for it to issue Jewish identity cards to non-Jews was a wholly unacceptable breach of Judaism. "Disturbing abuses have already occurred and the potential havoc is a threat to our survival," he warned. "This dangerous law removes the distinction between Jew and non-Jew, promotes intermarriage and assimilation, and jeopardizes the identity and essence of the Jew, the Jewish family, and the Jewish people as a whole. As a result of this outrageous decree, our own children may some day face the dilemma of not knowing whether they are marrying a Jew!"

The law states that anyone who has been converted is a Jew; but what is a conversion? Does it require a 'rabbi' to make a conversion? Then who is a 'rabbi'? There are several individuals in the United States calling themselves 'rabbis' who . . . are avowed atheists! Reasoning a little further, if one who denies God altogether can still call himself a 'rabbi,' surely a non-Jew who *does* believe in God and is sympathetic to the Jewish faith could be called a 'rabbi.' Now, let us say that this non-Jewish 'rabbi' issues a slip of paper which he calls a 'conversion certificate' to another non-Jew. This would make the second individual a Jew according to the Israeli Law of Return! Is this right? Does it make sense? Or is it inherently absurd?"

Partly as a result of the Lubavitcher Rebbe's persistence, a campaign within Israel to amend the Law of Return—and explicitly sanction only Orthodox conversion as valid—was instituted. When Menachem Begin became Prime Minister in 1977, he pledged himself to be an ally of this campaign, in exchange for support of the religious parties in the new coalition he was patching together.

In each subsequent year, the Knesset has failed by close margins to amend this law. However, more than a million Israeli citizens have signed a petition urging the Knesset to do so, and the Lubavitchers are confident that the lengthy controversy will soon be satisfactorily resolved.

As part of his vision of strengthening Jewish observance throughout the Holy Land, the Lubavitcher Rebbe began sending emissaries from the United States in 1976, three years after the nearly calamitous Yom Kippur War, which had inflicted heavy casualties and a marked loss of self-confidence among the Israeli people. Countless Israelis were disappointed and disillusioned with their leaders, who had almost led them into destruction. A young, extroverted country of pioneers and immigrants, Israel had plunged into a psychologically unfamiliar state of inner brooding and soul-searching.

From the Rebbe's perspective, though, every situation in life carries within it sparks of divine opportunity. He therefore saw amid the sadness and gloom following the Yom Kippur War an encouraging potential for greater receptivity to Chabad's message: that Jews everywhere have a sacred mission to accomplish, certainly no less within the Holy Land than in the Diaspora. It was time to expand Lubavitcher outreach work there.

Most of the settlers sent by the Rebbe were either newly married couples or unmarried rabbinic students from Crown Heights. He had asked for volunteers among these two particular social groups—perhaps deciding that Israel's pressing situation particularly required the youthful traits of energy and zealous commitment.

The old town of Safed has become home to an active Lubavitcher community of nearly two hundred families. Not long ago, the town was important only for its connections with sages and mystics such as Isaac Luria and Joseph Karo. But under the Rebbe's encouragement, its Chabad Hasidim today see their presence in this remote area of the upper Galilee as a key mission of spiritual revitalization. They have established a variety of schools and educational programs such as the Machon Alte (Alte Institute) for Women and the Ascent Institute to reach disaffected Jews around the world.

The Rebbe, however, advised most of those arriving in Safed and

Jerusalem in the late 1970s to fan out into new habitations once their religious study was completed. Among the 180 Chabad Houses now spanning Israel is Rabbi Joseph Hecht's program in the southernmost city of Eilat, a shipping port and military outpost of some twenty thousand inhabitants whose major business is tourism. Glossy travel brochures depict an enticing beach scene. Originally, during the late 1960s and early '70s, Eilat had the reputation of being a swinging hot spot. Today it is a more staid community of young families. A few miles across the water lies the Jordanian city of Akaba, a ceaseless reminder of the fragility of Jewish life in Eilat.

Founded in 1980, the Chabad House here is one of the "older" such programs now flourishing in Israel; many have been in existence for only two or three years. Joseph Hecht serves as Eilat's official chief rabbi—a paid governmental post attached to the Ministry of Religious Affairs. Like other Lubavitcher emissaries, his daily activities reflect local concerns.

"Housing is a big difficulty in Eilat today," says Rabbi Hecht emphatically, from his modern office overlooking the center of town. "Not enough was built for the people here. Sometimes, a family with many children needs a bigger place to live. That can be very hard to find, and some families come to me for help. If I write a letter saying that there's a lot of tension in the family because its members are too crowded together, they may be more likely to get governmental approval. And sometimes, tensions get so bad, that I find myself carrying out marriage counseling."

Indeed, the Connecticut-born Lubavitcher finds family strains dismayingly prevalent in Eilat and elsewhere in contemporary Israel. "A woman may come in and say, 'Yesterday, we had a terrible fight, and hands were raised.' Then I call the husband, and find out what's bothering him, and why he behaved as he did. I try to talk to each of them about their dual responsibility to their children. How they must both overcome their anger and bitterness, and learn to live together and raise their children in a joint, proper manner. This is a very wide scope of our work here. Maybe fifty percent of our dealings are with family problems. If they don't come to us, they will probably end up in the divorce courts. I know families that have pulled themselves together through our efforts. Sometimes I feel despair that among our Jewish people here in Israel such problems should exist. The institution of the family is in decline, not only in Eilat, but all over the country. People have forgotten the responsibilities of marriage and family life."

Joseph Hecht describes his efforts to spread commitment to Judaism's traditional "family purity" laws, and mentions that, "When I got here, only a couple of dozen families used the mikveh. Now, it's more than three hundred. We've also built a new mikveh, which should be ready soon. I also place a strong emphasis on having proper *mezuzahs* [ritual objects placed on doorposts] and teaching the men to put on tefillin every day, even if they don't come to synagogue services in the morning. Though the newspapers may describe the city as secularized, anyone who has lived in Eilat during the past fifteen years knows that it has changed. The synagogues are much more full now. On Friday nights, you now see men wearing yarmulkahs and walking, whereas before, they were driving in their cars. There's no doubt that there's a definite upsurge of religious awareness today in Eilat."

As for the intense economic and social pressures on local families, Rabbi Hecht views his Hasidic training as invaluable in making him an effective counselor. "Chabad teaches us to understand what life is all about, and what true happiness means. This awareness automatically helps a Jew to overcome certain difficulties in family matters, and in all aspects of life."

In the small, tense land of Israel today—from Jerusalem to the Negev, Kiryat Gat to Eilat and elsewhere—such an approach seems eminently characteristic of Lubavitcher activities. Sometimes, though, the Hasidic group has found itself called upon to explain its very presence in the contemporary world. Not long ago, an unusual and important court case involving the Lubavitchers within the United States provided a vivid example of such a situation.

IX

A LIBRARY ON TRIAL

Make your books your companions, let your cases and shelves be your pleasure-grounds and gardens.

—Judah Ibn Tibbon

FOR SEVERAL GENERATIONS, THE LUBAVITCHERS HAD POSSESSED an immense library of Judaica, including the most extensive and valuable collection of Hasidic works in existence. Especially after the Holocaust, when so much of the literature of Eastern European Jewry vanished in the flames, the Lubavitchers cherished their library as a vital part of their contemporary mission in the world. Jews have always been known as the People of the Book. They were among the first to take advantage of the new technology of the printing press in the late fifteenth century, and some of the earliest books printed were Hebraica. Throughout their wandering and persecution, Jews have always managed to make books available for study.

The Lubavitch library itself has a fascinating history. During the Russian Revolution, the Bolsheviks confiscated the fifth Rebbe's sizable book collection and to this day, its exact whereabouts are unknown. Several years later the sixth Lubavitcher Rebbe began to rebuild the library, making purchases throughout Europe and appealing to his Hasidim for book donations and financial support. When the Soviet government in 1927 commuted his death sentence to permanent exile, he refused to leave without taking his library, but later, when he moved in 1933 from Latvia to Poland, some of his books were lost en route. Then when he fled Nazi-occupied Warsaw in 1939 for the United States, the library was confiscated again. After the end of the war, the Rebbe managed to secure some of his books from Poland with the help of the United States government and the Joint Distribution Committee in New York City. He continued to augment the library until his last days.

Some twenty years later, Rabbi Yehuda Krinsky—board member of Agudas Chabad (one of Lubavitch's chief administrative organizations) learned that some of the late Rebbe's book collection seemed to have survived the Shoah. Through European intermediaries, Krinsky was sent microfilm copies of Hasidic manuscripts and asked whether he could identify them. He immediately realized that these were copies of Lubavitch manuscripts long thought to be lost. The agents refused to reveal where the copy manuscripts were, but Krinsky believed that if he could discover their whereabouts, the manuscripts themselves might be found in their original form. Investigation subsequently revealed that the microfilms had been processed in Warsaw, where there was a Jewish institute with thousands of rare Judaica books and manuscripts, including many from the late Rebbe's library. The microfilms had been processed on behalf of a foreign national library.

Rabbi Krinsky sent an emissary to the Jewish institute who confirmed the presence of many Lubavitch-owned manuscripts. The emissary also learned that about fifty books and manuscripts had already been given away as souvenirs to American tourists. The bulk of the collection, though, was still intact.

Through the help of the U.S. State Department, Krinsky and Chabad director Avraham Shemtov spent three years in negotiation with the Polish government. Finally, the Polish government was ready to release the books to Lubavitch, provided they published a thank-you notice in four major American newspapers. This seemed a reasonable request and the following notice appeared in *The New York Times, The Washington Post,* the *Los Angeles Times,* and the *Chicago Tribune:*

We thank the Polish authorities and our friends in Poland, for their efforts in preserving the invaluable and irreplaceable collection of Lubavitcher books and manuscripts. We also profoundly thank our Polish-

American friends, whose contacts in Poland made this gift possible. These religious books and manuscripts will now become a valuable addition to the Lubavitch movement's library in the United States.

When the Rebbe recovered from his heart attack in 1977, his first visit out of his home was to the Lubavitch library nearby. There he spent many hours perusing the newly returned books and manuscripts. As Krinsky recalls, "It must have been very pleasing and invigorating for him." Soon after, Agudas Chabad began extensive renovations and hired new staff to maintain the library and catalogue the books.

In the winter of 1985 Lubavitch library staff noticed valuable books were disappearing from the shelves. Before long, it became obvious that some of the rare Kabbalistic and biblical commentaries were missing.

All efforts to find out who who had been taking the books were fruitless, until a hidden camera was installed. For several weeks, the camera's videotape was blank, then the image of the Rebbe's nephew Barry Gourary appeared, entering the library's basement late at night and leaving shortly afterward with a full shopping bag.

Krinsky and his colleagues knew Barry Gourary as a grandson of the previous Lubavitcher Rebbe. His father, Rabbi Samarius Gourary, was a leading Lubavitcher educational administrator. But as a New Jersey management consultant in his early sixties, Barry Gourary had long since parted ways with the Lubavitcher movement and with Jewish Orthodoxy as well. Apart from visits to his elderly parents who lived in an apartment at Lubavitcher headquarters, he had minimal contact with its leadership or rank-and-file members.

When Barry Gourary was asked to return the books he refused, arguing that his mother and aunt (the latter being the Rebbe's wife, known as the Rebbetzin) had both granted him permission to take whatever he wished from the library. The books were his, he insisted, and he intended to sell them at a good price. When asked about any permission she might have given Barry Gourary to take the books, the Rebbetzin denied the account as totally false. Chabad's directors immediately had the library's locks changed and a substantial security system was installed.

Meanwhile, they learned that Barry Gourary had already begun selling some of the four hundred books he had taken from the library. Dealers in Europe, Israel, and the United States were very much interested in them. One illuminated Passover Haggadah dating back to 1757 was sold for $69,000 to a Swiss book dealer who soon found a private buyer to pay nearly $150,000 for it. Later, Lubavitchers learned that Barry Gourary had approached Christie's auction house in Manhattan, but staff became suspicious and turned him away.

When Barry Gourary repeatedly refused to return the books, despite his own father's urging, the Rebbe himself intervened and asked for the return of the books quickly and amicably. "They belong to the community and ultimately will certainly be restored to their rightful owner," he insisted.

On July 3, the Rebbe again reminded his audience of the tremendous dangers to which his father-in-law had exposed himself in order to retrieve the library from Soviet and then Nazi hands. The sight of the books on the open market for private gain moved him to comment, "Because we are living in exile, terrible things indeed happen." He promised that any innocent buyer who had unwittingly purchased an item from the Lubavitch library would be fully reimbursed.

At the same time, several wealthy supporters tried to negotiate a settlement with Barry Gourary. Their efforts failed. Gourary maintained that the books were his personal property. The Lubavitchers could not possibly agree. To them, his stance represented a brazen act to appropriate books belonging to the Jewish community. In an even larger sense, Barry Gourary's claim to own the library attacked the unique basis of the Rebbe-Hasid relationship and the very foundation of the Lubavitcher worldwide community.

What should Agudas Chabad do? Yehuda Krinsky sensed that the next step was up to them. Here was a man who had taken illegally hundreds of rare books, selling them like any ordinary merchandise. Some had already been sold and were in the hands of collectors here and in Europe. All the books could go at any time and would be irretrievable.

Barry Gourary was then asked to appear before a Jewish court but refused. Krinsky consulted rabbinic authorities on Jewish law who advised him that appeals can be made to a governmental court if justice cannot be effectuated in a Jewish court. On legal advice the Lubavitchers decided to obtain a temporary restraining order in the hope that this would resolve the matter.

By now, it was midsummer, and many federal judges for the Federal Court of the Eastern District at Brooklyn's Tillary Street were on vacation. Krinsky decided to work with Nathan Lewin, a prominent attorney in Washington, D.C. On Monday, July 29, they went to the Brooklyn courthouse. Before considering any legalities, the judge asked Barry Gourary to have the matter dealt with by the Jewish courts. Gourary refused, giving no alternative to Agudas Chabad but to proceed with the restraining order.

A court messenger was immediately dispatched to Barry Gourary informing him of the restraining order and enjoining him from selling any more books. Those in his possession were then placed in an escrow account in a bonded warehouse under attorney supervision. Krinsky waited eagerly for Gourary to return the books, but he did not. Accordingly, on August 5, Lewin filed a lawsuit on Chabad's behalf, asking for recovery of the books, and alleging "conversion and trespass."

On August 23, Barry Gourary counterclaimed for a judgment that all four hundred books, as well as everything else in the entire Lubavitcher library, belonged to him and his mother. His argument was simple: as the late Rebbe's grandson and natural heir, he was entitled to the library, which was his grandfather's private property. On September 23, he filed an "answer and counterclaim" with his mother involving herself as an intervening party. On October 2, he filed for a jury trial, but the court denied this. On October 23, his mother filed and demanded a jury trial on all issues, but her motion was likewise denied.

Agudas Chabad retained two legal firms—Miller, Cassidy, Larroca & Lewin of Washington, D.C., and Schnader, Harrison, Segal & Lewis of Philadelphia. The two chief attorneys were Nathan Lewin and Jerome Shestack respectively, and Seth Waxman, a law partner of Nathan Lewin; Shestack had assisted Agudas Chabad several years before in its efforts to retrieve long-lost books from Poland. Joining these two law firms were members of a third: Schlam, Stone & Dolan of New York City. Meanwhile, the Lubavitchers unobtrusively continued to buy back the 120 books that Gourary had already sold.

The case was assigned to Judge Charles P. Sifton, who had once been married to the daughter of theologian Reinhold Niebuhr. He saw the case as important and far-reaching—more than an internal dispute between the followers of a prominent deceased Jewish leader and his heirs for possession of a priceless library. Sifton recognized that the disagreement not only directly involved the Lubavitchers but also touched on a far more fundamental question: Are Jewish leaders, particularly spiritual leaders of a generation, essentially private individuals able to do as they wish with funds given to them, or are they, rather, figures entrusted with a sacred, enormously responsible task and therefore responsible to the community?

The Lubavitchers knew that the traditional Jewish answer was unequivocal. It was unthinkable that the previous Rebbe, who had sought to live his entire life in accordance with Jewish precepts, had amassed a magnificent library of Judaica out of communal funds for his own personal gain and that of his immediate family.

Yet Chabad's board members and attorneys knew that it would not be easy to prove this in court. For one thing, more than thirty-five years had passed since Rabbi Yosef Yitzchak Schneersohn's death, and it was doubtful whether the pertinent documents would be available. Furthermore, this kind of legal case had few precedents, and it was hard to tell how Judge Sifton, unfamiliar with Hasidism and Lubavitch's history, might interpret the facts. Finally, Agudas Chabad had decisively rejected any notion of compromise with Barry Gourary on the issue of the library's ownership. It would be necessary to win a complete and unequivocal verdict in Lubavitch's favor.

That fall, Chabad's attorneys advised the library staff, under the direction of Rabbi Sholom Levine, to find all pertinent documents to substantiate their claim to ownership of the library. It was a challenging and initially bewildering task, Levine remembers. "At first, I had little idea what we were even supposed to be looking for, but after we met the attorneys, I had at least some sense of what they considered to be important and what might be helpful. Then we began looking."

The late Rebbe had been an amazingly prolific correspondent, and had composed more than one hundred thousand letters over the last forty years of his life. Copies of about half of these were in the library's archives. Did any relate to the library, and if so, could they effectively back up the claim that the library was communal and not private property? That was Levine's first focus. Recalling that the previous Rebbe had been the subject of top-level American governmental intervention at the time of his rescue from Nazi-occupied Poland, attorney Lewin also initiated archival research at the Library of Congress.

By late autumn, hundreds of items and documents were found to buttress Chabad's argument, and the attorneys became more confident that they now had a solid case to present. They had amassed documents showing that the late Rebbe had publicly appealed for book donations to Chabad (rather than himself) in the 1920s, 1930s, and 1940s, and that book purchases had been made out of several of Chabad's organizational accounts rather than personal funds. They also found evidence that books continued to be bought for the library in the name of Chabad even after Rabbi Yosef Yitzchak Schneersohn's death in 1950.

In particular, they found a Hebrew letter written by the late Rebbe on February 25, 1946, to Alexander Marx, a prominent professor at the Jewish Theological Seminary:

> To the renowned scholar Dr. Alexander Marx:
> Greetings and blessings!
> After the Nazi occupation of Poland in [1939], the evildoers confiscated several crates full of aged manuscripts and valuable books which had been kept in my library in Otwock. These manuscripts and books—besides others added later—were the personal library of the well-known librarian Shmuel Wiener from whom I bought it.
> Manuscripts: Three large boxes of aged manuscripts were confiscated, as mentioned, by the Nazis. Among these manuscripts are some from the author of the *Tanya* and from the five generations of Chabad leaders coming after him, during a period of about 150 years. These manuscripts are on the subject of Hasidism and also Jewish law . . . letters and correspondence—which are a packed treasure house on the subject of our people's history in the land of Russia during the past two centuries.
> These manuscripts are registered under the names of the Rabbis, members of Agudas Chasidei Chabad, Rabbi Israel Jacobson, and his son-in-law Rabbi Shlomo Zalman Hecht, both American citizens, [who are] the official owners of this property.
> Books: Several thousand books, among them many ancient books

of great value and very rare. These books are the property of Agudas Chasidei Chabad of America and Canada.

Before the United States entered the War, the State Department conducted negotiations with Berlin concerning the return of this property to its owners, citizens of the United States of America. The boxes were stamped by the police and were kept until an opportune time for sending them to the U.S. However, after the U.S. entered the War, the negotiations stopped, and after the War, the negotiations were resumed. . . .

In order that the State Department should work energetically to locate these manuscripts and books in order to return them to their owners, the State Department needs to understand that these manuscripts and books are great religious treasures, a possession of the nation, which have historical and scientific value.

Therefore, I turn to you with a great request, that as a renowned authority on the subject, you should please write a letter to the State Department to testify on the great value of these manuscripts and books for the Jewish people in general and particularly for the Jewish community of the United States to whom this great possession belongs.

After Lubavitch library staff had sifted through hundreds of thousands of archival documents, attorneys Lewin and Shestack were given the opportunity to consult with the Rebbe. At the meeting, the Rebbe described his father-in-law's letter to Marx as a crucial piece of evidence, constituting a clear and unequivocal statement as to the nature and ownership of the library. The Rebbe recommended that it become a prominent part of their legal argument.

Lewin and his co-attorneys next began to plan for expert witnesses to testify on Lubavitch's behalf. They wished to establish irrefutably that among Hasidim in general and Chabad adherents in particular, it was unthinkable for Rebbes to spend communal funds on personal property; specifically, to collect a private library for personal gain. Their choice of witnesses included Nobel Laureate writer Elie Wiesel, and such renowned scholars of Jewish studies as Toronto's Immanuel Schochet and London's Dr. Louis Jacobs. Another key line of argument was to show that Agudas Chasidei Chabad had been an active organization since the mid-1920s, and that the books were its possession, not the previous Rebbe's.

On November 22, Judge Sifton ruled that a trial should proceed

without a jury and scheduled opening arguments to begin on December
2. For the Lubavitcher, the date could not have been more auspicious.
It marked the anniversary of their founder's release from czarist prison
in 1798 and has been celebrated annually (on the nineteenth day of the
Hebrew month Kislev) ever since. To those more mystically inclined,
it seemed wholly impossible that with such an omen, they could lose
the case. Barry Gourary tried to change the date, but failed.

The trial lasted twenty-three court days and was a fascinating
spectacle. Each morning, an old yellow school bus arrived at the federal
courthouse in downtown Brooklyn and disgorged dozens of men dressed
in the distinctive clothing of the Lubavitcher Hasidim. They lingered
in the hallway, reading prayers and psalms from little black books, then
filed into the courtroom.

Throughout the trial proceedings, a tableau of striking images was
presented. The Stars-and-Stripes at the rear of the courtroom contrasted
dramatically with the black garb of the Lubavitcher, who had drawn lots
to see who would be privileged to attend the trial. As in an Orthodox
Jewish synagogue, men and women sat on opposite ends of the courtroom. Bearded old men shuffled through space-age metal detectors. The
courtroom was jammed with Jews—litigants, spectators, and even the
court reporter—all presided over by a non-Jew: Judge Charles P. Sifton.
Much of the testimony, depositions, and archival material such as the
late Rebbe's correspondence was in Hebrew or Yiddish. Translations
into English were necessary, and had to be done precisely. Indeed,
interpreting fine nuances of specific Hebrew or Yiddish words created
a constant battleground between the opposing attorneys.

Most of the testimony involved each side's calling of witnesses to
bolster its interpretation of the facts, which were themselves little disputed. Though the Lubavitchers felt that they had a strong case, they
knew that little precedent existed with respect to its basic issues. Judge
Sifton sat impassively throughout the voluminous testimony and gave
neither side any clues as to his personal reaction.

Perhaps the most moving and poetic testimony came from Elie
Wiesel, who was testifying for the first time in an American courtroom.

Appearing at the end of the trial, he had agreed to speak on behalf of the Lubavitchers as an expert witness on Hasidic life, refusing any fee for his time. Wiesel had long been an admirer of the Rebbe and had met with him privately on many occasions. Wiesel commented during his testimony, "Although I am not a member of Chabad, still I felt that its place in history is incommensurate, and to this day, I feel close to it."

Wiesel emphasized that Hasidic life decisively rejects the notion that Rebbes may acquire personal wealth as a sign of their unique status. Rather, "the attitude of the Rebbe toward personal wealth was one of disdain," he commented. "First, because he didn't have it. And even if he had it, he never kept it. Numerous stories existed of Rebbes who whenever they received a ruble from a Hasid, would give it away. Most Hasidic masters claimed that money never stayed in the house overnight. From the time they received it and the time they went to bed, they had already found the opportunity to give the money away to the poor. And there were poor people enough in Eastern Europe."

Commenting on the subtleties of the Hasid-Rebbe relationship, Wiesel continued, "Strangely enough, the choice [of involvement] is made by the Hasid and not the Rebbe. It is not the Rebbe who chooses the Hasid. It is the Hasid who chooses the Rebbe. But once that choice is made, it is boundless. It is total, total loyalty. But, therefore, the Rebbe owes the Hasid total loyalty.

"So, the Rebbe must have for the community [not only] total loyalty, but total generosity [and] compassion. Even more, total responsibility. That's why he is a Rebbe."

Wiesel concluded, "I have seen followers of Chabad do for others with self-sacrifice things that I cannot even repeat because they were too dangerous."

In March 1986, the two sides completed their post-trial submissions, and awaited a decision. Judge Sifton was by reputation methodical and careful. He promised a judgment within three to four months.

This seemed like a long time to wait. Then, almost immediately, Sifton presided over a Mafioso criminal trial, and months began to drag by without a verdict.

On January 6, 1987, the forty-one-page decision was issued. It was a most unusual document, offering a capsule history of Hasidism and

Chabad, and peppered with Hebrew and Yiddish phrases. In first describing the collection of books and manuscripts at issue, Judge Sifton gave his opinion that "both . . . were undoubtedly, in their origins, personal property of the Rebbe, albeit property used to serve the purposes of Chabad Chasidism."

Sifton dismissed Barry Gourary's position that no trust relationship existed between the late Rebbe and Chabad. In Sifton's view, a legally enforceable relationship had indeed been created, "not because of the demands of his followers, but . . . as a result of the Rebbe's need to avail himself of the assistance of the United States government in getting the books out of Poland." In other words, the previous Rebbe decisively established the communal rather than private nature of the library once he involved the American government in retrieval efforts.

In ruling that the library was not the late Rebbe's personal property at the time of his demise in 1950, Sifton observed that a fundamental change in the Chabad movement had taken place: it had adapted to the modern industrial-legal world through historical exigency. In his view, the library became "a community asset . . . delivered [by the previous Rebbe] into the custody of Agudas Chasidei Chabad with an express declaration that it was to be held . . . in trust for the benefit of the Chabad Hasidic community. . . . The fact of the matter is that the library was never held by the Rebbe as personal property for his personal benefit and his private, as opposed to religious, purposes.

"The Rebbe did not . . . hesitate to convey his valuable library to be held in trust for the community when the events of World War II and its aftermath made that step advisable for the community's welfare. . . . What the record makes poignantly clear is the drastic change in the Rebbe's affairs brought about by World War II and his rigorously honest acceptance of the realities which those events forced him to recognize."

As one piece of evidence for this view, Sifton noted that by 1938, when Agudas Chabad sought to acquire in its name a prospective Brooklyn home for the late Rebbe, "the increasing sophisticated regularization of Chabad Chasidism's legal status" had already started to occur. Sifton further found it legally significant that in the same period of time, from 1940–46, when the late Rebbe was articulating the movement's relation to the library, he was also "regularizing his position with the State of New York by seeing to the acquisition of his residence at 770 Eastern Parkway in the name of Agudas Chabad." In short, the late Rebbe had entered into a legally enforceable relationship with his Hasidim not due to their demands, but "by the events of the mid twentieth-century."

As the present Rebbe had recognized in the legal-strategy meeting, his father-in-law's letter to Marx at the Jewish Theological Seminary proved to be the decisive evidence. Sifton described it as "an extraordinary letter which sets forth clearly and unambiguously the relationship between the books, their owners, and the community." It convinced Sifton that the previous Rebbe had realized that Chabad had to adapt from its preindustrial, Old World ways to survive and grow in the complex legal-administrative nexus of America.

Sifton rejected Barry Gourary's view that the letter was duplicitous and intended to mislead Marx in a self-serving way. Rather, Sifton commented, "Not only does the letter, even in translation, ring with sincerity. It does not make much sense that a man of the character of the Sixth Rebbe would, in the circumstances, mean something different than what he says, that the library was to be delivered to [Agudas Chabad] for the benefit of the community."

In short, the landmark decision not only upheld Lubavitch's full ownership of the library but affirmed it in a manner its adherents found gratifying: the mutual and reciprocal relationship of Rebbe and Hasid as partners in a sacred community.

It was late morning when the exciting news reached Crown Heights. Within a few hours, Lubavitch's global network had spread the word far and wide, by fax transmission, telephone, and word of mouth from Australia to Rio, from Jerusalem to Detroit. In Crown Heights yeshivas, students placed their hands upon each other's shoulders and circled in dance, joined by hundreds of others as they rushed, still dancing, to Lubavitcher headquarters on Eastern Parkway. Soon, Yiddish bands were playing and loudspeakers blaring as the celebratory dancing intensified.

Hundreds of Lubavitcher emissaries and supporters throughout the world flocked aboard flights, on their way to Crown Heights to participate in the rejoicing and express their solidarity.

The Rebbe himself did not seem interested in encouraging the exuberant celebration. Instead, after leading afternoon synagogue prayers as usual, he emphasized the trial's moral implications.

"To spur us to reach inner heights, there had to be an opposition created in the form of an attack. What was it? The charge that Agudas Chasidei Chabad is inactive, that we are not studying the manuscripts and books, and that we are not strengthening Judaism. These arguments were presented in an American courtroom to provide a basis for answering the legal question 'To whom do these things belong?'

"The broader implication of the court's decision is not only that such charges are wholly false, but that we must do more! We must now *expand* the library and make maximum use of its books. We must be filled with great joy which bursts all limitations and nullifies all restrictions on our spiritual life! This joy must infuse our action and influence all that we do to become messengers of God and transform every Jew to be an emissary of righteousness!

"Start by making your own home a place where Torah study is increased. So, too, increase prayer and all mitzvahs, beginning with charity and good deeds. All of you will accomplish great things for the sake of heaven!"

Since they had won the case, the Lubavitchers requested that Sifton allow the books to be released, but he refused: an appeals process had first to be completed.

The appeals presentation took place on June 25, several weeks later than anticipated, and was very brief. Each side had only twenty minutes to present its arguments. To the Lubavitchers, the three highly experienced judges all seemed very perceptive. For example, one sharply remarked to Gourary's attorney, "Do you know what *surreptitious* means? Do you know that your client was removing the books at night?"

Nevertheless, summer turned to fall, fall to winter, and still no decision was issued. The long wait brought considerable tension to the Lubavitcher community. Had its case presentation somehow been faulty? Was it possible that the appellate court was considering a reversal of Sifton's favorable ruling?

On November 19, the United States Court of Appeals for the Second Circuit issued its unanimous decision. The three judges fully upheld Justice Sifton's verdict. "The precise question before us is whether the evidence before the district court was sufficient to demonstrate a settlor's [the previous Rebbe's] unequivocal intent to convey the library in question to appellee [Agudas Chasidei Chabad] as trustee for charitable purposes. We acknowledge that some of the evidence is, standing alone, equivocal. But, as is often the case, a person's actions sometimes speak even more plainly than his words. Such is the case here. When the settlor's actions and words are viewed as a whole, the district court's findings of an unequivocal intent to create a charitable trust—far from being erroneous—is in our view rightly decided."

Citing Elie Wiesel's testimony, the appellate court ruled even more strongly than had Sifton that the late Rebbe had collected a communal, not a personal, library. They vigorously rejected the argument that his letter to Marx had been a deception. "It simply defies reason and common sense to believe that a religious leader of the [previous] Rebbe's stature, whose life was dedicated to expounding the spiritual values of truth and morality, would deliberately write letters of misrepresentation regarding the ownership of a valued and to him sacred national treasure in order to feather his own nest."

Concurring with Sifton, the appellate court also concluded that "the cataclysmic events of World War II irretrievably altered the prior, informal relationship that had existed between the [previous] Rebbe and the community he served."

Finally, the three dismissed on technical grounds the Gourary contention that a jury trial had been legally required for the case.

Once more, there was jubilation in Crown Heights and throughout Lubavitch's worldwide community. The exciting international convention of Chabad emissaries was under way in Crown Heights, and the following evening many participants analyzed the wider implications of the decisive ruling. Among these was England's Rabbi Faivish Vogel. "What does the trial represent?" he rhetorically asked the gathering. "Surely not only books, but also possession and title, which, in turn, is all about the Rebbe's capacity to influence the finite, material, physical world. This decision is a statement, and a demonstration that there can be no barrier between the spiritual and the material. Those who rose unwittingly or otherwise against that concept touched the most raw nerve: because to deny that capability is to deny God's purpose. And to deny God's purpose in the world is to render the three thousand years of Jewish sacrifice meaningless."

As before, the Rebbe too stressed the moral implications of the victory.

At last, the books could be returned home and the next day, Chabad sent an armored van to bring them back. Among them was a rare fifteenth-century Kabbalistic work entitled *Derech Emunah (The Way of Truth)* by Rabbi Meir ibn Gabbai. The Rebbe immediately urged that the book be republished and completely reset with a biographical sketch of Gabbai and detailed references to other Kabbalistic, Hadisic, and Jewish philosophical works. Two days later the staff of the Chabad Research Center and Lubavitch's publishing house had produced the work ready for sale in bookstores.

In his monthly address the following Sabbath, the Rebbe explained certain passages from the newly reissued work, and showed how Gabbai's discourse sheds much light on key issues in Jewish philosophy. On the first anniversary of Judge Sifton's verdict on the library, the Rebbe put the trial into perspective.

Today our theme is, "our cause has prevailed." Last year on this day, we were blessed with the favorable judicial decision and saw the benevolent Divine Providence of God that brought the books back. The books, of course, are part of the library of Agudas Chasidei Chabad-Lubavitch which was founded and expanded by the previous Rebbe while he was still in the Soviet Union. After his liberation from Soviet prison, this spiritually priceless collection left the country with him, eventually to reach these shores. Here the library of Agudas Chasidei Chabad-Lubavitch was reestablished by the previous Rebbe. It has grown and continues to grow.

Since we speak of a library of international importance which represents an invaluable treasure for all of Torah Judaism, it is clear that the liberation of these books represents a victory and a salvation for Torah Judaism. This includes the activities of spreading Torah, Judaism, and the wellsprings of Hasidism, including the teaching of the previous Rebbe.

In a peaceful way, we must overcome all obstacles and win over even those currently opposed to the just path of Torah. The Book of Esther [9:29] tells us, 'These days are remembered and come into being in every generation.' This means that every year on the anniversary of that day, one must remember and do those actions that occurred the first time. So we must establish this as an auspicious day and a time of goodwill in all aspects connected to the teachings contained in the books.

How do we celebrate the victory of the books? It is the books that were victorious. So let us ask the books. Their clear answer is: to study them and live by their teachings.

X

DAYS ARE COMING

And it shall come to pass in the end of days
That the mountain of the Lord's House
Shall be exalted at the head of the mountains
And exalted above the hills
And peoples shall stream to it.
And many nations shall go and say:
Come, let us go up to the Lord's mountain
And to the House of Jacob's God
And He shall teach us of His ways.

Micah 4:1–4

I see him, but not now.
I behold him, but not from nigh. . . .

Numbers: 24–17

THERE IS A FESTIVE, ALMOST EUPHORIC, MOOD IN CROWN
Heights. Few Hasidim heading for Sabbath services seem
even aware of the gray November skies as they cross from their homes
to the main synagogue on Eastern Parkway. Dominant among the animated conversations along the busy streets is the international convention for Chabad's emissaries.

During the past few days, hundreds of rabbis, some accompanied
by their families, have been arriving in Brooklyn. During the past
decade, the emissary conventions have grown tremendously in size, and
this year's is clearly the largest one ever held. Lubavitchers who live

near the Rebbe have long become accustomed to the constant stream of visitors to their community and regard such visits as proof of the successful Jewish outreach that the Rebbe has fostered for forty years. Indeed, the attitude of the Rebbe's local followers is that of bemused pride as they recount the latest Hasidic outpost established by their worldwide movement. But this week's spectacle of fellow Hasidim flying in from all parts of the United States and abroad is on an unprecedented scale. Predisposed to find mystical portents within the commonplace, local Lubavitchers regard the emissary convention as a harbinger of good things to come.

The main synagogue is packed full. Suddenly, senior members of the movement appear, escorting the determined figure of Rabbi Menachem Schneerson to his customary place next to the Torah ark. Throughout the ensuing Sabbath morning prayers and Torah reading, an atmosphere of impassioned fervor reigns in the synagogue.

There is a short recess, for lunch, but within the hour, the throngs begin forming again, for seats are on a first-come basis and most people will be obliged to stand for hours once all seats are filled. The occasion is the weekly Sabbath celebration—an intense afternoon of communal meeting with the Rebbe.

Most people who regularly participate in the Rebbe's celebrations find them inspiring, not merely for the philosophical content of his discourse, but for the entire atmosphere. In previous years, when the Rebbe addressed far smaller, national gatherings of Chabad emissaries, his words had left an enduring mark. Besides praising them warmly for strengthening Jewish self-identity in their host countries, he had explicitly related their outreach work to the ultimate goal of hastening the advent of the messianic age. In one such talk, the Rebbe had observed the close similarity between the Hebrew words for "emissary" *(shaliach)* and "messiah" *(moshiach).* Now these emissaries, comprising the largest global gathering of their far-flung minions ever organized, are filled with special anticipatory excitement.

The Rebbe reenters the synagogue, strides to the center of the makeshift dais and immediately begins his discourse in Yiddish. As usual, he draws inspiration from the Torah's weekly portion. This week, it is the passage from Genesis relating how Jacob is directed by Isaac to journey to the distant settlement of Haran to escape the vengeance of Esau. There, hundreds of miles to the north of the Holy Land in which his family lives, Jacob will carry out his mission: to find a suitable wife among his mother's kinfolk and raise a family in holiness.

"According to the teachings of the Baal Shem Tov," the Rebbe begins, "everything happens in this world by Divine Providence. Therefore, every Jew must learn from all that he sees and hears. How much more is this notion applicable to the Torah portion of the week! As the Lubavitch founder stated, we should all 'live with' the biblical portion of the week."

The Rebbe explains that Jacob's mission in Haran represents the first emissary role mentioned in the Torah. Sharply delineating both in philosophical and practical terms the difference in Jewish law between an emissary and a servant, he urges the emissaries gathered today to view themselves as free and independent agents of God, striving to realize their unique creative capacities. Yet, he stresses, an emissary's work is definitely not intended simply to gratify his own ego.

"Hasidism teaches us that God created the universe in order to have a dwelling place in the lower worlds. Why this is so, the Torah says we do not know. But it emphasizes that our entire purpose here until the Moshiach comes is to create a dwelling place for God. We do this by using our own nature, and converting and sanctifying this material world into a holy dwelling place."

Next the Rebbe compares Jacob's mission—leaving the exalted Holy Land for the darker realm of Haran—to the larger mission of the Jewish people as a whole: spreading the light of Torah throughout the world and thereby helping to bring about the long-prophesied messianic age. He reminds his audience of the Talmudic precept that one who teaches Torah to a fellow Jew is likened to having given birth to him. In this sense, the Rebbe observes, Isaac's directive to Jacob to marry and "to be fruitful and multiply," can be interpreted from a higher perspective: that Chabad emissaries, like all Jews, have a special duty to be "fruitful" by spreading the Torah's divine wisdom wherever they may be.

The Rebbe discusses several other subjects emanating from this single passage within Genesis. He explains the significance of the fact that Jacob, after gathering stones for his pillow in the wilderness, declares that these will some day become part of a House of God. "Here is a further lesson for us: that even before Jacob reached his destination he was uplifting and transforming his environment into a place of Godliness. He was striving to accomplish this with the very lowest, most material, and most physical aspects of his environment, symbolized by stones, which are not even organic. Everything on earth is thus meant to be elevated and become sacred."

It is late afternoon, more than three hours later, before the Rebbe concludes his final discourse. As has been the case for all others, he ends with a brief prayer for the imminent coming of the Messiah. Leaving the makeshift synagogue podium, he smiles and nods, gesturing with encouragement to several Hasidic youngsters who crowd to look at him as he passes up the aisle. Meanwhile, the Rebbe's audience bursts into sustained singing, clapping, and swaying. They continue long after he has left the synagogue. The singing continues, swelling and then abating, then swelling again, for more than half an hour. As Lubavitcher Rabbi Daniel Goldberg recalls, "I had seldom seen such excitement in nearly twenty years of attending these celebrations. The singing went on and on. It was really unbelievable. It was as if by the dancing and singing, and the joy, they were trying to bring down Moshiach into our world right then!"

The Lubavitchers approach the subject of messianism from a historical context. The essence of their underlying attitude is perhaps best conveyed in the poignant joke that Minnesota's Rabbi Manis Friedman currently tells audiences when he speaks on "We Want Moshiach Now":

> Michael, a sincere, young Jewish man, joined a cult, to the horror of those who knew him. It was only after great difficulty that Michael's family succeeded in extricating him. When he was asked why he had joined the cult, Michael replied: "Because Judaism doesn't have any of those great, inspiring spiritual teachers like Christianity does."
>
> "Such as?" his family challenged.
>
> "Oh, you know," he answered impatiently, with irritation. "Isaiah, and Jeremiah, and people like that!"

It is undeniable, as they rightly point out, that the twin concepts of exile and redemption have for millennia been an integral aspect of

Judaism. Modern scholars believe that the Hebrew term *moshiach*—of which "messiah" is the anglicized form—preceded the messianic outlook by many centuries. Originally, in biblical usage, *moshiach* simply meant "anointed one" and referred to Aaron and his sons, who were anointed with oil and thereby consecrated as priests to the service of God.

Subsequently, the High Priest of each generation was called "the Anointed" of God. When the Jewish monarchy was established with the reign of Saul, the same appellation was applied to successive kings. Each was called "the Anointed of the Lord," because he was installed in his exalted office by receiving the sacrament of anointment. Still later Elijah was commanded by God to anoint Jehu as king of Israel, and to anoint Elisha as prophet in Elijah's own place.

In the early days of the monarchy, leaders who were "the Anointed of the Lord" came to be venerated as holy. To cause them harm, or even to curse them, were capital offenses. Jews also adopted the notion that God provides special protection to their anointed king. For example, the Psalms contain several allusions to the concept of divine intervention on behalf of "the Anointed of the Lord," the idealized Davidic king. When the beloved King David ruled Israel in the tenth century B.C.E., the Jewish people believed that his House would rule forever, not only over Israel but also over all the nations.

Some two centuries later the Hebrew prophets began to shift their gaze from their own troubled present to a more inviting future. Isaiah was active in the eighth century B.C.E., a time when the Northern Kingdom of Israel was annexed to the Assyrian Empire while the Kingdom of Judah lay uneasily in its shadow as a tributary. Isaiah envisioned a future age of universal peace that would be ushered in by "a shoot out of the stump of Jesse": namely, a king of the Davidic line. During the eighth century B.C.E., the first explicit written reference within Judaism to the resurrection of the dead also appeared, in a single tantalizing line in the Book of Isaiah.

Later, in visionary writings filled with dazzling symbols and signs, the prophet Daniel described "a time [of great trouble] when shall arise Michael, the great prince of [our] people. . . . And [our] people shall be delivered, every one whose name shall be found written in the book. And many of those who sleep in the dust of the earth shall awake, some to everlasting life, and some to shame and everlasting contempt. And those who are wise shall shine like the brightness of the firmament, and those who turn many to righteousness [shall shine] like the stars for ever and ever."

The books of the other Hebrew prophets shared the same eschatological vision: that a Redeemer would come forth from the House of David, that he would bring about the restoration of the Temple to its magnificent glory, that Jews everywhere in the oppressive exile of the Diaspora would be gathered back to the Holy Land, and that there would be a resurrection of the dead. This powerful constellation of images became very deeply ingrained in Jewish consciousness; and, as the Lubavitcher Hasidim today bear witness, it has never vanished from the Jewish psyche. During the Maccabean period of the second century B.C.E., in apocryphal texts, the "End of Days" vision was given new emphasis and described in much fuller detail. For the next two centuries in the Holy Land, messianic expectations ran high.

Jewish messianic fervor peaked during a hundred-year period marked by three abortive revolts against their despotic Roman rulers, and subsided in the decades following the final unsuccessful revolt in 132–135 C.E. At that time Judaism underwent an extremely powerful and enduring change of emphasis. In today's language, one might almost say that a paradigm shift took place. Initially, many Jews expected and then hoped that the Second Temple, destroyed by Rome in the year 70 C.E., would be rebuilt in their lifetime.

Leading scholars, unfamiliar with the intricacies of political wheeling and dealing, periodically led delegations to high Roman officials, but they met with continual disappointment. In *The Ethics of Our Fathers*, these sages advised future generations: "Be on guard in your relations with the ruling power, for they bring no man near to them except for their own interests; seeming to be friends such time as it is to their own advantage, they stand not with a man in his hour of need."

Apocalyptic teachings about an approaching Judgment Day also aroused much excitement at first. Even the great Rabbi Akiba, the dean of his contemporaries, at first proclaimed the Judean soldier Bar-Koziba the Messiah (renaming him Bar-Kochba, or Son of the Star), when he won a few early victories against Rome.

However, the brutality and horror that accompanied the Roman suppression of Bar-Kochba's revolt decisively convinced the Jewish people that no quick reversal of their political situation was at hand. Indeed, they could hardly afford another apocalyptic bid for national independence. As punishment for the revolt, the Romans forbade teaching the Torah, observing the Sabbath, and circumcision as capital offenses. Thousands were sold into slavery. Jerusalem was rebuilt as Aelia Capitolina and no Jew was allowed within its gates. The Emperor renamed the country Palestine (Land of the Philistines), a label deliberately chosen to signify that the territory was no longer considered Judean. Soon after the rebellion was put down, Rabbi Akiba and other leading scholars were executed for violating the ban on teaching the Torah. Simon bar Yochai—Rabbi Akiba's leading disciple—and his son went into hiding for thirteen years. In 139 C.E., Antoninus Pius began to ease conditions, but the Jewish people were indisputably in exile.

During this era, the significance of Torah learning came to occupy a central position in Judaism. The Torah academies deliberately put apocalypse aside. In order for Judaism to survive, its spiritual leaders stressed, it was necessary to accept the nation's fate and strive for individual closeness to God. The Temple had been the Holy House. But now the synagogue was a miniature holy place. With the Temple in ruins and Jerusalem a forbidden city, each Jew would become a High Priest, seeking heavenly favor for the nation and for individuals.

Study of the Torah—that is, the Bible and the oral tradition based upon it—became regarded as vital to God's plan. Through sacred study, the sages declared, the divine order becomes clear and explicit. Torah study also became respected as a mystical activity, permitting Jews to draw nearer to the Almighty. Thus, inevitably, the scholars came to be viewed as holy figures, capable of working wonders. Some were extolled as seers and masters of arcane knowledge. But nearly all were venerated as teachers to guide men and women through the straits of everyday life. Indeed, the Hebrew appellation *rabbi*, which originated in this period, literally means "my teacher."

As a result of this situation, Jewish emphasis on the practical aspects of personal growth and daily spirituality became paramount. Messianic speculation receded to the background of Judaism, for the rabbis were far more concerned with the patient, step-by-step path of inner ascent. Clearly reflecting this outlook, the Mishnah, the foundation of Jewish law, was completed and put into writing in the early third century C.E.

Yet, faith in a divine redemption never vanished from Judaism. Rather, evidence from the Talmud clearly shows that scholars believed that in every generation there is one Jew whose piety, mystical prowess, and Torah scholarship mark him as the potential Messiah, should God decide that the prophetic time has come. For example, the Talmud records a conversation in which each sage names his own particular teacher to be the (potential) Messiah of their time. In these discussions, the sages agreed that such a Jew will be conceived, born, and raised in a normal, nonmiraculous way. Made of flesh and blood like any other human being, he would mature physically in a normal way as well. They further suggested that he might not need to demonstrate supernatural powers: The proof that he actually *was* the Messiah would come only when he had brought about the restoration of the Temple in Jerusalem and the Jewish people's ingathering to the Holy Land to dwell there unharmed and unhindered.

By the third century, the dominant Jewish belief was that all the events forseen by Daniel, Isaiah, and the other prophets were literally true and would eventually occur, but no human knew how or when. The sages declared that the Messiah might come at any moment in any generation; and that Jewish study, ritual observance, and the performance of good deeds would surely hasten his arrival.

It is now Sunday afternoon in Crown Heights, and the Lubavitcher international emissary convention is in progress. The sidewalks seem especially gray under the chilly, overcast skies, but there is light in the eyes of the Rebbe's emissaries as they head toward the Oholei Torah Jewish Center on Eastern Parkway.

Though it valiantly displays fresh coats of paint here and there, the Oholei Torah Jewish Center has clearly seen better days. Its high walls, ceilings, and floors look in need of renovation; the basement rooms are decidedly shabby. Perhaps the hundreds of rabbinic emissaries filling the drafty rooms throughout the large building do not notice its condition, or perhaps they try to see beyond it.

Half a dozen workshops are beginning, and groups of emissaries crowd into their respective meeting places. In the first floor banquet hall, Rabbi Sholom Lipskar gazes round his audience of colleagues before launching into a talk about the Aleph Institute, its philosophy and history. He will be joined by fellow Chabad rabbis from California, Illinois, Iowa, and Michigan to discuss the problems and practicalities of outreach to Jewish prisoners. Also present at the workshop will be a former Jewish federal inmate, now paroled in South Florida, who gratefully participated in many Aleph Institute activities.

The panel on prison outreach is followed without a break by one concerned with a very different segment of the world Jewish community: the elderly. A pair of Lubavitcher emissaries, from Los Angeles and New York City respectively, discuss their efforts to help as well as to spread Jewish study and observance among those in nursing homes, adult congregate facilities, senior citizen centers, and other institutions. Such outreach work, they remind their fellow emissaries, is inspired by the Rebbe's statement that retirement has no place in Judaism. Several years ago, the Rebbe—already past eighty—spoke for hours with considerable emotion on the importance of providing meaningful Jewish education to retirees, especially those spending endless hours playing cards or watching television to keep themselves busy. But Rabbi Menachem Gerlitzky warns his rabbinic audience, "When you start going into nursing homes to do outreach, you're going to find it's not what you expected. They are mostly women. And don't think you'll be leading intense, high-level Jewish classes either." The audience smiles in agreement.

"One of the biggest successes I've had recently," says Menachem Gerlitzky, "was when one woman in her nineties begged me to get her a Yiddish newspaper. She said to me, 'I haven't had anything Yiddish to read in the ten years I've been here.' When I got her a Yiddish newspaper to read, you should have seen the look on her face! That's what your work will generally be like."

Meanwhile, in one of the largest chambers upstairs, several dozen Lubavitcher emissaries are listening to a panel discussion on "The Menorah: Practical and Legal Ramifications." The panelists come from all over the United States, including St. Louis, south Florida, and Rochester, New York. But the speakers share a common conviction with their audience, that the placing of Chanukah menorahs in public places is important and worth defending vigorously through the American legal system. Many emissaries are proud to hear how the U.S. Supreme Court recently upheld the Lubavitcher view in a Pittsburgh case. But, the panelists stress, the Supreme Court ruling was not decisive; indeed, "mainstream" Jewish organizations in many local communities are continuing unabated their efforts to block Lubavitcher menorah activity involving public places.

Most of the emissaries in the room now appear tense: while they are undoubtedly committed to do all that is legally possible to fight for the menorahs, court action is obviously not to their taste.

Down a long, dimly lit corridor on the same floor yet another workshop is taking place on the topic of "Spiritual Welfare of Emissaries' Children." Joined by colleagues from Houston, Texas; Grand Rapids, Michigan; and Madrid, Spain, Rabbi Sholom Weinberg describes his difficulties in struggling to raise his children as proper Hasidim in Kansas City. To supplement the non-Hasidic Hebrew day-school education they receive, Sholom Weinberg relates, he spends one to two hours every morning privately tutoring them at home. "I have learned to make this a pattern that I never, never deviate from," he declares. "Because if you're doing this work as an emissary of the Rebbe, and your own children start to suffer, that's clearly no good. The work of the parents can't be done at the expense of the children."

"What if you try and try, and you just can't give a proper Jewish education to your kids?" asks a young emissary.

Several panel members note that such situations are rare and describe the sensitivity and understanding—as well as religious strength—instilled in children of emissaries even at tender ages. "When I saw what was available for my kids," relates Houston's Shimon Lazaroff, "I started my own Orthodox day school, and now, thank God, many children attend, and it's growing day by day."

In still other meeting places around the Oholei Torah Jewish Center, similar workshops are progressing on a variety of other issues. Emissaries from London and Vienna, joined by a Los Angeles colleague, are leading a discussion about administering Hebrew day-school programs. Downstairs, the largest panel, composed of emissaries from Indiana, Maryland, Texas, Virginia, and other states, heads a workshop on "Getting Started: A Chabad House in a New Community." Before an animated audience of some fifty rabbis, the panel leaders provide colorful stories of how they won religious and financial support in places that were at first indifferent, or even hostile, to their Hasidic presence.

The panelists banter with one another and with the audience. They have all discovered that there are no quick solutions to the manifold problems of becoming, in effect, religious entrepreneurs in a highly decentralized worldwide organization. Rather, they have learned the importance of a sense of humor in defusing the tensions of their daily outreach work.

But behind the healing power of such self-deprecatory laughter there is an underlying mood of urgency. For underlying these discussions, and sometimes explicitly stated, is the Lubavitcher belief that we are living on the edge of messianic times, when, as Maimonides wrote more than nearly eight centuries ago, our slightest deed may tip the balance of the entire world toward triggering the long-awaited redemption.

The twelfth-century Jewish philosopher and legal codifier, Moses Maimonides, had much to say about messianism. His codification of more than a thousand years of Talmudic and other pronouncements has long been considered Judaism's major source for practical law on this important topic. Indeed, as the Lubavitcher Rebbe likes to point out, no Torah scholar since Maimonides has ever disputed his basic formulations about the Messiah, hence they remain authoritative even today. Because the Lubavitchers' messianism derives specifically from Maimonides's teachings, it may be useful to outline them briefly.

In essence, Maimonides wrote in his *Mishne Torah (The Second Torah)* that an individual of Davidic lineage will one day arise and restore the ancient kingship of the Jewish people to its former glory. This person, who will certainly be of flesh and blood and known to the world for his piety and scholarship, will bring about the gathering of all Diaspora Jews to the Holy Land and the rebuilding of the Temple. Thereupon, all the Bible's laws will be the law of the land once more, including those pertaining to the Temple. All nations will finally and peacefully recognize their oneness as God's children. Strife will end, and the Jewish people will lead humanity in divine homage and obeisance: "In that time, there will be neither hunger nor war, neither jealousy nor competition, but goodness will spread over everything. All delights will be as common as dust, and the whole world will have no other occupation but to know the Lord."

Maimonides further declared that after several decades of this messianic period, a "new age" will begin with the resurrection of the dead. The world will become miraculously and unimaginably transformed. Because the nature of earthly existence—and our physical perceptions—will be radically altered, Maimonides, like all other sages, insisted that we lack the capability to describe, much less comprehend, what he termed the "World to Come" after the messianic era.

Though supernatural events might occur during the unfolding of the messianic era that precede the "World to Come," this is not essential. "Think not that the Messiah must perform signs and portents and bring about new things in the world, or that he will resuscitate the dead, or the like," Maimonides explained, citing as proof that Rabbi Akiba initially believed Bar-Kochba was the Messiah, though he accomplished nothing even remotely supernatural.

Rather, Maimonides emphasized in a passage that has at times been given a symbolic interpretation, "If there should arise from the House of David a king who studies the Torah and occupies himself with its commandments . . . and if he compels all Israel to follow the Torah and observe its rules; and if he fights the wars of the Lord—then he must be *presumed* to be the Messiah. And if he succeeds in his acts, and rebuilds the Temple in its place, and gathers the exiled of Israel—then he certainly *is* the Messiah."

To Maimonides, this outlook was not mere speculation, but an inherent part of Judaism. He saw messianic faith as essential to humanity's ultimate spiritual evolution. In fact, he explicitly named belief in the Messiah's coming and belief in the resurrection of the dead as two of the thirteen essential principles of the Jewish faith:

"I believe with a complete faith in the coming of the Messiah; and even though he tarry, nevertheless I await him every day that he should come." And, "I believe with a complete faith that there will be a resurrection of the dead at a time when the [Creator wills it] . . . blessed be His name, and may His remembrance be exalted for all eternity."

Maimonides was aware that world Jewry had already experienced several abortive messianic movements during the preceding centuries. One major episode had occurred in fifth-century Crete, for many Jews had believed that the Messiah would come exactly four hundred years after the destruction of the Second Temple, corresponding to the supposed duration of the Jewish exile in Egypt before the Exodus. There had also been messianic frenzies in eighth-century Persia and Syria. Still later, incidents had taken place in the years 1096 and 1146, during the time of the first two Christian crusades, when anti-Jewish sentiment ran to unprecedented levels and left thousands dead or wounded. Indeed, Maimonides recorded one such pseudomessianic episode, related to him by his father, that had occured relatively recently in Spain.

Although the Messiah had failed to come through countless generations and no end to the eleven-hundred-year Diaspora was in sight, Maimonides was unshaken in his faith: "He who does not believe in [the Messiah], or he who does not longingly await his coming, denies not only the prophets, but also the Torah."

The Lubavitcher emissaries have seated themselves around the many tables, and the convention banquet is about to begin. The opening speaker, Rabbi Yehoshua Rosenfeld, emissary in Bogotá, Colombia, quotes the Talmudic adage that when Jews perform their religious duties, they bring divine favor to all peoples. "The nations of the world thank God because they know that through our effort and concern, the word of the Almighty will reach everyone. May the Almighty grant us many blessings and success in spreading the Rebbe's Torah teachings to all the different corners of the world, not only to the Jewish people, but to all those in the world, to the final blessing: the coming of Moshiach speedily in our days."

Yehoshua Rosenfeld is not the only speaker who voices hope for the imminent advent of the messianic age. Virtually all emissaries addressing their colleagues express confidence that through the Lubavitchers' devoted spiritual outreach around the globe, the long-awaited redemption will finally come.

Many speakers emphasize the vital role that Jews must play in promulgating the "Seven Noahide Laws" to all humanity. These injunctions, according to Jewish tradition, were given to Noah by God, discussed by the Talmudic sages and later codified by Maimonides. They comprise six prohibitions of human behavior: idolatry, blasphemy, cruelty to animals, crimes of theft, incestuous acts, and murder. The seventh "law of Noah" calls for establishing local systems of justice to enforce the six prohibitions.

In recent years, the Lubavitcher Rebbe has urged Jewry in the West to help spread worldwide observance of these moral laws. In his view, Jewish well-being in the United States now carries a special and historically unprecedented opportunity to bring "the light of Torah" to all. Never before in the history of the Diaspora have the Jewish people been secure enough to preach religious morality to others without fear of vicious retaliation.

"Until quite recently," the Rebbe has observed, "there was great potential danger involved in this kind of activity, for it could be misconstrued as an attempt to proselytize. In our generation, however, there is no misunderstanding in this respect, and it will increase the honor and respect shown to Jews among the nations. For they will see that the Jews are concerned with the welfare of *all* peoples, for the world was 'created in order to be filled with holiness,' which will only be achieved when it follows the divine plan.

"In this country, there is an additional incentive, since President Reagan issued a proclamation that urged and encouraged the observance of the Seven Noahide Laws. He indicated that only in this way can the world remain civilized. This proclamation lends support to disseminating the Seven Noahide Laws among all humanity, for the proclamation has made it easier for every Jew to influence non-Jews whom he meets through his business, profession, or social group."

Deliberately stressing the international character of the contemporary Lubavitcher movement, this evening's program includes rabbinic speakers from South Africa, Brazil, and England. As dinner is slowly served, each speaker at the lectern discusses some of the specific problems in local Jewish outreach, as well as those common to all Hasidic emissary activity. The chief emissary from London, a bespectacled middle-aged man, touches on a problem facing Lubavitch emissaries all around the world. "There is a certain ambiguity, an uncertainty, a question mark over our position and role. We go into a Jewish community, certainly in the Western world, where everything is beautifully organized. There are synagogues, there are welfare agencies, educational

organizations, legal-defense organizations, there are many other group-
ings. And when the emissary enters the host community, there is a
question: 'Who are you and where do you belong? Where do I slot you
in?

The answer is that Lubavitch cannot be slotted in, because it stems
from a much higher perspective and it radiates and generates breadth,
depth, and purpose into all of the aforementioned agencies."

After the expulsion of the Jews from Spain and Portugal in the
1490s Jewish messianic fervor was dramatically increased. There was
a sense of urgency now. The two countries had long been liberal and
tolerant toward their Jews. If such tolerance could so decisively turn to
utter hatred, there seemed little hope for Jewish survival anywhere in
the Diaspora and Jewish leaders began to look to divine intercession for
salvation. Among these was Don Isaac Abavanel, who wrote a trilogy
on the messianic theme. Living in Italy among his fellow Iberian exiles,
Don Isaac recorded extant messianic expectations. On the basis of his
own interpretations of biblical and Talmudic literature, historical
events, and astrological calculations, Don Isaac predicted that the prophetic age of redemption would begin in 1503 and be completed by
1531.

The most significant messianic outburst since ancient Jewish times
was unquestionably the Sabbatian movement of the mid-seventeenth
century. Large numbers of Jews, including prominent rabbis and scholars, became convinced that the Messiah had arrived in the person of
Sabbatai Zevi. The exuberant movement began in the region of Gaza
in the Holy Land, spread to communities throughout the Diaspora, and
reached a fever pitch early in 1666, when Zevi sailed from Smyrna to
Constantinople. Countless supporters sold their possessions and abandoned their livelihoods to await the ecstatic moment when Zevi would
remove the crown from the sultan, assume his dominance over the
Ottoman Empire, and inaugurate the messianic era. While Zevi was en
route, the Turkish authorities intercepted his ship, arrested him, and
threatened to behead him unless he immediately converted to Islam.
Sabbatai Zevi capitulated, and for the next ten years he remained under

house arrest and then imprisonment before his death in 1676. The episode had a catastrophic effect on Jewish morale, and rabbinic authorities thereafter sought to suppress mystical and messianic longings among the masses. Another such debacle, they reasoned, and Judaism might utterly collapse.

The advent of Hasidism under the charismatic leadership of the Baal Shem Tov some sixty years later was viewed with alarm by many rabbinic leaders. His opponents suspected him of harboring Sabbatian messianic tendencies and sought to burn Hasidic writings and even excommunicate its adherents. It seems clear, however, that the Baal Shem Tov did not believe that the Great Sabbath would come in his time. This is made clear in a remarkable letter, housed today in the Lubavitcher main library in Brooklyn, that modern scholars acknowledge as authentic.

The Baal Shem Tov describes how, in the year 1746, he experienced a mystical "ascent of the soul" to paradise. Beseeching the Messiah to reveal when he would at last come to earth, the Hasidic founder was told: "By this shalt thou know it: when thy teaching will become renowned and revealed throughout the world, and when thy wellsprings [will] be dispersed abroad." The Besht idealistically added, "I was bewildered at this response. I had great anguish because of the length of time [the Messiah implied it would take, and I wondered] when it would be possible for this to occur."

Messianic longings were prominent among many Hasidic leaders, who sought through joy and ritual observance to hasten the long-prophesied age. In accounts that have come down to us, some Rebbes, seized with religious ecstasy and devotion, went to bed each night literally expecting the Messiah's coming before dawn. Several narratives exist about other Hasidic leaders who before their synagogue congregants publicly challenged God above to answer why persecution of the Jews had been allowed to continue for so long.

In the fall of 1814, three great Hasidic figures tried to "force" the Messiah's coming by such methods. The Lubliner, Rimanover, and Medzybozer Rebbes, doubtless aware of traditional warnings against such attempts, together made a pact to compel the divine arrival, but further details are lacking from historical records. All three died within the year. The Lubavitcher Rebbes did not attempt to hasten the coming of the Messiah by mystical techniques, but encouraged followers to accomplish the task through their ardent devotion to Judaism. In general, each Hasidic group regarded its particular Rebbe as the "sage of the generation" and, hence, as its potential Messiah. This outlook has characterized the Lubavitchers.

Outside the Hasidic communities, though, messianism during this era began to fade from the consciousness of Western Jews. A key event occurred in 1791, when Napoleon bestowed citizenship upon all French Jews and legal emancipation was subsequently extended to many other European regions controlled by his forces. After Napoleon's defeat, the rulers of Europe's leading nations reinstated legal restrictions upon Jewish inhabitants, but segregation was significantly reduced. Though Jews often remained subject to official civil disqualification and occupational exclusion until late in the nineteenth century, they were no longer isolated in ghettos, barred from major towns, or restricted to a few despised occupations.

With the gradual removal of barriers between Jews and non-Jews, the majority of Western Jewry eagerly sought entry into wider society. To achieve this goal, many began to declare, sincerely, that they were no longer simply Jews, but were now "Germans of the Mosaic Faith," "Englishmen of the Jewish persuasion," and so on. Yet, many Christians and Jews alike recognized that this redefinition of Jewish identity in strictly religious terms appeared to be incompatible with the age-old Jewish prayers for the Messiah's advent and return to the Holy Land. Christians who opposed Jewish emancipation frequently cited such messianic prayers as evidence that Jews could not be loyal citizens. At the same time, in the industrial age that was dawning, mystical visions concerning messianic times and the "World to Come" seemed outmoded, and no longer germane to daily life.

As a measure of the growing psychological distance many Jews now placed between themselves and traditional messianism, they started to treat the subject with humor. A representative joke began to circulate:

> One day a Jewish shopkeeper rushes home to tell his wife the exciting news: the Messiah has finally arrived, and they will all be transported miraculously to the Holy Land almost momentarily. With a fierce look, his wife retorts, "And how about Mendel's huge unpaid debts

to us? What will become of those? And, Moishe also owes us, and other customers, too. And what about the goods sitting in our shelves that we paid for? And the shipment we just bought that won't be getting here until next week? We'll be ruined!"

The two look at each other ruefully for a few seconds. Then the shopkeeper's face brightens. Smiling triumphantly, he tells his wife, "God has saved the Jewish people from so many calamaties in our history. So, He'll save us from the Messiah, too!"

The founders of Reform Judaism in Germany undertook the first major reformulation of the messianic prayers. At a Frankfurt conference in 1845, participants resolved that "the messianic idea should receive prominent mention in the prayers, but all petitions for our return to the land of our fathers and for the restoration of a Jewish state should be eliminated." This became the policy in German Reform Jewish congregations.

Ten years later, a Reform leader in the United States echoed a growing refrain among his colleagues when he told his congregation, "We Israelites of the present age do not dream any longer about the restoration of Palestine and the Messiah crowned with the diadem of earthly power and glory. America is our Palestine; here is our Zion and Jerusalem; Washington and the signers of the glorious Declaration of Independence—of universal human rights, liberty and happiness—are our deliverers, and the time when their doctrines will be recognized and carried into effect is the time so hopefully foretold by our great prophets."

Among Eastern European Jewry, the small, wealthy merchant class was the chief agent of cultural change. This elite group of "privileged" Jews in Austria, Poland, and Russia held similar views to the Reform adherents in Germany, and helped spread to their less affluent brethren faith in the efficacy of political rather than religious action. By the late nineteenth century, millions of Eastern European Jews were ready to see a far better world, if not the prophesied age, through parliamentary means or emigration to the United States. Some historians suggest, too, that traditional Jewish messianism during this era became rechanneled into two specific currents: left-wing radicalism and Zionism.

Yet messianic belief remained integral to Hasidism. Over the succeeding generations, Lubavitcher Rebbes and their followers remained loyal to the ancient beliefs that Maimonides had systematized. They were also skeptical that Jewish redemption could be realized through political methods, even in such seemingly liberal and "enlightened" countries as Germany. To them, the conviction among their many fellow Jews that Jewish well-being ultimately lay in assimilation seemed extremely misguided and even dangerous. After all, had not God clearly explained millennia earlier the consequences of rejecting His path?

Thus, soon after arriving in the United States following his nightmarish experience in Nazi-occupied Poland during 1939, the previous Lubavitcher Rebbe publicly urged all Jews to embrace the Torah as completely as possible. "The walls of exile are burning down around us now," he warned with great urgency, "and the Messiah will soon be coming if a full return to Judaism takes place." But after issuing four such proclamations in 1941, Rabbi Yosef Schneersohn did not raise the subject again in this manner.

His son-in-law and successor, Rabbi Menachem Schneerson, returned increasingly to this theme, especially after the Israeli victory of the Six Day War in 1967 and the return of Jerusalem to Jewish sovereignty for the first time in almost two thousand years. The Rebbe urged Jews to speed the advent of the Great Sabbath by encouraging Jewish commitment and observance in every city and village on the globe, beginning with simple rituals such as men's putting on tefillin, women lighting Sabbath candles. Children too would have an important role to play in bringing about the messianic age. Those younger than bar mitzvah or bat mitzvah age would be encouraged to participate in a children's "army of God" through which Jewish observance would be stressed.

In this way, by carefully planned and directed "mitzvah campaigns" on a scale never before seen in history, the contemporary Lubavitch movement would help the words of the Messiah come true: "By this thou shalt know it: when thy Hasidic teaching will become renowned and revealed throughout the world, and when thy wellsprings will be dispersed abroad."

Tonight's banquet at the Oholei Torah Jewish Center is moving into its final hour. Speaking now before the rapt audience is Rabbi Avraham Shemtov, emissary on Capitol Hill. As part of his outreach activity, he has devoted nearly twenty years to communicating effectively the Lubavitcher perspective to Jews as well as non-Jews on the national political scene. A regular visitor to the White House since the late 1960s, Rabbi Shemtov developed a particularly friendly relationship with former President Reagan, and informs the delighted assemblage tonight that he has already begun to form a similar relationship with President Bush.

He reminds his colleagues of the international recognition the Rebbe has received from figures like prime ministers Margaret Thatcher and François Mitterrand of England and France respectively, and Spain's King Juan Carlos. In the United States as well as other countries, the Rebbe's birthday in April has become the occasion for official declaration as a day to honor education.

"For several years now, each President of the United States has signed the International Scroll of Honor that pays tribute to the Lubavitcher Rebbe as a force for moral education throughout the world. This is no accident. There are people in all parts of government who recognize that the Rebbe knows where our government is supposed to go, and there is a willingness to listen that I sense nowadays in traveling to government circles that is unbelievable.

"Now, if we as Jews enjoy such prosperity, this is not just to make life more comfortable for us. The condition, rather, brings about and calls for a renewal or an expansion of our role in the world. Whereas until recently our role and mission was to preserve Judaism and to be able to survive ourselves, the doors have now been opened for us to reach out to the whole world. When we say we want Moshiach now, it is not only a matter of belief and faith. It is a matter that we ourselves can turn this prayer and wish and hope into a reality. 'Moshiach now' is a reality which is reachable. It's at hand, it's up to us to reach it. We here can do it."

Next, a well-known Soviet émigré speaks emotionally on Chabad's behind-the-scenes efforts within his former homeland to help bolster Jewish identity and religious involvement. He stresses the importance that the Rebbe attaches to Soviet Jewry and its urgent spiritual needs. "Many years ago," he recalls, "when nobody spoke about them, the Rebbe did. Day by day, he demanded the things that we in Russia were denied in our everyday lives. Nobody knew at that time. It had to be done extremely secretively. But its influence was felt. Jews in Russia felt that somebody—and they knew who it was, though they dared not say it openly—was thinking about them.

"Then, when the gates of Russia opened a little bit more, the Rebbe was the only one who helped set up organizations, sometimes openly and sometimes very quietly, secretly, discreetly on behalf of Soviet Jews."

There are a few more short speeches, echoing the earlier sentiments of program chairperson Rabbi Moshe Kotlarsky, who seems to have best summed up the purpose of this entire convention. "We honor tonight the emissaries of the Rebbe, but especially the Rebbe who has motivated us and who guides us, and who gives us the courage to go out throughout the world and turn on the lights of Judaism and morality. May the Rebbe have success in all his endeavors, everything that he wants to accomplish. There is one thing really that he wishes to accomplish: to brighten up this world, so that the Messiah should be able to come not tomorrow, not the day after tomorrow, but tonight as we sit here by this banquet. Moshiach, Moshiach now!"

It is now nearly two in the morning, and the international Lubavitcher emissary banquet is over. In the drafty lobby of the Oholei Torah Jewish Center, weary wives greet their husbands to drive home, or stay overnight with local family and friends. The New York City night is cold and damp. Few people are foolish or courageous enough to venture alone into these dark streets at this hour. But as the Lubavitchers stream out of the Oholei Torah Jewish Center and across Eastern Parkway, their faces are aglow with excitement, even euphoria, they are beyond mere fatigue. In just a few hours another busy day lies ahead with Hasidic discourses, pragmatic workshops, and outreach planning sessions. But convinced that the final premessianic countdown depends on the fervor and commitment of all Jews to Judaism, they are hopeful, even confident that the long-prophesied age of universal peace will soon be here.

INDEX

Aaron (Hebrew high priest), 197
Abavanel, Don Isaac, 207
Abraham (Old Testament patriarch),
    68–69
ACLU (American Civil Liberties
    Union), 109, 132, 133
Aelia Capitolina. *See* Jerusalem
Afghanistan, 78
Agency for International
    Development, 168
Agudas Chasidei Chabad, 178–84,
    187–91
Agudat Israel, 169
AJC (American Jewish Congress),
    109, 132, 133, 135
Akiba, Rabbi, 30, 153, 198, 199,
    204
Alaska, 57
Aleichem, Sholom, 78
Aleph Institute, 103, 106, 108–15,
    201
Alpert, Richard ("Ram Dass"), 72
Alte Institute. *See* Machon Alte for
    Women

America. *See* United States
American Civil Liberties Union. *See*
    ACLU
American Jewish Congress. *See* AJC
American Jews
    and anti-Semitism, 135, 142
    assimilation of, 142
    vs. Israeli Jews, 91–92
    and Lubavitch menorah campaign,
        136
    secularization of, 137
    and separatism, 139, 141
    See also Jews
Amish, 23
Ann Arbor (Mich.), 66
Anti-Defamation League, of B'nai
    B'rith, 132, 135
Anti-Semitism, 135, 142
Antoninus Pius, 199
Apollo flights, 126–27
Applebaum, Dr. Sholom Zev, 117–19
Arabs, 20, 154, 156, 158, 160, 161,
    162, 164, 165, 167
Argentina, 43, 49

Ascent Institute, 173
Ashkenazi Jews, 157, 158
Assyrian Empire, 197
Auschwitz concentration camp, 61
Australia, 26, 43, 49, 155, 168, 169, 188
Austria, 155, 210

Baal Shem Tov (Besht) (Israel ben Eliezer), 16–19, 21, 30, 67, 123, 126, 157, 195, 208
Baer, Rabbi Dov, 18, 20–21
Baer, Rabbi Sholom Dov, 22, 41, 177
Bailey, Dr. Stephen, 59, 62
Bais Chana Women's Institute, 77–89, 92–102
Barash, Rabbi Yitzchak, 78
Bar-Kochba (Bar-Koziba), 198–99, 204
Begin, Menachem, 172
Bel Air (Calif.), 61
Belgium, 66
Belorussia. See White Russia
Ben-Gurion, David, 155, 171
Ber, Dov, 36, 40
Berkeley (Calif.), 60, 66, 94
Beth Rivkah Girls High School and Girls Vocational Schools (Israel), 159
Beverlywood (Calif.), 58, 61, 62
B'nai B'rith, 115, 116
    Anti-Defamation League, 132, 135
Bobover Hasidim, 146
Bogotá (Colombia), 205
Bolshevik Revolution, 23
    See also Russian Revolution
Bolsheviks (Soviet), 177
Book of Esther, 192
B'or Ha'-Torah (In the Light of Torah), 123
Borough Park (Brooklyn), 146
Boschwitz, Rudy, 79
Boston, 70, 84, 98
Branover, Dr. Herman, 123, 124–25, 149–50, 151, 152
Brazil, 30, 43, 206

British, 139, 154
    See also England
Brooklyn, 63, 66, 77, 79, 85, 133
    See also Borough Park; Brownsville; Crown Heights
Brooklyn Jewish Center, 143–44
Brown, Dennis, 59
Brownsville (Brooklyn), 144
Buddhism, 92
Buenos Aires, 57
Buffalo, 66, 67, 75, 96, 97
Burger, Warren, 135
Burger Court, 135
Bush, George, 212

California, 51, 53–63, 201
Camp David agreement, 165
Canada, 40, 155, 184
Capland, Chaim, 114
Caracas (Venezuela), 129
Carlson, Allan C., 91
Carter, Jimmy, 130
Castro, Fidel, 100
Catholics, 137
Central Europe, 144
Chabad
    and aesthetic creation, 119–22
    cause of, 162
    emissaries of, 112–14
    message of, 173
    yeshiva students, 144
    See also Hasidism
Chabad Houses, 19, 60, 66, 67, 72, 74, 80, 85, 123, 152, 155, 174
Chabad Research Center, 191
CHAI (Chasidic Art Institute), 121
Chanukah, 57, 113, 167
    meaning of, 67
    menorah campaigns, 127, 129–33, 136, 138, 140, 143, 201–2
Chase, David, 50
Chasidic Art Institute. See CHAI
Chicago, 74
Chicago Tribune, 178
Christianity, 142, 196, 209
Christie's auction house, 180

Codes of Jewish Law, 36, 162–65
Colombia, 205
Columbus (Ohio), 66
"Come, my beloved." *See* "Lekha Dodi"
Commentary, 44
Communist Party (Soviet), 37
    Yevsektsia, 23, 24
Congress (U.S.), 133, 134
Constitution (U.S.), 133–34, 139, 140
Coolidge, Calvin, 24
Cornell University, 65, 67, 69, 70, 73, 74, 75
Crete, 204
Crown Heights (Brooklyn), 27, 51, 104, 105, 121, 173, 200
    celebration in, 188–89, 190, 193–96
    Lubavitch world headquarters in, 26, 29–30, 46–47, 49, 53, 54, 158
    preservation of, 143–48
Crusades, 141, 205
Cuba, 100
Culver City (Calif.), 60, 61
Cunin, Mendel, 57
Cunin, Rabbi Shlomo, 53–54, 55–63

Dalfin, Rabbi Chaim, 54, 55
Daniel (Hebrew prophet), 197, 200
David, King, 85, 197, 198, 203, 204
Dayan, Moshe, 161
Declaration of Independence, 133, 139, 210
de Gaulle, Charles, 160
Denver, 66
Derech Emunah (The Way of Truth) (Gabbai), 191
Detroit, 74, 78, 79, 86, 188
Dreyfuss, Richard, 58
Dylan, Bob, 58

Eastern Europe, 15–18, 21–23, 26, 30, 144, 153, 157, 166, 177, 186, 210
Eastern religion and philosophy, 71, 72, 92, 119, 122

Eban, Abba, 160
Ecclesiastes, 111
Egypt, 130, 160, 163–65, 205
Eilat (Israel), 174–75
Eliezer, Israel ben. *See* Baal Shem Tov
Elijah (Hebrew prophet), 197
Elijah of Vilna, Rabbi, 18
Elisha (Hebrew prophet), 197
"End of Days" vision, 198
England, 26, 43, 50, 81, 155, 190, 206, 209, 212
    See also British
Enlightenment. *See* Haskalah
Esau (brother of Jacob), 195
Essay on Population (Malthus), 91
Establishment clause, of First Amendment (Constitution), 133, 134, 135, 139
Esther (Jewish heroine), 68
Ethics of the Fathers. See Pirkey Avoth, The
Europe, 22, 25, 26, 39, 47, 56, 82, 87, 142, 143, 152, 155, 177, 180, 209
    See also Central Europe; Eastern Europe; Western Europe
Exodus, 205

Feller, Mindy, 79, 85
Feller, Rabbi Moshe, 77–79, 80, 98, 101–2
Festival of Lights, 129–32
Finger Lakes (N.Y.), 66
First Amendment to Constitution, Establishment Clause of, 133, 134, 135
First International B'Or Ha'Torah Conference, 123
Florida, 100, 103, 104, 113, 115, 201
Fogelman, Rabbi Mendel, 57, 58
France, 20, 24, 25, 38, 39, 43, 155, 158, 209, 212
Frankfurt, 210
Frankl, Dr. Viktor, 119
Friedman, Chana, 79, 89

Friedman, Rabbi Manis, 57, 79–83, 84, 87–89, 92–97, 99, 101, 196
Friedman, Murray, 141

Gabbai, Rabbi Meir ibn, 191
Galilee (Israel), 173
"Gan-Israel" (Garden of Israel) summer camps, 158
Gaza Strip, 160, 162, 207
Genesis, 68, 69, 109, 125, 194, 195
Georgia (Soviet), 166
Gerlitzky, Rabbi Menachem, 201
Germany, 22, 23, 24, 25, 33, 37, 38, 39, 40, 155, 209, 210, 211
    See also Nazis
Gödel (mathematician), 124
Goetz, Bernhard, 67
Golan Heights, 162
Goldberg, Arthur, 140–41
Goldberg, Rabbi Daniel, 196
Goldberg, Whoopi, 58
Goldstein, Stanley, 60
Goldwater, Barry, 145
Golombevitz, David, 159–60, 161
Golombevitz, Shifra, 159–60, 161–62
Gould, Elliott, 58
Gourary, Barry, 179–81, 182, 185, 187, 188, 189, 190
Gourary, Rabbi Samarius, 37, 42, 179
Graham, Bill, 130
Grand Rapids (Mich.), 202
Greeks, 130
Groner, Rabbi Yitzchok, 169
Gross, Elye, 121
"Guardians of the City." See Neturei Karta brigade
Gutnick, Rabbi Yoseph (Yossi), 151, 168–69
Gutnick, Sterelle, 169

Harvard University, 84, 85
Hasidism
    and aesthetic creation, 119–22
    essence of, 157
    exuberance of, 32, 35, 196
    faith of, 122
    leadership of, 30–31
    mind-set in, 84
    outreach, 156–57
    and personal wealth, 186
    philosophy of, 67–72
    and Rebbes, 18, 21–22, 97
    and sexuality, 74
    stereotypes about, 74
    stories, 81–82
    teachings of, 195
    transcendental aspects of, 98
    and women, 84, 85, 86, 100
    See also Bobover Hasidim; Chabad; Lubavitch
Haskalah (Enlightenment), 21
Hasofer, Avraham, 123
Hatamim (The Upright), 38
Hebrew prophets, 197, 198
Hebron, 21, 121, 153, 154
Hecht, Rabbi Joseph, 174–75
Hecht, Rabbi Shlomo Zalman, 183
Helms, Jesse, 168
Herberg, Will, 139, 141, 142
Hertzberg, Arthur, 135–36
Hillel (Jewish teacher), 30
Himmelfarb, Milton, 141
Hinduism, 92
Hitler, Adolf, 33, 38, 39
Holocaust, 26, 33, 39, 43, 50, 62, 92, 119, 144, 177
Hong Kong, 49, 129
Hope, Bob, 58
Horenstein, Rabbi Menachem, 25, 39–40
Houston (Tex.), 202
Hungary, 162
Hussein, King of Jordan, 160

Illinois, 201
India, 73
Indiana, 202
Industrial Revolution, 88
In The Light of Torah. See B'Or Ha'-Torah
Inquisition, 141

Iowa, 201
Iran, 157
Irish, 143
Isaac (Hebrew patriarch), 68, 69, 194, 195
Isaiah (Hebrew prophet), 196, 197, 200
Islam, 207
Israel, 21, 26, 27, 30, 31, 43, 49, 73, 121, 125, 137, 148, 149–75, 180, 210
  ancient, 197, 204
  Knesset, 169–73
  Law of Return, 170–72
  and Sinai War, 159
  and Six Day War, 161, 162, 211
  Soviet emigration to, 150–54, 155–56, 159
  and Yom Kippur War, 163, 173
Italy, 26, 39, 43, 155, 207
Ithaca Journal, 70
Ithaca Chabad House, 68, 72, 73, 75
Ithaca College, 65, 69, 70, 74

Jacob (Hebrew patriarch), 194–96
Jacobs, Dr. Louis, 184
Jacobson, Rabbi Israel, 183
Javors, Irene, 119–20
Jefferson, Thomas, 134
Jehu (king of Israel), 197
Jeremiah (Hebrew prophet), 196
Jerusalem, 21, 153, 154, 156, 162, 165, 174, 175, 188, 210, 211
  Soviet emigrants to, 151–52
  Temples of, 130, 149, 198, 199, 200, 203, 204, 205
  Western Wall, 149
Jesse (father of King David), 197
Jewish Chronicle (London), 161
Jewish Federation, 132, 138
Jewish Federation Council Task Force on the Homeless, 56
Jewish Theological Seminary, 183, 188
Jews
  alienated, 72–73
  American vs. Israel, 91–92

  discipline of, 126–27
  and family stability, 76
  and Messiah, 195–213
  and Seven Noahide Laws, 205–6
  See also American Jews; Ashkenazi Jews; Sephardic Jews
Johnson, Lyndon, 145, 160
Joint Arab Command, 160
Joint Distribution Committee, 178
Jordan, 160, 165, 174
Joseph (son of Jacob), 109
Juan Carlos, King of Spain, 212
Judah (kingdom), 197

Kansas City, 202
Karo, Rabbi Joseph, 22, 173
Kfar Chabad agricultural collective (Israel), 154, 156, 157–59, 161–62, 166
Kfar Chabad Bet (Israel), 159
KGB, 150
Kiryat Gat (Negev), 165–68, 175
Knesset (Israel), 169–73
Kollek, Teddy, 152
Kotlarsky, Rabbi Moshe, 213
Krinsky, Rabbi Yehuda, 132, 178, 179, 180–81
Kristol, Irving, 141

Latin America, 78
Latvia, 24, 25, 37, 178
Laval, Pierre, 39
Lazaroff, Shimon, 202
Lazaroff-Schaver, Emma, 157
Leib, Israel Aryeh, 36
"Lekha Dodi" ("Come, my beloved"), 22
Levine, Rabbi Sholom, 156, 158–59, 182, 183
Lewin, Nathan, 181, 184
Lieberman, Hendel, 120, 121
Lipchitz, Jacques, 120
Lipskar, Rabbi Sholom, 103–8, 111–12, 113, 114–16, 201
Lithuania, 18, 23
London, 30, 148, 202, 206
Long Island, 86, 122

Los Angeles, 53, 54, 56, 57, 59, 60,
    63, 65, 101, 129, 201, 202
Los Angeles Times, 178
Lubavitch
    and Chanukah menorah campaigns,
        127, 129–33, 136, 138, 140,
        143, 201–2
    on criminal offenders, 109–11
    and Crown Heights, reversing
        abandonment of, 146–48
    in Eastern Europe, 22–23
    and family stability, 76
    grass-roots approach, 78
    and high technology, 122
    in Israel politics, 169–70
    large families for, 89
    library, 177–92
    and Messiah, 196–213
    mystical foundation of, 42, 194
    network of centers, 56, 60
    nonsectarian humanitarian
        programs, 58
    prison outreach work, 112–15
    psychological perspectives of,
        118–19
    refugees, 155–56
    and ritual observance, 167
    role of, 43–44
    values of, 84–85
    world headquarters, 26, 29–31,
        46–47, 49, 50, 53, 54, 62,
        63, 98, 158
    See also Hasidism
Lubavitch Drug Rehabilitation Center
    for Women, 60–62
Lubavitcher Homeless Program for
    Los Angeles, 56, 59
Lubavitch Residential Drug Treatment
    Center for Men, 58–59
Lubavitch Women's Organization, 86
Lubavitch Youth Organization, 130
Lubliner Rebbe, 208
Luria, Isaac, 153, 173
Lutherans, 22

Maccabean period, 198
Maccabees, 130

Machne Israel, 49, 50
Machon Alte (Alte Institute) for
    Women, 173
Madrid, 202
Maggid of Mezritch, 19
Maimonides, Moses, 22, 23, 30, 33,
    49, 109, 116, 137, 153,
    203–5, 210
Malthus, Thomas, 91
Marin County (Calif.), 54–55
Markowitz, Vladimir, 121
Marx, Dr. Alexander, 183, 184, 188,
    190
Maryland, 202
Maslow, Abraham, 72
Medzybozer Rebbe, 208
Meir, Golda, 155
Melbourne, 129, 169
Mendel, Rabbi Menachem, 22
Mennonites, 23
Miami, 74, 78, 100, 106, 107
Miami Beach, 103, 104, 105, 106,
    108, 109, 115
Michael (archangel), 197
Michigan, 201, 202
Mill, John Stuart, 91
Miller, Cassidy, Larroca & Lewin, 181
Milwaukee, 66, 96, 97
Minnesota, 45, 57, 98, 196
    Twin Cities of, 78–80, 85, 101–2
    See also Bais Chana Women's
        Institute
Mishnah, 40, 200
Mishne Torah (The Second Torah)
    (Maimonides), 203–4
Mitnaggedim (Opponents), 18, 21
Mitterrand, François, 212
Morocco, 43, 157, 166
Morristown (N.J.), 60
Moses (Hebrew prophet), 30, 105,
    122
Moussia, Chaya, 25, 37, 38, 39,
    44–45

Nachalat Har Chabad, 159
Nachman of Bratslav, Reb, 78
Nachshon, Baruch, 121

Napoleon, 20, 209
Nasser, Gamal Abdel, 160
Nazis, 25, 39, 143, 178, 180, 183,
    211
Negev (Israel), 165–68, 175
Neturei Karta brigade ("Guardians of
    the City"), 162
New Jersey, 60
New York City, 31, 45, 70, 78, 86,
    101, 129, 130, 144–46, 148,
    150, 162, 201
    See also Brooklyn
New York State, 66, 188
New York Times, The, 145, 162, 178
Niebuhr, Reinhold, 182
Nixon, Richard, 145
NKVD, 24, 25, 37
Noah (Old Testament patriarch),
    205–6
Nunes Ranch (Calif.), 55

Ohio, 114
Oholei Torah Jewish Center, 49,
    200–202, 211–13
Oppenheimer, Dr. Susan, 56–57
Opponents. See Mitnaggedim
Ottoman Empire, 207

Pale of Settlement, 15
Palestine, 199, 210
Palestine Liberation Organization. See
    PLO
Palestinians, 160
Palnik, Paul, 121–22
Paris, 129
Passover, 40, 73, 113, 130, 146,
    154, 167, 180
Perelman, Ronald, 151
Peres government, 170
Persia, 205
Pétain, Philippe, 39
Pfeffer, Leo, 135–36
Philadelphia, 78
Philistines, 199
Phoenix, 66
Pirkey Avoth, The (Ethics of the
    Fathers), 86, 198

Pittsburgh, 66, 202
PLO (Palestine Liberation
    Organization), 160, 170
Poland, 15, 21, 23, 24, 25, 38, 39,
    143, 178–79, 181, 183, 187,
    210, 211
Portugal, 25, 207
Potiphar (Egyptian), 109
Poughkeepsie, 94
Project Aleph, See Aleph Institute
Project Pride, 60
Protestants, 135, 137
Psalms, 197
Purim, 167

Rabinowitz, Avi, 124
Rachel (wife of Jacob), 153
Reagan, Ronald, 206, 212
Rebbe (seventh), the. See Schneerson,
    Rabbi Menachem Mendel
Regents Prayer, 134, 141
Return, The (Branover), 125
Rimanover Rebbe, 208
Rio, 188
Ritchie, Lionel, 58
Rochester (N.Y.), 201
Roman Catholics, 135
    See also Catholics
Romans, 198–99
Rosenbloom, Paul, 124
Rosenfeld, Rabbi Yehoshua, 205
Rosh Hashanah, 25, 56–60, 68, 72,
    113
Rubashov, Schneur Zalman. See
    Shazar, Zalman
Russia, 16, 18, 19, 20, 36, 38, 40,
    47, 48, 50, 100, 104, 135,
    153, 158, 169, 183, 210
turmoil in, 22–25
    See also Soviet Union
Russian Revolution, 177
    See also Bolshevik Revolution
Ruth (Moabite), 68

Sabbatian movement, 207, 208
Sadat, Anwar, 165
Safed (Israel), 173

Saks, Dr. Zvi, 124
Salem witch-hunt trials, 135
San Diego, 60
San Francisco, 54–55, 130
San Rafael (Calif.), 55
São Paulo (Brazil), 30
SATEC, 149–50, 152, 168
Satmar group, 162
Saul (king of Israel), 197
Schahach from London, 206–7
Schlam, Stone & Dolan, 181
Schnader, Harrison, Segal & Lewis,
    181
Schneersohn, Sheine, 25
Schneersohn, Rabbi Yosef Yitzchak
    (sixth Rebbe), 41, 211
  in Crown Heights, 143–44
  death of, 26–27, 182, 183
  in Israel, 153–54, 155
  leadership of, 23–26
  library of, 177–88, 190, 191
Schneerson, Chana (née Yanovsky),
    36, 40
Schneerson, Levi Yitzchak, 36
Schneerson, Rabbi Menachem Mendel
    (seventh Rebbe), 24, 25, 26,
    27, 40, 41, 54, 97, 144, 158
  on artistic creation, 120–21
  and assimilation, 142
  birth of, 36
  and Camp David agreement, 165
  on change, 156
  and Chanukah menorah campaign,
    130, 131, 140
  and Codes of Jewish Law, 162–65
  on Creation, 125–26
  dedication of, 44–46
  discourses of, 94, 194–96
  early years, 36
  on family planning, 89–90
  on individual capability, 75
  inspiration of, 100–101
  and Israel, 155, 170, 173, 211
  on Jewish discipline, 126–27
  on Jews, 105
  and joy, 62–63
  to Kfar Chabad, 159
  and Lubavitch library, 179, 180,
    186, 188–91
  marries Chaya Moussia, 37
  meeting, 47–49, 50–51
  and mental health, 117–19
  on moment of silence, 137–38
  recognition for, 212, 213
  on retirement, 106, 201
  on ritual observance, 161
  and Seven Noahide Laws, 206
  as seventh Lubavitcher Rebbe, 27,
    42–43
  and Soviet emigration, 150–51
  studies of, 38–39
  and Talmud, 152
  and technology, 123
  and Torah, 132, 146–48, 157,
    159, 160, 171, 194, 195, 205
  at TV celebration, 30–35
  and Who Is a Jew controversy,
    171–72
Schochet, Immanuel, 184
Second Torah, The. See Mishne Torah
Sephardic Jews, 81, 93–94, 157,
    158, 166, 167
Seryebranski, Rabbi Zalman, 169
"Seven Noahide Laws," 205–6
SHAMIR (organization), 125, 152
Shamir, Yitzhak, 170
Shanghai, 25
Shazar, Zalman (Schneur Zalman
    Rubashov), 158
Shemtov, Rabbi Avraham, 49–50,
    178, 211–12
Shestack, Jerome, 181, 184
Shmuel, Rabbi, 22
Shochet, Rabbi Immanuel, 67
shtetls, 15, 16
Shulchan Arukh, 19
Siberia, 25, 37
Siegel, Seymour, 141
Sifton, Charles P., 181–82, 184–85,
    186–88, 189, 190, 191
Silberstein, Chana, 66, 68, 70,
    73–74, 75
Silberstein, Rabbi Elie, 65–76
Sinai Desert, 160

Sinai oil wells, 164
Sinai War, 159
Six Day War, 161, 162, 211
SOLMECS, 168
Sonoma County (Calif.), 55
South Africa, 81, 206
Soviet Union, 125, 160, 177
    emigration from, 26, 40, 150–56,
        159, 166, 212–13
    imprisonment in, 30, 104
    Jewish identity in, 32–33
    and Lubavitch library, 180, 191
    See also Communist Party; Russia
Spain, 202, 205, 207, 212
Stackhouse, Max L., 139–40
Stalin, Joseph, 36, 154
Stanford (Calif.), 60
State Department (U.S.), 178, 184
St. Louis, 201
Succoth, 39, 69
Suez Canal, 161
Supreme Court (U.S.), 133, 134, 137,
    141, 202
Sweden, 25
Switzerland, 49
Syria, 205
Syrian Greeks, 130

Talmud, 36, 39, 68, 74, 77, 123,
    147, 152, 165, 195, 200,
    203, 205
    importance of, 15–18
Tammuz, 30, 34
Tanya (Zalman), 19, 71, 104, 109,
    183
Task Force on Jewish Population, 92
Tasmania, 168
Tel Aviv, 154, 155, 156, 165
Teldon, Chaya, 86–87
Teldon, Rabbi Tuvya, 86, 122–23
Texas, 113, 202
Thatcher, Margaret, 212
Tiberias (Israel), 168
Torah, 32, 33, 38–39, 49, 50, 68,
    69, 89, 101, 104, 130, 131,
    159, 160, 163, 192, 200,
    206, 211

emissary roles in, 194–95
and Hasidism, 157
and homosexuality, 96
and imprisonment, 109–11
and Jewish customs, 62
Judaism, 191
and Messiah, 203–5
principles of, 146–47, 148
for prisoners, 107–8
and science, 124, 125
and sexuality, 95
significance of, 199
and tradition, 171
Torat Emet yeshiva, 153
Toronto, 67, 104
Treblinka, 25, 40
Tunisia, 43, 78, 166
Turkey, 20, 26, 153, 157, 207

UAHC (Union of American Hebrew
    Congregations), 132, 133
UCLA, 53, 57, 58, 94
Ukraine, 15, 21
UN (United Nations), 160
Union of American Hebrew
    Congregations. See UAHC
Unitarians, 98
United Nations Declaration on Human
    Rights, 140
    See also UN
United States, 26, 34, 38, 39, 47,
    56, 82, 83, 130, 134, 135,
    153, 158, 168, 173, 180,
    184, 188
    art collections in, 121
    emigration to, 23–25, 155, 178,
        210, 211
    Founding Fathers in, 139–40
    and International Scroll of Honor, 212
    and Israel, 152, 156, 163, 164
    and Lubavitch library, 187
    small families in, 90–91
    suburbanization in, 144
Upright, The. See Hatamim
U.S. Court of Appeals for the Second
    Circuit, 190
U.S.S.R. See Russia; Soviet Union

Vassar College, 94
Vienna, 202
Vietnam, 130
Virginia, 202
Vogel, Rabbi Faivish, 148, 190–91
Voight, Jon, 58, 62

Warren Court, 134, 135
Warsaw, 178
Washington Post, The, 178
Waxman, Seth, 181
Way of Truth, The. See Derech Emunah
Weinberg, Rabbi Sholom, 202
Weinstein, Jack, 112
Weintraub, Jerry, 58
Weizmann, Chaim, 155
West Bank, 162
Western Europe, 26
Westwood headquarters (Calif.), 53, 56–63
White Russia, 15, 19–21, 23
Who Is a Jew controversy, 170–72

Wiener, Herbert, 44
Wiener, Shmuel, 183
Wiesel, Elie, 184, 185–86, 190
Wilson, Harold, 160
Wolpo, Chana, 166
Wolpo, Rabbi Sholom Ber, 166–168

Yemen, 26, 157
Yevsektsia, of Soviet Communist Party, 23, 24
Yochai, Shimon ben, 153
Yochai, Simon bar, 199
Yom Kippur, 57, 58, 60, 68, 72
Yom Kippur War, 163, 173

Zalman, Rabbi Schneur, 18–20, 71, 157
Zern, Chaya, 84–85
Zevi, Sabbatai, 207–8
Zionists, 170, 210
  Labor, 166
Zusya, Reb, 122